Gold and Jade Filled Halls

Monies, Markets, and Finance in East Asia, 1600–1900

Edited by

Hans Ulrich Vogel

VOLUME 3

The titles published in this series are listed at brill.com/mmf

Gold and Jade Filled Halls

A Cognitive Linguistic Study of Financial and Economic Expressions in Chinese and German

By

Shelley Ching-yu Hsieh

with the collaboration of

May Hsin-mei Huang, Lydia Yu-ling Chang,
Sophia Chen-ying Wu and Carrie Hsin-wen Tseng

BRILL

LEIDEN • BOSTON
2013

Cover illustration: A collage of documents on financial linguistic expressions. Photo by Shelley Ching-yu Hsieh.

Library of Congress Cataloging-in-Publication Data

Hsieh, Shelley Ching-yu.
Gold and Jade Filled Halls : a Cognitive Linguistic Study of Financial and Economic Expressions in Chinese and German / By Shelley Ching-yu Hsieh ; with the collaboration of May Hsin-mei Huang, Lydia Yu-ling Chang, Sophia Chen-ying Wu and Carrie Hsin-wen Tseng.
pages cm.—(Monies, Markets, and Finance in East Asia, 1600-1900 ; VOLUME 3)
Includes index.
ISBN 978-90-04-24433-7 (hardback)—ISBN 978-90-04-24434-4 (e-book) 1. Intercultural communication—China. 2. Intercultural communication—Germany. 3. Cross-cultural orientation—China. 4. Cross-cultural orientation—Germany. 5. Economics—Dictionaries. 6. Economics—Dictionaries—Chinese. 7. Economics—Dictionaries—German. 8. Finance—Dictionaries. 9. Finance—Dictionaries—Chinese. 10. Finance—Dictionaries—German. 11. Comparative linguistics—East Asia. I. Title.

P94.65.C6H75 2013
401'.47—dc23

2012047371

This publication has been typeset in the multilingual "Brill" typeface. With over 5,100 characters covering Latin, IPA, Greek, and Cyrillic, this typeface is especially suitable for use in the humanities. For more information, please see www.brill.com/brill-typeface.

ISSN 2210-2876
ISBN 978-90-04-24433-7 (hardback)
ISBN 978-90-04-24434-4 (e-book)

This book is printed on acid-free paper.

CONTENTS

LIST OF FIGURES AND TABLES

Figures

Tables

PREFACE

This book is a collection of papers examining linguistic issues introduced in the Brill's MMF book series. A hall full of gold and jade pictures the theme of wealth, fortune and longevity. This is one of the most popular symbols of wealth in Chinese society, and is wished for by many, either for themselves or for their friends and family, as is suggested in the idiom, *jin1yu4 man3tang2* 金玉满堂 'gold and jade filled halls = wealth.' We hope this book, a collection of papers examining financial and economic expressions in Mandarin Chinese and German from the perspective of cognitive linguistics, will simultaneously attempt to both illuminate and draw more attention to the research on the issue of financial linguistic expressions in language.

Motivated by research work on financial linguistic expressions, this book gathers a number of studies which focus on the metaphorical reasoning of various financial linguistic expressions with the goal of generating a better understanding of the significance behind these linguistic expressions. In other words, clarifying the cognitive, pragmatic and cultural factors which are involved in the generation and propagation of financial linguistic expressions is the major concern of the present research. Moreover, this collection not only investigates the financial linguistic expressions in Mandarin, but contrasts these expressions to homologous or contrastive expressions used in German, to unravel the resemblances and differences between them.

This collection is comprised of two parts: the first part, chapters 3 to 8, gathers the research on financial linguistic expressions in Mandarin. The second part, from chapter 9 to 11, collects pertinent ideas from comparative studies contrasting German and Mandarin. The collection is organized as follows: Chapter 1 explains the methodology used in the collecting of data and explains the theoretical framework of the project; Chapter 2 gives a review of previous research; Chapter 3 analyses the idea of *huang2jin1* 黃金 'gold;' Chapter 4 is a close study of the connotations of *jin1qian2* 金錢 'money;' Chapter 5 studies *yin2* 銀 'silver;' Chapter 6 is concerned with *pin2qiong2* 貧窮 'poverty;' Chapters 7 and 8 explain *gu3shi4* 股市 'stock market' jargon; Chapter 9 delves into *buy, sell* and *charge*; Chapter 10 deals with *business* in both Mandarin and German; Chapter 11 is concerned with financial linguistic expressions in embodiment, followed by the conclusion in Chapter 12.

Preliminary versions of several chapters have been presented at different conferences: Chapter 3 "The metaphorical interpretations of *huang2jin1* 'gold' " was presented at the *The 11th International Symposium on Chinese Languages and Linguistics* (IsCLL-11), National Chiao Tung University, Hsinchu, Taiwan in 2008. Chapter 4 "Mandarin speakers' perception of *jin1qian2* 'money' " was presented at *Workshop on Monies, Markets and Finance in China and East Asia, 1600-1900*, Heidelberg University, Germany in 2008, and at the *2nd Intercollegiate Theses Presentation Conference*, National Kaohsiung Normal University, Kaohsiung, Taiwan in 2009. Chapter 5 "The metaphorical expressions of *yin2* 'silver' " was presented at *American Association of Corpus Linguistics* (AACL), Brigham Young University, Provo, Utah in 2008. Chapter 7 "Stock market jargons in Mandarin: related metaphors and their source domains" and Chapter 8 "Stock market jargons in Mandarin: related collocations and the cognitive strategies" were presented at the *12th International Conference on Processing of East Asia Related Languages*, National Cheng Kung University, Tainan, Taiwan, 2007 and at the *American Association of Corpus Linguistics* (AACL), Brigham Young University, Provo, Utah in 2008. Chapter 9 "Financial linguistic verbs in German" was presented at the *Lernen und Lehren: Deutsche Sprache, Literatur und Kultur*, Fu Jen University in 2009. Chapter 10 "*Geschäft* in German newspaper reports" was presented at *Foreign Language Pedagogy and Practice: Language, Literature, and Culture*, Soochow University, Taipei, Taiwan in 2010. Chapter 11 "The financial linguistic expressions in embodiment" was presented at the *International Workshop on Monies, Markets and Finance in China and East Asia, 1600-1900: Global and Comparative Perspectives*, Eberhard Karls University of Tübingen, Germany in 2011. Chapters that have previously been published in journals will acknowledge the original publications in a footnote at the beginning of the chapter.

ACKNOWLEDGEMENTS

This book is based on research within the project *Monies, Markets, and Finance in China and East Asia, 1600-1900: Local, Regional, National, and International Dimensions*, under the sub-project No. 54, titled *A cognitive semantic & pragmatic study of Mandarin Chinese, Taiwanese & German fixed expressions of money, wealth & poverty*. I wish to thank Professor Dr. Hans Ulrich Vogel for his kind invitation to participate in this international project that is mainly supported financially by the Deutsche Forschungsgemeinschaft. Many thanks also go to my editing assistant May Hsin-Mei Huang for her patience and hard work. Of course the contributors of the book chapters made the completion of this book possible. They are May Hsin-Mei Huang, Lydia Yu-ling Chang, Sophia Chen-Ying Wu, and Carrie Hsin-wen Tseng, whose addresses and contact info can be found in the List of Contributors of this book. I also would like to thank Seth Pankhurst for his careful proofreading of the English and helpful comments. The advice and stimulating discussions with Dr. Chin-fa Lien, Dr. Chao-chih Liao, Dr. Shu-miao Huang, Dr. Hui-Chen Hsiao, Dr. Shu-Ping Gong, Dr. Jung-hsing Chang, and Dr. Yu-Fang Wang provided insight to various issues in this book. Finally, I wish to express my gratitude to Brill Academic Publishers for their kind permission to print this book. I am responsible, without a doubt, for any deficiencies that remain in the book.

LIST OF CONVENTIONS AND ABBREVIATIONS

Conventions

capitalized: conceptual metaphor; elements of semantic frames,
e.g., *JIN1QIAN2* IS WATER, POSSESSION

italicized: target words/phrases (FLEs),
e.g., *jin1, kaufen, gu3shi4*

single quotation marks: English meaning; animal/plant vehicles
e.g., 'society'; 'pig'

Abbreviations

ASP	aspect marker, e.g., *le* 了, and *zai4* 在
CIN	Conceptual Integration Network
CMM	Conceptual Mapping Model
FLE	financial linguistic expression
GCB Metaphor	Great Chain of Being Metaphor
INT.	interrogative marker, e.g., *ma* 嗎, and *ne* 呢
MP	mapping principle
PART	particles, e.g., *o* 喔, *ba* 吧, and *jiu4* 就
POSS.	possesive marker, e.g., *de* 的, *zhi1* 之
SD	source domain
SUMO	suggested upper merged ontology
TD	target domain

LIST OF CONTRIBUTORS

Shelley Ching-yu Hsieh
Department of Foreign Languages and Literature
National Cheng Kung University
No. 1, University Rd., East Dist., Tainan city, Taiwan (R.O.C.)
Email: shelley@mail.ncku.edu.tw

May Hsin-mei Huang
No. 239, Sec. 1, Fuqian Rd., West Central Dist., Tainan city, Taiwan (R.O.C.)
Email: plum0910@yahoo.com.tw

Lydia Yu-Ling Chang
522-0222 Shiga province Hikone City, Minamikawase Town 815-1 Berufore, Japan
Email: lm864012@msn.com

Sophia Chen-Ying Wu
3F., No. 25-2, Ln. 381, Jiuru 1st Rd., Sanmin Dist., Kaohsiung City, Taiwan (R.O.C.)
Email: smallsophia999@yahoo.com.tw

Carrie Hsin-Wen Tseng
No. 239, Junwei St., West Central Dist., Tainan city, Taiwan (R.O.C.)
Email: ilc888888@yahoo.com.tw

CHAPTER ONE

METHODOLOGY

Shelley Ching-yu Hsieh

The global Economic Crisis in 2008 overwhelmed much of the world. The negative influence of the turmoil on the global economy began to accelerate and grow from the day Lehman Brothers shut down, September 15. Directly or circumspectly, economics plays an important role in daily life, and people in different countries, with different cultures, and speaking different languages all, whether they are aware of it or not, integrate the concepts of business and finance into their daily language.

This chapter introduces how the data used in this study were collected and analyzed. The data collection is introduced in 1.1. The theoretical framework is presented in 1.2. A summary of this chapter will be given in 1.3.

1.1. Data Collection

Mandarin Chinese is the official language of three countries: Taiwan, People's Republic of China, Singapore. There are regional differences in how ideas are expressed in various regions.[1] For example, *huan4tie3* 換帖 'change-card' in Taiwan is an expression used to mean close and intimate friends, while the same meaning is expressed by *bai4ba3zhi* 拜把子 'worship-handle-suffix' in Mainland China. This book concentrates on the Mandarin spoken in Taiwan (hereafter Mandarin). We will point out some regional variations in footnotes in our later discussion, when necessary.

Most of the data have been collected from corpora, electronic newspapers, Chinese dictionaries, and everyday spoken utterances. The materials for the metaphorical examination are therefore up to date. The gathered data for each chapter are introduced as follows.

[1] For the linguistic differences of regional or dialectal Mandarin usage in other regions, see Fluck, Li and Zhao (1984), Li and Thompson (1989), Qiu (1990), Tang (2001), Schmidt (2003), and Klein (2007).

For Chapter 3 on *huang2jin1* and Chapter 4 on *jin1qian2*, the data were collected simultaneously. The majority of the financial linguistic expressions (hereafter FLEs) were gathered from (1) *Academia Sinica Balanced Corpus Mandarin Chinese* (Chen and Huang 2001), the first segmented Chinese corpus, with a total of 4,892,324 lexical items taken from articles on six topics: philosophy, science, social studies, arts, literature, and life from 1981 to 2007, (2) *Mandarin Chinese Knowledge Network*, (3) *Lin Yutang's Chinese-English Dictionary of Modern Usage, and* (4) *Mandarin Chinese Flexible Usages dictionary* (Zhou and Qiu 2004). A minor portion (4%) of the data has been gathered from other sources, such as newspapers, e-newspaper, radio broadcasts, TV programs on economic topics, and books. Table 1.1 presents the raw data collected for the metaphorical expressions.

Table 1.1. Data collection of *jin1qian2* and *huang2jin1*.

	FLEs	N	Metaphorical Expressions
jin1qian2 金錢	'gold-money = money'	331	101
huang2jin1 黃金	'yellow-gold = gold'	323	94
	Total	654	195

There are 331 expressions of *jin1qian2*. 101 of these are metaphorical and these are the ones which will be discussed. In the other 323 expressions of *huang2jin1*, 94 are metaphorical. The metaphorical tokens were first identified and discussed personally by one of the authors and a Mandarin native speaker with a major in linguistics. The identification and modification were then checked by the authors and six other native speakers and finally confirmed by the authors. In total, 654 expressions of *huang2jin1* and *jin1qian2* were gathered, and 195 of them are metaphorical.

The collected data for *yin2*, the focus of Chapter 5, is divided into two parts: the fixed expressions, such as *bin4fa3ru2yin2* 鬢髮如銀, meaning 'elderly people,' and metaphorical clusters, such as *hu2gua1 nü3er2 ta4shang4 yin2se4lu4* 胡瓜女兒踏上銀色路 'Mr. Hu's daughter is going into show business.' The data for *yin2* was collected from two sources: a dictionary base for *yin2* fixed expressions, and a mass media base for *yin2* metaphor clusters. The data sources of the dictionary base are (1) *Chinese Mandarin Online Dictionary* (3rd edition) (Committee of Official Language Promotion 1994)[2] and (2) *Great Dictionary*. The mass media based

[2] The Ministry of Education indicates that the editing of the original version of the Chinese dictionary was finished in 1945. The revised version of the Chinese dictionary was

data sources are (3) *Newspapers in Taiwan* and (4) TV programs, broadcasts and books, which make up a certain percentage of our materials. Table 1.2 contains the raw data of *yin2* fixed expressions and *yin2* metaphor clusters.

Table 1.2. Data collection of *yin2*.

FLEs	Data Source	N	Total
Fixed expressions	On-line dictionary	210	251
	Paper dictionary	41	
Metaphor clusters	Electronic database	352	582
	Media (TV, radio, book)	230	

N refers to the number of collected data items. There are in total 251 *yin2* fixed expressions, consisting of 210 online-based terms and 41 paper-based terms. After cross-checking the data, 25 duplicated terms were deleted. Therefore, our final data set consists of 226 instances of *yin2* fixed expressions for examination. In addition to the fixed expressions, there are 352 metaphor clusters of *yin2* culled from electronic databases and 230 sentences and utterances taken from the media, either from TV programs, radio broadcasts or books. After incorporating all the instances of fixed expressions and metaphor clusters of *yin2*, we have in total 808 terms for our investigation.

The data used for *pin2qiong2, pin2* and *qiong2* which is used in Chapter 6 have been collected from the *Newspapers in Taiwan Database* in which *jing1ji4ri4bao4* 經濟日報 'Economic Daily News' served as the primary source of our data collection because it focuses on economically related news, making it an excellent match for this research. In addition, the periods of data collection were limited to before and after the Financial Crisis, which happened during late 2008 to 2009. The utterances of *pin2, qiong2* and *pin2qiong2,* three quasi-synonyms referring to the same general concept of 'poverty,' used during these two distinct periods of time, February 16th to September 15th in 2008 and September 16th in 2008 to April 15th in 2009 have been compared. Table 1.3 shows the quantity of the raw data and the number of collected expressions.

extended to six volumes and did not come out until 1981. Later, Corrected Versions of the Chinese Dictionary (Ministry of Education 1994) were revised several times and promoted in an online version.

Table 1.3. Data collection of *pin2qiong2, pin2* and *qiong2.*

FLEs	Before the Financial Crisis		After the Financial Crisis	
	raw data	collected expressions	raw data	collected expressions
pin2qiong2	410	117	328	102
pin2	1592	349	1628	323
qiong2	1834	626	1712	473
Total	3836	1092	3668	898

The total number of instances of the three expressions, *pin2, qiong2* and *pin2qiong2* (all expressing ideas related to the concept of 'poverty') is 3,836 before the Financial Crisis and 3,668 after it. Among these instances, 1,092 items were collected before the Financial Crisis, while 898 instances gathered after the Financial Crisis. We got a total of 410 expressions of *pin-2qiong2* out of which 117 were collected before the Financial Crisis, 1,592 expressions of *pin2* in which 349 were collected before the Crisis, and 1,834 expressions of *qiong2* of which 626 were collected before the Crisis. Similarly, we got a total of 328 expressions of *pin2qiong2,* 1,628 expressions of *pin2* and 1,712 expressions of *qiong2* out of which 102, 323, and 473 were collected after the Financial Crisis, respectively.

For the stock market metaphors used in Chapters 7 and 8, we used 113 stock market jargon as keywords, such as *zhi3die2hui2sheng1* 止跌回升 'bounce back from a slump' and *zhang3ting2ban3* 漲停板 'limit up.' These example sentences were collected during the period from 1995 to 2008. They have been chosen via a two-step process. We (1) collected familiar stock jargon from stock-related articles in newspapers, and then (2) checked whether the collected stock jargon was found in the stock-related articles of newspapers from the database of *Newspapers in Taiwan* (新聞知識庫). If yes, we can say that this stock jargon originates from the stock market. The *xin1wen2zhi1shi4ku4* 新聞知識庫 'Newspapers in Taiwan Database' (http://newspaper.ntl.gov.tw) is a corpus consists of 13 domestic Taiwanese newspapers, such as *lian2he2bao4* 聯合報 'United Daily News,' *zhong1guo2shi2bao4* 中國時報 'China Times,' *shi4jie4 ri4bao4* 世界日報 'World Journal,' etc. In total, the corpus contains over 20,529,489 lexical items up to the year 2010. The total number of sentences which met our economic terminology criteria is 1512, of which 178 sentences have been excluded because of unclear mapping domain and insufficient tokens to form a conceptual metaphor group. In total, 1334 utterances qualify for data analysis.

Finally, for Chapters 9 to 11, we carried out 3 comparative studies on FLEs in Mandarin and German. The Mandarin data have been collected from *Academia Sinica Balanced Corpus Mandarin Chinese* (Chen and Huang 2001). The German data are taken from the *Corpus Search, Management and Analysis System* (COSMAS II) (Institut für Deutsche Sprache 2008), *Deutscher Wortschatz* (Universität Leipzig 2006), and Google search. The main data are newspaper articles searched from COSMAS II. COSMAS II is a German corpus system that is designed and managed by Institut für Deutsche Sprache, which was built in 1993 and has been updated regularly since then. Data for the present study was collected from the version COSMAS II WIN 2008, which comprises 86 corpora and contains a total of 3.6 billion words. *Deutscher Wortschatz* is a corpus dictionary designed in 1998 by Universität Leipzig, Germany. This system not only presents the utterances with the lexeme but demonstrates the collocations along with giving the frequency of usage. This corpus has been collected from German newspapers and randomly adopts linguistic data from German language websites. So far, they have assembled about 30 million German sentences. In the present study, we use the utterance collocations from *Deutscher Wortschatz* to help analyze our data.

For the study performed in Chapter 9, 5677 tokens were retrieved from COSMAS II: *kaufen* 2,810, *verkaufen* 2,631, and *bezahlen* 236 from 2006 and 2007. About ten thousand tokens were gathered from *Deutscher Wortschatz* for the right and left collocations (see Table 9.2). For Chapter 10, 8456 instances of German *Geschäft* were collected from COSMAS and 160 *Geschäft* collocations were collected from *Deutscher Wortschatz*. For Mandarin, 289 instances of *shenglyi4* were collected from *Academia Sinica Balanced Corpus Mandarin Chinese*. In addition, 253 *shenglyi4* collocations (from the same corpus) were collected (see Table 10.1). For Chapter 11, 419 Mandarin and 262 German FLEs of embodiment were collected for further analysis.

1.2. Theoretical Framework

This book analyzes linguistic data of various topics on FLEs. Six theories are adopted for different chapter topics. We will introduce Lakoff and Johnson's (1980) conceptual metaphor in 1.2.1, Kövecses' (2002) interpretations of metaphor in 1.2.2, Ahrens' (2002) Conceptual Mapping Model in 1.2.3, Lakoff and Turner's (1989) Great Chain of Being Metaphor in 1.2.4, Fauconnier and Turner's (1998) Conceptual Integration Network in 1.2.5, Hopper's (1987) Emergent Grammar in 1.2.6, Niles and Pease's (2001) suggested upper merged ontology (SUMO) in the 1.2.7, and Fillmore and Atkins' (1992) Semantic Frame in 1.2.8.

1.2.1. *Lakoff and Johnson (1980) Conceptual Metaphor*

When people talk, each word in their utterances contains a lexical form and pairs with one meaning. The brains of both interlocutors start to combine words along with their meanings which have been said or heard. These form-meaning pairs are the common and basic processes of linguistic coding. However, some utterances go beyond their literal expressions. For instance, *I don't know which path to take*, and *he works his way round many obstacles*. These are the examples of the conceptual metaphor LIFE IS A JOURNEY. They convey not only the surface meanings (people are on a trip or have direction problems), but also the underlying meaning that a person's entire life is like the many stages of a journey. Such a metaphorical usage comprises the source domain (hereafter SD) and the target domain (hereafter TD), where the SD provides the means to describe the TD. Thus, in the conceptual metaphor LIFE IS A JOURNEY, journey (the SD) is mapped onto life (the TD) (Lakoff and Johnson 1999–2006; Šeškauskienė and Urbonaitė 2007). More on SDs and TDs will be given in 1.2.2.

The focus of the present book is on the metaphorical applications of the FLEs in Mandarin, with the last three chapters on German as well. Metaphor, as a type of figurative language, refers to literally unacceptable but nevertheless meaningful expressions (Carroll 2004: 137–138). As Fromkin and Rodman (1998: 187–188) state, "metaphorical use of language is language creativity at its highest." Lakoff and Johnson (1980: 3) first proposed an innovation that our conceptual system is metaphorically structured, suggesting that "metaphor is pervasive not just in language but in our thought and action." Accordingly, metaphors display a powerful communicative strategy in people's daily life by which a relatively abstract or unstructured concept becomes vivid and comprehensible in terms of concrete or well-structured subject matter (Lakoff 1993; Su 2000; Chung 2008; Tsao, Tsai and Liu 2000; Ahrens, Chung and Huang 2004; Chung, Ahrens and Huang 2003, 2004, 2005; Chung, Ahrens and Sung 2003; Chung, Huang and Ahrens 2003).

According to previous research that sheds light on the present book, living organisms are preferred SDs when FLEs are perceived. For instance,

Smith (1995) discusses the metaphorical descriptions of *stock market* trading related to economic activity in Hong Kong. The research result shows that human characteristics are stock markets. Charteris-Black (2000) investigates *economy* and *market* in English and reports that ECONOMY IS A PERSON, since economy is attributed to have social interaction, physical condition and mental process. In addition, Charteris-Black and Ennis (2001) target financial reports in English and Spanish. In this work, the FLE metaphors are perceived in terms of an organism because they have psychological and physical health. Later, White (2003) examines economic activities in terms of *growth* and suggests that ECONOMY IS LIVING ORGANISM, such as humans, animals, or plants.

Likewise, Charteris-Black and Musolff (2003) point out that THE EURO IS A PATIENT, indicating *the euro* is perceived passively for the euro is 'weak' and is in need of 'support' to 'recover' from its difficult unhealthy condition. Further, Chung, Ahrens and Huang (2003) perform a cross-linguistic corpora analysis to show how similarly or differently *economy* is demonstrated in English and Chinese. Their study reports that ECONOMY IS PERSON for people have a life cycle and economy has a growth cycle. All the above suggest that the SD, living organisms, are the prototypical operations in structuring the metaphors of FLEs. The use of animated metaphors is not just the preferred operation when an FLE is perceived; moreover, it denotes dominance and control as Charteris-Black (2000: 160–163) points out the use of animated metaphor implies dominance and control. For example, economy is perceived animatedly, whereas market is inanimated for economists view themselves as the experts who are able to predict, control, and foresee economic trends, but free from the dynamics and uncertainty of markets.

1.2.2. *Kövecses' (2002) Interpretations of Metaphor*

Metaphor is a cognitive strategy by which people compare concrete objects to abstract ideas (Lakoff and Johnson 1980; Goddard 1998). According to Kövecses (2002), metaphor involves four concepts: (1) TD, (2) SD, (3) mapping and (4) conceptual metaphor. We draw Figure 1.1 (see p. 8) to illustrate Kövecses (2002) interpretation of metaphor.

The TD, which is the concept being explained, is the linguistic proposition that the speakers would like to address. However, since the TD is an abstract idea in most cases, it requires more elaboration. Therefore, in order to make an abstract idea more easily accessible, a vivid and concrete object is selected and employed. The concrete object is the SD, which

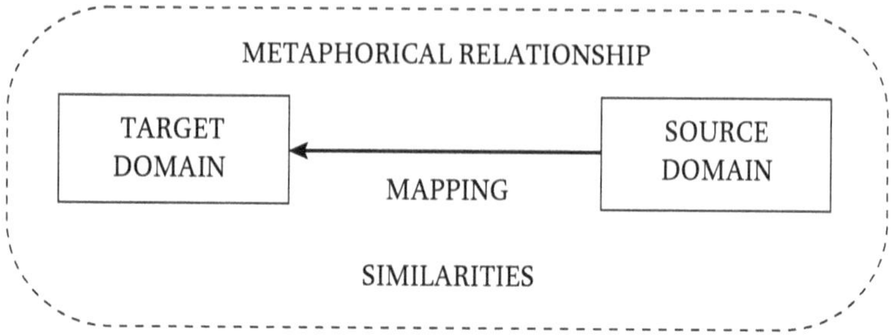

Figure 1.1. Metaphorical relationship.

is the concept that helps construct the TD. When the lexical correspondences are found between the SD and the TD, mapping takes place. Conceptual metaphor, which is dependent on people's schematic knowledge, will constrain the mappings into a single shared concept. For example, AN ARGUMENT IS A BUILDING, given by Ungerer and Schmid (2006: 123) will help explain the terms discussed above, and is exemplified in (a) and (b) below.

(a) We have got a framework for a solid argument.
(b) With the groundwork you've got, you can construct a pretty solid argument.

The argument referred to in (a) and (b) is the TD that needs to be made more concrete. It appears to be the proposition, or the TD, addressed by the speaker. As an argument is an abstract concept, it therefore requires a concrete object to characterize its properties. The necessary concrete object, defined here as the SD, is the building. The lexical correspondences that contribute to the mappings between an argument and a building are "the framework" and "solid" in (a), and "the groundwork" and "construct" in (b). Based on our schematic understanding of a building, we compare the concrete attributes of a building with the abstract reasoning of an argument. The notion of SD and TD will be applied in some chapters in this book, such as Chapters 3, 4, 5, 7.

1.2.3. *Ahrens' (2002) Conceptual Mapping Model*

Based on Lakoff and Johnson's (1980) Traditional Conceptual Mapping, Ahrens (2002) further examines the mappings between the SD and the TD in terms of three subcategories: (a) entities, (b) qualities, and (c) functions.

The theory she proposes is the Conceptual Mapping Model (hereafter CMM).

Table 1.4 presents how a metaphor is analyzed by means of the CMM (Ahrens 2002: 276–279), which was revealed by progressing through a series of five steps. First, the informants generated all the examples about a proposed TD based on their linguistic intuition. Second, the informants work on the SD. That is, they brainstorm and answer the three sets of questions (1a)–(1c) by accessing the schematic knowledge of the SD in their mind. Third, the informants address the lexical correspondences between the SD and the TD by observing the entities, qualities, and functions that correspond between two domains by answering (2a)–(2c). Fourth, the informants map their schematic knowledge of the SD onto the interpretation of TD as questions (3a)–(3c) suggest. Finally, based on the most frequent lexical choices, the underlying reason of the metaphor is postulated by the mapping principle (hereafter MP).

Table 1.4. The Conceptual Mapping Model analytical procedures.

CMM Analytical Procedures	The Corresponding Schematic Knowledge
Real world knowledge about SD	(1a) What entities does the SD have? (1b) What qualities does the SD have? (1c) What does the SD do or what does the subject or the object do to or in the SD?
The lexical correspondences between the SD and the TD	(2a) What entities correspond between the SD and the TD? (2b) What qualities correspond between the SD and the TD? (2c) What functions correspond between the SD and the TD?
Actual mapping between the SD and the TD	(3a) What entities does the SD have mapped onto the TD? (3b) What qualities does the SD have mapped onto the TD? (3c) What does the SD do or what does the subject or the object do to or in the TD?
The postulation of the MP	What are the most frequent lexical choices?

The following examples (c)–(f) demonstrate Ahrens' (2002: 279–283) postulation of IDEA IS BUILDING in Mandarin by means of the CMM.

(c) *zhe4 ge li3 lun4 jia4 gou4 hen3 song1 san3*
這 個 理 論 架 構 很 鬆 散
'The framework of this theory is loose.'

(d) *ni3 de lun4 dian3 gen1 ji1 shi4 shen2 me*
你 的 論 點 根 基 是 什 麼
'What is the foundation of your argument?'

(e) *zhe4 qun2 wen2 ren2 zheng4 nu3 li4 jian4 gou4 yi2 tao4 li3 lun4*
這 群 文 人 正 努 力 建 構 一 套 理 論
'This group of scholars is working hard at constructing a theory.'

(f) *ta1 de si1 xiang3 jia4 gou4 kuai4 cheng2 xing2 le*
他 的 思 想 架 構 快 成 形 了
'His thought's framework is taking shape.'

During the first step, people access their schematic knowledge about the SD, buildings. For instance, a building is something that has a base, is strong when it is well built, and is a place people stay or live in.

Second, people address the lexical correspondences between the SD and the TD by observing the entities, qualities, and functions that motivate the mapping between two domains. For example, one of the primary entities that make up a building is its 'foundation' or 'base.' One of the qualities a building may have is its stability: i.e. strong and stable, or weak and unstable. And one of the functions a building has—in terms of something being built—is that they 'take shape,' and so on.

Third, people continue to categorize the attributes of the SD, such as foundation, stability, or construction, by specifying the lexical correspondences between the building and ideas into three categories: entities, qualities, and functions. For instance, in (c), *jia4 gou4* 架構 'framework' is classified under entities, and *song1 san3* 鬆散 'loose' is classified under qualities. In (d), *jian4 gou4* 建構 'build' is classified under functions.

Fourth, people formulate an underlying principle that contributes the conceptual mapping by designating the most frequent lexical choices. For example, that a building is an object that has a structure appears most frequently in the lexical correspondences of framework, foundation, layout or construct. Therefore, Ahrens (2002: 279) formulates the MP which states that: "idea is understood as building because buildings involve a (physical) structure and ideas involve an (abstract) structure."

The CMM works on the conceptual principle, aiming at the underlying reasoning that contributes to mapping from the SD onto the TD. The CMM is powerful because it gets us a step closer in our examination of the lexical correspondences and more vividly explains the reason that a certain SD, but not others, is picked. In other words, the CMM not only discusses the general mapping between the SD and the TD, but also examines the very basic level schematic knowledge involved with the SD and the TD. Later, we will demonstrate how we adopt these theories into the analysis of our data in the chapter topics on *huang2jin1* 'gold' (Chapter 3), *jin1qian2* 'money' (Chapter 4), stock market jargons of *gu3shi4* (Chapters 7 and 8), and *Geschäft* 'business' (Chapter 10).

1.2.4. *Lakoff and Turner's (1989) Great Chain of Being Metaphor*

Lakoff and Turner (1989: 160–213) propose that the Great Chain of Being Metaphor (hereafter GCB Metaphor) as the working mechanism explaining why and how a number of seemingly irrelevant conceptual metaphors fit together in a certain domain. It is also a hierarchy in which the corresponding conceptual metaphors are organized from top to bottom. It is divided into two kinds of conceptual hierarchies: (1) basic and (2) extended. Figure 1.2 (see p. 12) demonstrates the diversity between the basic GCB Metaphor and the extended GCB Metaphor.

The basic GCB Metaphor is defined by typical attributes and behaviors in a hierarchy, and its highest level reaches to humans. The extended GCB Metaphor spreads its metaphorical level from humans up to the relations of society, universe and god.

In the hierarchy system, it is implied that the higher level is superior to the lower level. That is to say, the human level is superior to the animal level by mental and character attributes. The animal level is superior to the three lower levels of plants, complex objects and natural physical things by their possessing all the attributes of the three lower levels. Further, at the same level, the lower entity can be conceptualized as the higher entity. On the other hand, the higher entity can also be understood metaphorically in terms of the lower entity.

A particular level of the GCB Metaphor hierarchy can also be used to conceptualize another kind of level. Kövecses (2002: 127–29) suggests that the society level can be characterized as "Abstract Complex Systems", including economic systems, careers, society, companies and all the related entities fitting into the concept of abstract complex systems. For instance, 'money talks' indicates that money is compared to a person,

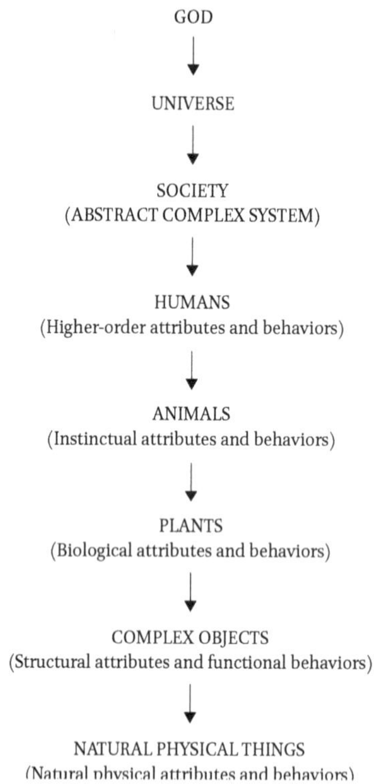

Figure 1.2. The hierarchy of Great Chain of Being Metaphor.

who has the power to speak. In other words, the GCB Metaphor provides us with a sketch of how a series of irrelevant conceptual metaphors are conceptualized with each other. It also reveals why the SDs and TDs can be constituted to form a cognitive hierarchy by people's perception. Further, it can allow us to better understand the entities' relationships within the hierarchy.

Above all, the GCB Metaphor helps us to gain insight into lay people's perception. Since the order of its components at each level is irreversible, the chain illustrates dominance and subordination. Beings or substances at the higher levels are always superior to those at the lower ones (Shao 2008: 75–76). As a consequence, the GCB Metaphor illustrates the relationship of domination or subordination. In this viewpoint, if the beings at the lower level are attributed in terms of those in the higher level, they are upgraded or complimented, while "it may be abused if they become the TD of the beings at the lower level" as Sun (2009: 31–) has stated.

GCB Metaphor will be used in the analysis of chapters 4, 5, 7 and 8.

1.2.5. *Fauconnier and Turner's (1998) Conceptual Integration Network*

This section presents the Conceptual Integration Network model (hereafter CIN) that will be applied in the chapter on *yin2* 'silver' (Chapter 5). The network model proposed by Fauconnier and Turner (1998: 142) "is concerned with online, dynamic cognitive work that people do to construct meaning for the local purposes of thought and action." It focuses on conceptual projection as an instrument of people's speech. Fauconnier and Turner (1998: 137) propose the CIN, "the input structures, generic structures, and blend structures in the network are all called mental spaces." The mental spaces go through two processes: the steps for process 1 are composition, completion and elaboration; the step for process 2, compression, is also called blending. In the following, we adopt the example and the explanation from their study to clarify the original necessary elements and processes of the CIN. Consider a classic puzzle of inferential problem-solving:

> A Buddhist monk begins at dawn one day walking up a mountain, reaching the summit at sunset, where he meditates for several days until one dawn when he begins to walk back down to the foot of the mountain, which he reaches at sunset. Making no assumptions about his starting or stopping point or about his pace during the trip, there is a place on the path which he occupies at the same hour of the day on the two separate journeys (Koestler 1964).

In the example of the monk, there are four mental spaces, as Fauconnier and Turner (1998: 137–138) explain: the two inputs (going up the mountains and going down the mountains), the generic (moving individual, his position, a path linking to the summit of the mountain, motion in direction), and the blend (each of the trips going up and down mountains projects to the same single mountain). Fauconnier and Turner (1998: 142) also propose that "background frames are recruited to build these mental spaces, such as the background frame of two people approaching each other on a path. This is a minimal network. Networks in other cases of conceptual integration may have more input spaces and may even have multiple blended spaces."

According to Fauconnier and Turner (1998), the CIN has two process stages. Stage 1 consists of three operational elements: composition, completion and elaboration. In Stage 1, the CIN requires at least one element before reaching to Stage 2. Blending is the second stage for the CIN. Fauconnier and Turner give a composition example in the monk riddle and they (1998: 144) state that "the composition yields two travelers making two journeys. Fusion is one kind of composition. Counterparts may be brought into the blend as separate elements or as a fused element." In the example of the monk, the two days in different inputs fused into one single day as can be drawn in Figure 1.3:

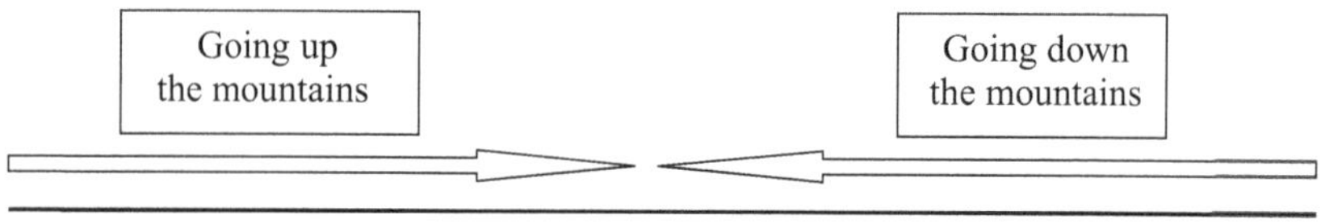

Figure 1.3. The composition process in Stage 1.

Fauconnier and Turner (1998: 144) explain that blends sign up a large background conceptual structure and knowledge but the language users do not recognize it and so "a composed structure is completed with another structure". As for realization in the monk example, "the structure achieved through composition is completed by the scenario of two people journeying toward each other on a path, which yields an encounter" (Fauconnier and Turner 1998: 144), as Figure 1.4 shows:

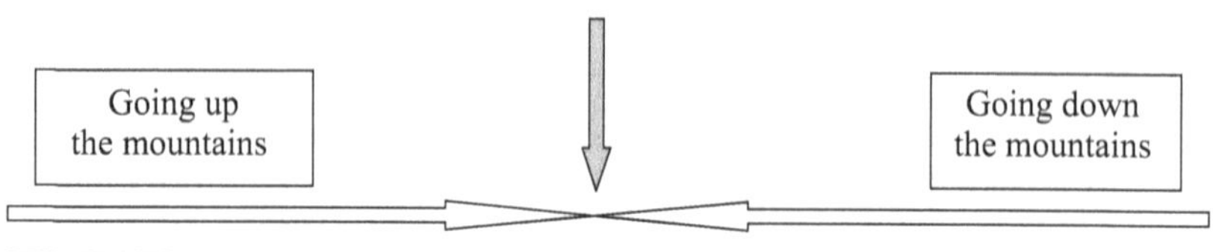

Figure 1.4. The completion process in Stage 1.

Fauconnier and Turner (1998: 144) also go on to elaborate that "we can 'run the blend' indefinitely: for example, the monks might meet each other and have a philosophical discussion about the concept of identity. Blended spaces can become extremely elaborate."

In Stage 2, a further space, the blend, which is projected onto from the two input mental spaces, is formed. Figure 1.5 shows how we conceptualized the example of the monk. "The two input spaces have two journeys completely separated in time; the blend has two simultaneous journeys" (Fauconnier and Turner 1998: 143).

As indicated by Figure 1.5, when the contexts in different mental spaces are composed, completed, and elaborated, blending occurs and conceptual metaphors are generated.

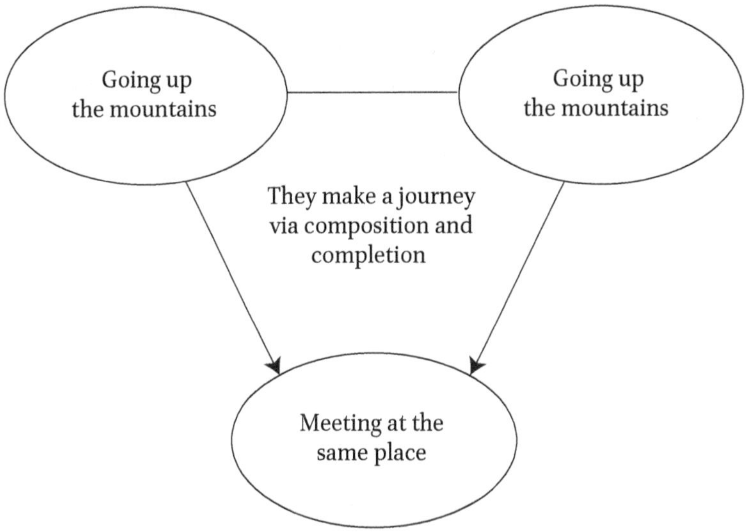

Figure 1.5. Blending in Stage 2.

1.2.6. *Hopper's (1987) Emergent Grammar*

Early theorization of Emergent Grammar can be traced back to Hopper (1987). It is believed that grammar together with speech is regarded as a kind of transient social phenomenon; grammar influences its structure which is seen as "a spreading of systematicity from individual words, phrases, and small sets" to become "emergent" (Hopper 1987: 142). Hopper defines Emergent Grammar as "a grammar which is not abstractly formulated and abstractly represented, but always anchored in the specific concrete form of an utterance" and further explains that "grammar is what results when formulas are re-arranged, or dismantled and re-assembled, in different ways" (Hopper 1987: 145). In addition, Hopper says that there are three doctrines which distinguish Emergent Grammar from A Priori Grammar. One is that there is not a clear boundary between grammatical or emergent regularity and rhetorical or formulaic regularity.

Another is grammaticalization, that is, Emergent Grammar does not present grammar that exists but grammar that changes (Hopper 1987). Additionally, Emergent Grammar provides a deeper understanding of modes of universal linguistic rules and grammaticalization to form discourses by examining the high frequency of clauses (Hopper 1987). Based on Hopper's theory, Emergent Grammar seems to be a good approach to explaining language. In sum, the phenomenon of blurring regularity, grammaticalization and the frequently appearing sentences in language shows that grammar is not fixed but always changing.

Emergent syntax is used as a tool to understand language function as well as complicated semantics (Schoenemann 1999). Tao's (2003) study is consistent with Schoenemann's claim. Tao (2003) provides three examples in light of Hopper's Emergent Grammar to prove semantics is also not fixed. The following paragraphs will demonstrate the principal claims of Hopper's Emergent Grammar and the examples of semantic lexical expressions provided by Tao (2003).

Tao (2003: 839–40) says that according to the explanation in the dictionary, the term *chu1chai1* 出差 'on business' refers to "an out-of-town activity related to business or industry assignments". However, in practical discourse, it can be regarded as "taking a tent, and a sleeping bag, and then you go out, you just sleep outdoors". The definition of *chu1 chai1* is rhetorical or formulaic, while the new meaning of *chu1 chai1* added to practical discourse is emergent. Both of these are acceptable, therefore it can prove that there is no fixed interpretation of the semantics of the expression due to the blurring line of the regularity. Figure 1.6 shows the emergent process of *chu1chai1*.

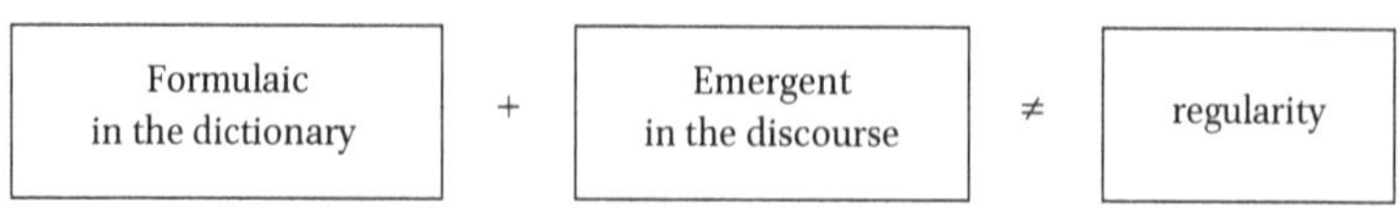

Figure 1.6. The emergent process of *chu1chai1*.

The formulaic meaning of *chu1chai1* found in the dictionary and the emergent explanation of *chu1chai1* in the discourse coexist in communication. People accept both usages in their daily life. Therefore, the line of the regularity becomes blurred.

On the other hand, the development of *shuo1* 說 'to say' exemplifies grammaticalization. At first, *shuo1* serves as a speech act verb to indicate the speech activity and a mental activity verb to indicate the act of thinking. Gradually, it loses its content meaning and serves as a quotative, a linking element or a complementizer (Tao 2003). The changing process of *shuo1* is so-called grammaticalization and shows that the meaning of a linguistic lexeme is not always the same and could develop gradually and be classified into different grammatical groups. Figure 1.7 shows the grammaticalization of *shuo1* 說 'to say.'

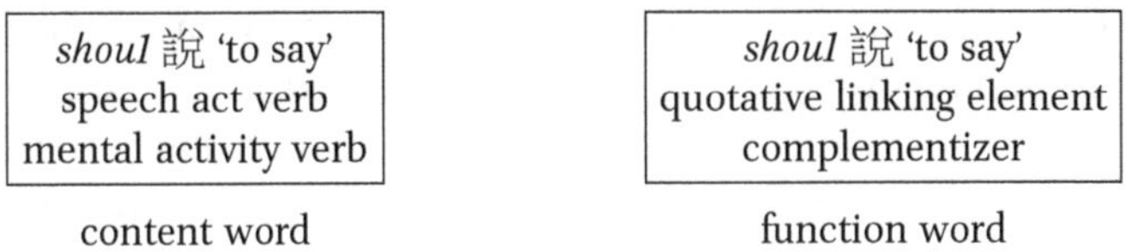

Figure 1.7. The grammaticalization of *shuo1*.

Figure 1.7 shows that *shuo1* is a content verb when serving as a speech act verb or a mental activity verb; that is, it has meaning. However, when developing toward grammaticalization, *shuo1* gradually becomes a function word, and its grammatical function in the context is much more emphasized than its meaning.

Finally, the frequency of similar expressions collocating with other terms can differentiate synonyms and show that synonyms which share a similar concept are emergent because they have a distinct concordance. Examples of the concordance of three synonyms, *chu1xian4* 出現 'to appear,' *chan3sheng1* 產生 'to produce' and *fa1sheng1* 發生 'to occur' can be found in Tao (2003).

As a result, Emergent Grammar can be applied not only to syntax, but also to semantic lexical expressions. Chapter 6 adopts Tao's (2003) method to interpret three quasi-synonyms of the same concept of 'poverty' from the perspective of Emergent Grammar.

1.2.7. *Niles and Pease's (2001) Suggested Upper Merged Ontology*

Suggested upper merged ontology (SUMO hereafter) is a superior ontological knowledge which is used for linguistic research. Niles and Pease (2001) state that Sumo serves as a foundational ontological knowledge to help define linguistic items. This section describes the extended research tool SUMO. In order to get the whole picture of it, Lakoff and Johnson's (1980) conceptual metaphor and McGlone's interpretation of Lakoff and Johnson's approach are introduced.

Metaphors are ubiquitous and present in language to help people explore conceptual mechanism (Lakoff and Johnson 1980). Lakoff and Johnson (2003: 4) give common usages in daily life such as: *your claims are indefensible, I demolished his argument* and *he attacked every point in my argument* to prove the existence of the conceptual metaphor ARGUMENT IS WAR. The above examples show that the words *indefensible, demolished* and *attacked* related to war and are used to describe an argument. Metaphorical expressions are understood in the human conceptual system. In other words, conceptual metaphors can reflect how people think. According to McGlone (1996), the major principle of conceptual metaphor is the correspondent relationship between the abstract TD and the concrete SD. That is to say, when discussing conceptual metaphors, the TD made up of people's abstract ideas and the corresponding concrete SD are two important elements to be concerned. McGlone's (1996) interpretation of conceptual metaphor is shown in Figure 1.8.

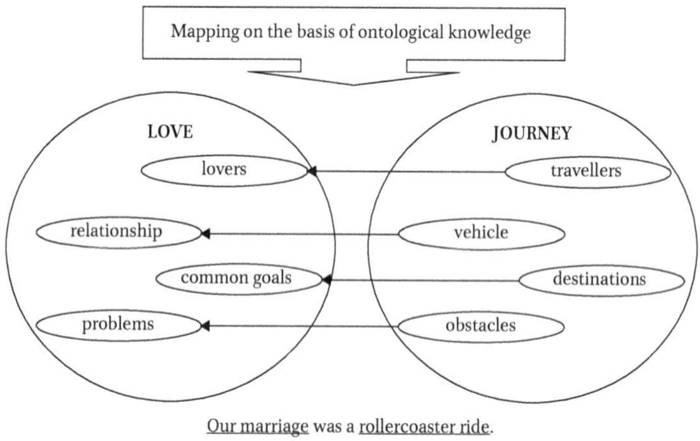

Figure 1.8. Metaphorical mapping process.

The example provided by McGlone (1996), OUR MARRIAGE WAS A ROLLERCOASTER RIDE explains the metaphorical mapping process based on ontological knowledge. The lexical expression *journey*, which is a concrete idea including four sub-concepts, *travelers, vehicle, destinations* and *obstacles*, in the SD is applied to understanding the abstract idea *love* in the TD. The concept of 'love' also has four related sub-concepts, *lovers, relationships, common goals* and *problems*, and each sub-concept respectively shares the similarity with other sub-concepts in the TD. Mapping should be regarded as "a fixed pattern of ontological correspondences across domains and may, or may not, be applied to a SD knowledge structure or a SD lexical item" (Lakoff 1993: 210). For example, *lovers* in the TD can be interpreted as human beings the same as *travelers* in the SD. That is, *lovers* in the TD have the same ontological knowledge related to humans with *travelers* in the SD.

In this example, the relationship referring to our marriage in the TD is the abstract concept that needs to be concretized. The concrete idea, a rollercoaster serving as a vehicle, is the SD mapping to the TD. According to the ontological knowledge, *relationship* belongs to the subclass of the intentional process that involves interactions between cognitive agents, while *VEHICLE*, a kind of transportation device, is a device which serves as the instrument in a transportation process to carry the patient of the process from one point to another. The similar ontological element, process, in these two domains explains their mapping connection. We conceptualize marriage as a kind of exciting process that can be experienced by taking a rollercoaster ride.

People understand abstract ideas like time, states and so on in our daily life by cross-domain mappings (Lakoff 1993). That is, people take advantage of mapping correspondences between the SD and the TD to understand complicated ideas. Based on this, Ahrens (2002) provides the CMM as a tool to further analyze how the metaphorical expressions in terms of the entities, qualities and functions map between an SD and a TD. At first, people figure out one concept in the TD and then classify the corresponding examples in the SD into several groups on the basis of similarity. Different SDs are mapped onto the same target concept. An ontology-based knowledge representation is used as a tool to clarify and restrain the scope of the SD in the conceptual model SUMO, which is advantageous to comprehending knowledge by reasoning automatically (Ahrens, Chung and Huang 2003).

Gong (2009: 6) explores "how metaphors are used in corpus data and what mapping theory can account for the distribution of metaphor patterns realized in corpus data." The TD related to the idea is the one she is concerned about and SUMO serves as one tool to help explore the verbs and nouns associated with the idea in the TD. Figure 1.9 shows the ontology of *ji1chu3* 基礎 'foundation' and *zhang3wo4* 掌握 'hold' that collocate with *li3lun4* 理論 'theory.' The former word *ji1chu3* is classified into entities while the later *zhang3wo4* is classified into qualities.

(A)	(B)
Ontology	**Ontology**
SUMO / OBJECTS	SUMO / QUALITIES
Superclass(es)	**Superclass(es)**
entity	entity
physical	abstract
object	attribute
self-connected object	relational attribute
corpuscular object	normative attribute
artifact	subjective assessment

Figure 1.9. The ontology of *ji1chu3* and *zhang3wo4* (Gong 2009: 6).

Based on SUMO, though the noun *ji1chu3* and the verb *zhang3wo4* both collocate with the concept of 'idea,' they are classified into different groups of the ontology. The lexical expressions *ji1chu3* and *zhang3wo4* in the SD which map onto the same complex concept of 'idea' can be further examined and determined in terms of SUMO. Ahrens, Chung and Huang (2003: 37) state that SUMO is suitable for both Chinese and English data. We also infer that SUMO can help clarify how people conceptualize the hidden reasons behind their concepts. In this book, the chapter topics on *pin2qiong2* 'poverty' in Chapter 6 and the collocation of *gu3* 'stock' and *shi4* 'market' in Chapter 8).

1.2.8. *Fillmore and Atkins' (1992) Frame Semantics*

Fillmore and Atkins (1992) put forth Frame Semantics. They said that it links to people's comprehension process. That is, how we understand meanings in context. Lexical meaning and grammatical characteristics "both with information about related words and with our general cultural knowledge about the world" (Goddard 1998: 69) work together in our comprehension process. The meaning of a word can be understood only against a background frame of experience, beliefs, or practices that "motivate the concept that the word encodes" (Fillmore and Atkins 1992). They give this set of verbs as an example: *buy, sell, charge, pay, cost,* and *spend.* To understand any of these verbs, we must understand a complete 'commercial transaction frame':

> in which one person acquires control or possession of something from a second person, by agreement, as a result of surrendering to that person a sum of money. The needed background requires an understanding of property ownership, a money economy, implicit contract, and a great deal more (Fillmore and Atkins 1992: 78).

In other words, this frame serves as a complex yet compact linguistic base for words such as *buy, sell,* and *charge* in a given society. People lacking this socioculturally determined linguistic frame would not understand the meaning of *buying* and *selling*; Tarzan, for example, would have such difficulty. Stated otherwise, it is through the compositionality of the concepts in the associated words and the background schematic knowledge of the society that we comprehend the words and expressions used in daily life. For example, to understand the three FLE verbs *kaufen* 'buy,' *verkaufen* 'sell' and *bezahlen* 'pay' in German also requires a complete commercial transaction frame in speakers' minds. In other words, the frame defines the commercial verbs and enables us to go on investigating the concepts they carry which are seemingly outside economic ideas. This approach will be applied in the analysis of the three financial verbs, *kaufen* 'buy,' *verkaufen* 'sell' and *bezahlen* 'pay' in German newspaper usage in Chapter 9.

1.3. Summary

This chapter has presented the data sources for analysis and theories to be applied in this book. Kövecses (2002: 6) defines metaphors succinctly as "a set of mappings." A metaphor is recognized when the correspondences between the SD and the TD are identified. Ahrens' (2002) CMM will be applied in Chapters 3, 4, 7, 8, and 10. The GCB Metaphor (Lakoff and Turner 1989) is another cognitive base that not only points out the levels, definitions and assigned features of each substance or being in our world, but also provides the present book a cognitive framework for how people evaluate or attribute an FLE as it is used to construe our finding in Chapters 4, 5, 7, and 8. The CIN (Fauconnier and Turner 1998) give us a concrete image for the abstract conceptual blending that occurs in our mind, which will be adopted to analyze the data in Chapter 5. Hopper's (1987) Emergent Grammar is a tool to understand a word or an expression in terms of its language function or its complicated semantics. By observing how the meanings of a word develop syntactically and semantically as Emergent Grammar is applied in Chapter 6 to observe how the word is interpreted. Another cognitive theory is SUMO (Niles and Pease 2001), which is the superior ontological knowledge, and is applied in Chapters 6 and 8. With SUMO, linguistic items can be defined and a conceptual metaphor can be generated. Frame Semantics (Fillmore and Atkins 1992) is a complex yet compact linguistic base for a set of words to make sense, such as *buy, sell,* and *charge,* and is adopted in Chapter 9 for it defines the commercial verbs and enables us to interpret the concepts appearing in non-economic ideas.

In short, metaphor is the access to comprehending one thing in terms of another in a systematic way. With the seven theories introduced above, how Mandarin and German speakers perceive and evaluate FLEs will be illustrated. The analysis of the data and the discussions of the categorizations of the FLEs are demonstrated in the following chapters.

CHAPTER TWO

LITERATURE REVIEW

Shelley Ching-yu Hsieh

This chapter introduces several previous research works on the following topics: studies of Mandarin phraseology, fixed expressions revealing modes of thought, studies within economic contexts, and FLEs showing cognition, society and culture.

2.1. Studies on Phraseology

There has long been research interest in Mandarin phraseology. Some delve into the etymology (e.g., Chen 1991; Yao and Mao 2006), some focus on specific classic masterpieces (e.g., Lin 1984; Hong 2001; Tsai 2004), some compile dictionary works (e.g., Shih 1979; Zhou 1994; Wang 2010), and some have performed linguistic analysis of Mandarin as well as comparisons with other languages (e.g., Fillmore, Kay and O'Connor 1988; Nunberg, Sag and Wasow 1994; Horn 2003; Lien 2007; Hsieh 2009a).

When attempting to illuminate a national culture through an analysis of language, certain types of expressions and phrases are particularly useful. Colorful expressions show evidence of conceptual thinking and cultural values. For example, the Mandarin *shu4yu4jing4er2feng1bu4 zhi3, zi3yu4yang3 er2qin1bu2dai4* 樹欲靜而風不止，子欲養而親不待 'tree-desire-stillness yet-wind-not-stop, son-desires-raise yet-parents-not-remain' voices a son's regret at not being able to take care of his parents after they are deceased, and shows the value of filial piety in Chinese culture. As *Ren2sheng1bu4du2shu1, huo2zhebu4ru2zhu1* 人生不讀書，活著不如豬 'people-life-not-read-book, live-not-as-pig' bluntly states that people who do not seek education (read) are almost sub-human (living as a pig), reflecting Mandarin speaking society's great respect for education and learning. Popular expressions like these serve as almost a magic window into a culture's values and living philosophy, and with this idea in mind Liu and Qin (2001) compare Mandarin Chinese and English expressions and attempt to use the knowledge they glean in the process to promote better understanding and communication between these two peoples. Similarly, Hsieh and Kolodkina (2011) prepared a study on expressions of emotion in three languages with the purpose of improving cross-linguistic communication.

The relationship of language and culture is one of the most investigated issues because language is closely connected to the way we think, the way we behave and the way we cope with society and the world (Kramsch 1998: 79). On the other hand, "the culture of everyday practices draws on the culture of shared history and traditions" (Kramsch 1998: 7). Vervaeke and Kennedy's research (1996: 278–79) on *Metaphors and Thought* states that "... a core concept of people controls and guides our selection and generation of metaphors to suit the fleeting purposes of the moment." That is to say, metaphors, a rhetoric, show people's thoughts and concepts. Hsieh (2006a) compares fixed expressions involving animals in Mandarin Chinese and German and in this manner reveals Mandarin speakers' holistic mode of thinking in contrast to German speakers' individualistic mode of thinking. Further, Hsieh, Lien and Meier (2005) focus on *flower*-related idiomatic expressions and find that people observe and perceive the world from different standpoints and express different concepts in their minds. Chinese tend to show visual perspective of the observation of the world in their language, while the Germans present more functional views.

2.2. Studies on FLEs

Within economic contexts, studies have been conducted related to FLEs from various perspectives (Smith 1995; Boers 2000; Charteris-Black 2000; Charteris-Black and Ennis 2001; Charteris-Black and Musolff 2003; Chung, Ahrens and Huang 2003; Chung, Ahrens and Sung 2003; Chung, Huang and Ahrens 2003; Chung, Ahrens and Huang 2004; Chung 2008; Henderson 2000; Schmidt 2002; White 2003; Xu 2006; Šeškauskienė and Urbonaitė 2007; Morris, Sheldon, Ames and Young 2007; Tseng and Hsieh 2007; Tseng and Hsieh 2008; Hsieh and Huang 2008; Huang and Hsieh 2008; Huang and Hsieh 2009). These research works do not aim at the financial meanings but concentrate on people's thinking behind the FLEs. They show evidence that although economy is a complicated idea, observing the use of metaphors or preferences for FLEs, we can understand the cognitive, social and cultural aspects of the language users.

The attributes or functions of the FLEs influence their metaphorical extension as construed by White (2003) since economy is the core of an industrialized society in which mechanical processes play a crucial role in industrial manufacturing and transportation. Economy in this case is perceived to be a dynamic mechanical process. The research of White (2003) demonstrates a lexicalized mainstream of an economic concept and provides evidence as to how humans interpret concepts through FLEs. Khalil (1998: 29) also notes that the "ecosystem" metaphor shows the order of markets and that is different from the order of organizations. Corning (1995) examines a set of FLEs in English and tries to determine whether these expressions are metaphors which help abstract reasoning or are merely new collocations.

Many research works focus on the use of conceptual metaphors of FLEs. The metaphorical interpretations of FLEs are influenced by the situations the language users are exposed to. This notion is demonstrateed in Charteris-Black and Musolff's work (2003) where the euro was investigated during the period the euro lost its value in the market. The research result shows that the euro is perceived passively. Obviously, the metaphorical perception and interpretations of the euro are influenced by economic situations. Likewise, White (2003) presents that economy is the juxtaposition of the natural and mechanical process. It is natural to construe economy as animated since the growth of organisms is signified by increase. Economy associated with growth gives rise to ECONOMY AS A MECHANICAL PROCESS for growth denotes a dynamic state. Henderson (1982), Resche (2001), Skorczynska and Deignan (2006) also delve into conceptual metaphors related to economics.

On the other hand, Šeškauskienėand and Urbonaitė (2007) point out that when describing political or economic difficulties, health metaphors, especially diseases or recovery, are comprised. Alejo (2010: 1139) quotes the central metaphors in macroeconomics as pointed out by Bradford DeLong (1999: 6): (1) hydraulic metaphors, related to the model of the circular flow, (2) the market describes the different 'processes of exchange,' (3) the concept of equilibrium, and (4) the use of graphs to stand for algebraic questions.

Alejo (2010: 1140) categorized conceptual metaphors occurring in economic texts from various linguistcs researchers. There are four types. The first type is THE ECONOMY IS A MACHINE (Boers 2000a; Resche 2002; Skorczynska and Deignan 2006; Boers and Demecheleer 1997; White 2003) as we can see in the phrases like *fine-tuning economic tools, economic levers,* and *tighten the screws on the economy*. The second type is THE ECONOMY IS A LIVING ORGANISM (Charteris-Black 2000; Resche 2002; Boers and Demecheleer 1997; Boers 2000b; López-Maestre 2000; White 2003).

Phrases indicating this concept are *economic growth*, a *healthy economy*, and *breakdown*. The third type is BUSINESS IS WAR/TRADE IS WAR (Boers and Demecheleer 1997; Boers 2002a; López-Maestre 2000; Charteris-Black and Ennis 2001; Eubanks 1999). These metaphorical concepts are expressed by *economic arm-twisting*, *the fight for market share*, and to *combat fraud*. The fourth type is BUSINESS IS A JOURNEY/THE PATH METAPHOR (Boers and Demecheleer 1997; López-Maestre 2000; Eubanks 1999) These metaphors are exemplified by *move toward privatization, the economy has shifted*, and *turning point*.

Social-linguistic phenomena are observed in the belief that it can benefit cross-cultural communication. Keesing (1981), an anthropologist, points out that culture is an ideational system, which means it is a pattern of the social behavior and social communication of a specific social group. Since culture comprises a value system, thinking, language, paralanguage, and presupposition (Stern 1993: 209; Nostrand 1978), different languages give their preferences in metaphorical reasoning. For example, Tendahl and Gibbs (2008) examine the language use in English and Lithuanian political and economic discourse. English has more health metaphors whereas Lithuanian tends to use specific diseases instead of a general character.

Though we see that culture-specific concepts are comprised in language, culture is a generalization, and it is almost impossible for two individuals to have the same perception of any given culture. In previous studies, similarity and difference of FLEs are exemplified cross linguistically. For example, Fukuda (2009) examines the usability of metaphors by comparing US dollars and Japanese Yen in the current economic conditions, presenting that US dollars, which are collocated with verbs, adjectives and adverbs, are only found in the metaphor s as mechanical processes. Such linguistic phenomenon is however not observed in Yen. Chung (2008) incorporates frequency counts into a combined semantic-grammatical analysis of 'market' metaphors and proposes a quantitative approach to compare these types of metaphors in three different language communities toward the economy of their countries. Moreover, in the work of Charteris-Black and Ennis (2001), economy is attributed in terms of a state of mental health in Spanish, whereas English prefers physical health. Likewise, the euro in English participates in physical combat as a battered hero, and such linguistic expressions are not found in German data. Chung, Ahrens and Sung (2003) examine STOCK MARKET IS OCEAN WATER in Chinese, English and Spanish. They construe that stock market is conceptualized differently in the three languages: Chinese emphasizes upward movement; English highlights the safety and calmness of the ocean; however, no systematic SD is discovered in Spanish, implying that its emphasis is on the unpredictability (Chung, Ahrens and Sung 2003). In other words, the same metaphor in different languages may employ different operations and cross-linguistic analysis of FLEs is practical and beneficial for cross-cultural communication.

From the above, we see various aspects of studies on phraseology, the related modes of thought, the investigation on FLEs within the domain of cognition, society and culture. People's cognitive and cultural backgrounds display important parts of their conceptualizations in phraseology such as FLEs. However, a more systematic research on FLEs in Mandarin as well a comparison with German is still in need. This book is conducted for this purpose.

PART ONE

IN MANDARIN CHINESE

CHAPTER THREE

THE METAPHORICAL USE OF *HUANG2JIN1* 'GOLD'

May Hsin-mei Huang & Shelley Ching-yu Hsieh

3.0. Introduction

The present study concentrates on the metaphorical reasoning of *huang2jin1* 黃金 'gold' with the aim at (1) the metaphorical process of *huang2jin1*, (2) the cognitive or cultural values that occur in the realizations and interpretations of *huang2jin1*. It is divided into three parts. First, we present the metaphorical extensions of *huang2jin1* in 3.1 by anaylzing data collected from *Academia Sinica Balanced Corpus Mandarin Chinese, Mandarin Chinese Knowledge Network, Lin Yutang's Chinese-English Dictionary of Modern Usage*, and *Mandarin Chinese Flexible Usages Dictionary* (Zhou and Qiu 2004) in terms of Ahrens' (2002) CMM. The CMM not merely analyzes the mapping between the SD and the TD. Section 3.2 further postulates an MP for each conceptual metaphor. With the MPs, we can demonstrate the conceptualization of *huang2jin1*[1] and unravel people's different perceptions, expectations, and language specific cultural values mattering in metaphorical depiction. Finally, the chapter has an discussion in section 3.3.

3.1. The Metaphorical Extensions of *Huang2jin1*

The section presents the analysis of the data in terms of Kövecses' (2002) interpretations of metaphor and Ahrens' (2002) CMM. *Huang2jin1* is found to be the SD which explains other abstract ideas. In addition, the conceptual correspondences between *huang2jin1* and its TDs are *huang2jin1*'s salient attributes. However, they are not denoted but inferred. Take *jin1 kou3* 金口 'the emperor's statements' for example. The conceptual

[1] In the following, we will omit Chinese characters and English translations to save space when they are the chapter focus, like *huang2jin1* 黃金 'gold' in this chapter, or when the examples have just been mentioned, such as the *jin1 kou3* 金口 'the emperor's statements' on the next page.

correspondence between *huang2jin1* and the emperor in *jin1 kou3* is the 'nobility' of *huang2jin1*. Nobility is not literally denoted but implied by *huang2jin1* as nobility is one of its salient attributes.

Therefore, *huang2jin1* will be analyzed in terms of its salient attributes. For example, when interpreting the metaphorical extensions of *huang2jin1*, we first present the conceptual correspondence, which is the attribute which contributes to the mapping, and then categorize the conceptual correspondence in terms of the CMM. Overall, eight clusters of metaphorical expressions are found in the present chapter: (1) Chinese emperor, (2) solidity, (3) eternity, (4) word, (5) literary work, (6) excellence, (7) perfection and (8) opportunity.

3.1.1. *CHINESE EMPEROR IS* HUANG2JIN1

The Chinese emperor is conceptualized as *huang2jin1* as shown in examples (1a)–(1b). Examples (1a), *jin1 kou3* 金口 'the emperor's statements,'[2] and (1b), *jin1 zhi1 yu4 ye4* 金枝玉葉 'the descendants of the royal family,' are the metaphorical expressions generated from *huang2jin1*. The nobility of *huang2jin1* is the conceptual correspondence and is the quality that corresponds between the SD and TD.

(1) noble: Quality
  a. *jin1 kou3* 金口
    gold-moth = 'the emperor's statements'
  b. *jin1 zhi1 yu4 ye4* 金枝玉葉
    gold-branch-jade-leave = 'the descendants of the royal family'

The emphasis on the nobility of the Chinese emperor allows us to postulate the MP.

(I) MP for CHINESE EMPEROR IS *HUANG2JIN1: Huang2jin1* is compared to the Chinese emperor because *huang2jin1* is a noble metal, which is metal of value, and the Chinese emperor who is the one with all the wealth in his kingdom, is highly valued and is thought to be at the very top of the world.

Many linguists assert that metaphor has to do with culture, e.g., Gibbs 1999; Su 2000; Charteris-Black and Ennis 2001; Charteris-Black and Musolff 2003;

[2] *Jin1 kou3* 金口 'gold-mouth' has two meanings: the Chinese emperor or a precious statement. The present exmpale here refers to the Chinese emperor (Zhou & Qiu 2004).

Chung, Ahrens and Sung 2003; Chung, Ahrens and Huang 2003; Deignan and Potter 2004; Ungerer and Schmid 2006. Here, the conceptualization of the Chinese emperor has cultural significance. First, *huang2jin1* and the Chinese emperor are assimilated to each other since they both represent wealth and power. *Huang2jin1* with its financial status is recognized as wealth and power since historically it was used as currency in ancient times, e.g. the Chin Dynasty. The Chinese emperor as the only lord of his people in Chinese society was born to have power and wealth. Since it is representative of wealth and power, *huang2jin1* and the Chinese emperor are comparable.

Second, both *huang2jin1* and the Chinese emperor are highly valued. *Huang2jin1* is a noble and valuable metal. For centuries, up until the late 20th century, the Chinese emperor was at the very top of Chinese society. It is obvious that the Chinese emperor has a significant social and cultural status in Chinese society. As a result of being highly valued, *huang2jin1* and the Chinese emperor are assimilated to each other. This cultural specific value is observed in the materials used in palace-building. The palace where the Chinese emperor conducts political affairs with his courtiers was *jin1 luan2 dian4* 金鑾殿 'gold-tinkle bell-palace' which is made of *huang2jin1* 'gold.' So far it has been suggested that metaphors, the significance of which will be addressed in later sections, have much to do with culture.

3.1.2. *SOLIDITY IS* HUANG2JIN1

Solidity is conceptualized as *huang2jin1* in examples (2a)–(2b). Example (2a), *gu4 ruo4 jin1 tang1* 固若金湯 'impregnable,' is the metaphorical expression. In this expression *huang2jin1* is a hard, solid metal. Solidity is the conceptual correspondence and is the quality that corresponds between the SD and TD. Example (2b), *jin1 cheng2 tang1 chi2* 金城湯池 'impregnable wall and moat,' is another example in which solidity is the quality that corresponds between the SD and TD.

(2) solid: Quality
   a. *gu4 ruo4 jin1 tang1* 固若金湯
      solid-like-gold-hot water = 'impregnable'
   b. *jin1 cheng2 tang1 chi2* 金城湯池
      gold-city-hot water-pool = 'impregnable wall and moat'

The emphasis on solidity allows us to postulate the MP.

(II) MP for solidity is *HUANG2JIN1: Huang2jin1* is compared to solidity because *huang2jin1* as a metal is solid and hard by nature.

3.1.3. *ETERNITY IS* HUANG2JIN1

Eternity is conceptualized as *huang2jin1* in examples (3a)–(3b). Example (3a), *jin1 shi2 zhi1 gong1* 金石之功 'everlasting exploit,' is the metaphorical expression. Because *huang2jin1* is a stable chemical element, it is the conceptual correspondence that contributes the mapping between eternity and *huang2jin1*. Stability here is identified as the quality that corresponds between the SD and TD. Example (3b), *jin1 lan2 zhi1 jiao1* 金蘭之交[3] 'durable relationship,' is another example in which the stability of gold is the quality that corresponds between the SD and TD.

(3) constant: Quality
 a. *<u>jin1</u> shi2 zhi1 gong1* <u>金</u>石之功
  <u>gold</u>-stone-zhi-exploit = 'everlasting exploit'
 b. *<u>jin1</u> lan2 zhi1 jiao1* <u>金</u>蘭之交
  <u>gold</u>-orchid-zhi-relationship = 'close and intimate friendship'

The emphasis on stability allows us to postulate the MP.

(III) MP for ETERNITY IS *HUANG2JIN1: Huang2jin1* is compared to eternity because *huang2jin1* is a stable, unchanging chemical element.

3.1.4. *WORD IS* HUANG2JIN1

Words are conceptualized as *huang2jin1* in examples (4a)–(4b). Example (4a), *yi1 yan2 qian1 jin1* 一言千金 'a solemn promise' is the metaphorical expression. Because *huang2jin1* is a noble metal, it is precious. This preciousness, which is the conceptual correspondence, is the quality that contributes the mapping between words and *huang2jin1*. Example (4b), *jin1 yu4 liang2 yan2* 金玉良言 'precious and beneficial statement,' is another example in which preciousness is the quality that corresponds between the SD and TD.

---

[3] For the difference between Mandarin spoken in Taiwan and in People's Republic of China, here is one example. When referring to close and intimate friends, it is *bai4ba3hi* 拜把子 'worship-handle-suffix' or *jie2bai4* 結拜 'bear-worship' whereas Taiwan Mandarin may use *jin1lan2zhi1jiao1* 金蘭之交 'gold-orchid-zhi- relationship,' *jie2bai4* 結拜 'bear-worship' or *huan4tie3* 換帖 'change-document.'

(4) precious: Quality
  a. *yi1 yan2 qian1 jin1* 一言千金
     one-statement-thousand-gold = 'a solemn promise, which deserves thousands of money'
  b. *jin1 yu4 liang2 yan2* 金玉良言
     gold-jade-good-statement = 'precious and beneficial statement'

The emphasis on the preciousness of statements allows us to postulate the MP.

(IV) MP for WORD IS *HUANG2JIN1: Huang2jin1* is compared to words because *huang2jin1* is a precious, noble metal, and because one's statement in Chinese culture needs to be truthful. We can infer that a person's statement is thought of as a kind of preciousness.

In line with 3.1.1 (CHINESE EMPEROR IS *HUANG2JIN1*), WORD IS *HUANG2JIN1* reveals cultural values. A cultural preference can be observed in the following examples. First, the Chinese word *xin4* 信 'trustworthiness' is composed of two Chinese radicals *ren2* 人 'people' and *yan2* 言 'word.' This word formation suggests that what people state should be reliable and credible, highlighting the quality of a person's words. This idea was supported by Confucius, who claimed that *ren2 er2 wu2 xin4 bu4 zhi1 qi2 ke3 ye3* 人而無信不知其可也 "person-but-without-credit-no-know-it-can-also = people can achieve nothing if they are not faithful to their words." This utterance clearly illustrates the importance of one's words, suggesting that Mandarin speakers place great emphasis on the truthfulness of one's statement. Moreover, *jun1 wu2 xi4 yan2* 君無戲言 'emperor-no-play-word = the emperor's words should be sincere and earnest' indicates that even the emperor should commit to what he says. Also, *da4 zhang4 fu1 yi4 yan2 ji4 chu1 si4 ma3 nan2 zhui1* 大丈夫一言既出駟馬難追 'big-husband-once-say-already-out-four-horse-hard-catch = one's word once spoken can never be taken back' similarly supports the concept of "what is said cannot be unsaid" by stressing the commitment to one's words. In line with the examples above, (4a) *yi4 yan2 qian1 jin1* and (4b) *jin1 yu4 liang2 yan2* similarly convey the important concept that one's statement is important in Chinese culture.

3.1.5. *LITERARY WORK IS* HUANG2JIN1

Literary works are conceptualized as *huang2jin1* in examples (5a)–(5b). Example (5a), *sui4 jin1* 碎金 'brief good writing piece,' is a metaphorical expression in which *huang2jin1* is a noble, precious metal. This preciousness provides the conceptual correspondence and is the quality that contributes the mapping between literary works and *huang2jin1.* Example (5b), *yi1 zi4 qian1 jin1* 一字千金 'a single word deserves thousands of dollars,' is another example in which preciousness is the quality that corresponds between the SD and TD.

(5) precious: Quality
  a. *sui4 jin1* 碎金
    fragment-gold = 'brief good writing piece'
  b. *yi1 zi4 qian1 jin1* 一字千金
    one-word-thousand-gold = 'a single word deserves thousands of money'

The emphasis on the great value of literary works allows us to postulate the MP.

(V) MP for LITERARY WORK IS *HUANG2JIN1: Huang2jin1* is compared to literary works because *huang2jin1* is a noble, valuable metal, and accordingly one's literary works in Chinese society are highly esteemed and are therefore considered to be precious.

3.1.6. *EXCELLENCE IS* HUANG2JIN1

Excellence is conceptualized as *huang2jin1* in examples (6a)–(6b). Example (6a), *jin1 sheng1 yu4 zhen4* 金聲玉振[4] 'Confucius's great virtue,' is a metaphorical expression in which *huang2jin1* is a metal with high quality. High quality is the conceptual correspondence which contributes the mapping between excellence and *huang2jin1.* The high quality of *huang2jin1* is identified as the quality that corresponds between the SD and TD. Example (6b), *jin1 tou2 nao3* 金頭腦[5] 'intelligent or brilliant people,' is another example in which the conceptual correspondence is identified as the quality that corresponds between the SD and TD.

(6) high quality: Quality
  a. *jin1 shen1 yu4 zhen4* 金聲玉振
    gold-voice-jade-vibrate = 'Confucius's great virtue'

---

[4] It indicates Confuscious' great virtues are like music playing (Zhou & Qiu 2004: 1995).

[5] Another difference between Mandarin in People's Republic of China and Taiwan is shown in the usage referring to a brilliant person. It is *tou2 nao3 ling2 guang1* 頭腦靈光 'head-brain-clever-light' in People's Republic of China, whereas *jin1 tou2 nao3* 金頭腦 'gold-head-brain' can also be used for the same meaning in Taiwan.

b. *jin1 tou2 nao3* 金頭腦
gold-head-brain = 'intelligent or brilliant people'

The emphasis on the excellence allows us to postulate the MP.

(VI) MP for EXCELLENCE IS *HUANG2JIN1: Huang2jin1* is compared to excellence because *huang2jin1* is a metal with high quality.

3.1.7. *PERFECTION IS* HUANG2JIN1

Perfection is conceptualized as *huang2jin1* in examples (7a)–(7b). Example (7a), *huang2 jin1 bi3 li4* 黃金比例 'golden ratio,' is a metaphorical expression of perfection. *Huang2jin1*'s perfect quality is the conceptual correspondence which contributes the mapping between perfection and *huang2jin1*. This perfectness of gold is the quality of *huang2jin1* that is identified as the quality that corresponds between the SD and TD. Example (7b), *jin1 xiang4 yu4 zhi2* 金相玉質 'the form and content of a writing piece can not be better,' is another example in which the conceptual correspondence is identified as the quality that corresponds between the SD and TD.

(7) best quality : Quality
a. *huang2 jin1 bi3 li4* 黃金比例
yellow-gold-compare-example = 'golden ratio'
b. *jin1 xiang4 yu4 zhi2* 金相玉質
gold-appearance-jade-property = 'the form or content of a writing piece can not be better'

In line with 3.1.6 (EXCELLENCE IS *HUANG2JIN1*), *huang2jin1* is the noble metal and a stable chemical element on earth with the best quality, which is compared and understood to be perfect. The emphasis on perfection allows us to postulate the MP.

(VII) MP for PERFECTION IS *HUANG2JIN1: Huang2jin1* is compared to perfection because *huang2jin1* is a noble, stable, and constant metal with the highest quality, which is thus understood to be perfect.

3.1.8. *OPPORTUNITY IS* HUANG2JIN1

Opportunity is conceptualized as *Huang2jin1* in (8a)–(8b). Example (8a) *gan1 ai2 zhi4 liao2 zhi3 you3 yi4 xiao3 duan4 huang2jin1 shi2 jian1* 肝癌治療只有一小段黃金時間 'a short period of time to cure liver cancer' is a metaphorical expression in which *huang2jin1* as a superior metal makes the abstract reasoning. Superiority is the conceptual correspondence that is identified as the quality. Example (8b), *ba3 wo4 zhong1 xue2 zhe4 duan4 xue2 xi2 de huang2jin1 shi2 duan4* 把握中學這段學習的黃金時段 'To make good use of one's prime time in middle school to learn,' is another example in which superiority is the quality that corresponds between the SD and TD.

(8) superior: Quality

a. *gan1 ai2 zhi4 liao2 zhi3you3 yi4 xiao3 duan4*
肝 癌 治 療 只 有 一 小 段
liver cancer cure only a limited
huang2 jin1 shi2 jian1
黃 金 時 間
gold time
'A short period of time to cure liver cancer.'

b. *ba3 wo4 zhong1 xue2 zhe4 duan4 xue2 xi2 de*
把 握 中 學 這 段 學 習 的
seize middle school this period study POSS.
huang2 jin1 shi2 duan4
黃 金 時 段
gold time interval
'Make good use of one's prime time in middle school to learn.'

The emphasis on the superiority allows us to postulate the MP.

(VIII) MP for OPPORTUNITY IS *HUANG2JIN1: Huang2jin1* is compared to opportunity because *huang2jin1* is superior to other metals.

As demonstrated above, *huang2jin1* is the SD, which attributes abstract reasoning. Overall, there are eight TDs and eight corresponding principles as presented in Table 3.1. In the next section, we further discuss the metaphorical assimilation of *huang2jin1*.

Table 3.1. The corresponding principles of the conceptualizations of *huang2jin1*.

No.	*Huang2jin1* for TDs	MPs
I	CHINESE EMPEROR	*Huang2jin1* is compared to the Chinese emperor because the Chinese emperor like *huang2jin1* is the one with all the wealth in his kingdom, is highly valued and is thought to be at the very top of the world.

Table 3.1. (*cont.*)

No.	*Huang2jin1* for TDs	MPs
II	SOLIDITY	*Huang2jin1* is compared to solidity because *huang2jin1* as a metal is solid and hard by nature.
III	ETERNITY	*Huang2jin1* is compared to eternity because *huang2jin1* is a stable, unchanging chemical element.
IV	WORD	*Huang2jin1* is compared to words because *huang2jin1* is a precious, noble metal and because one's statement in Chinese culture needs to be truthful. We can infer that a person's statement is thought of as a kind of preciousness.
V	LITERARY WORK	*Huang2jin1* is compared to literary works because *huang2jin1* is a noble, valuable metal that is valuable, and accordingly one's literary works in Chinese society are highly esteemed and are therefore considered to be precious.
VI	EXCELLENCE	*Huang2jin1* is compared to excellence because *huang2jin1* is a noble metal with high quality.
VII	PERFECTION	*Huang2jin1* is compared to perfection because *huang2jin1* is a noble, stable, and constant metal with the highest quality and is understood as existing in a perfect state.
VIII	OPPORTUNITY	*Huang2jin1* is compared to opportunity because *huang2jin1* is superior to other metals.

3.2. The Conceptualization of *Huang2jin1*

In the previous section we exemplified the metaphorical extensions of the FLEs *huang2jin1*. This section aims to answer the following research questions: (1) what is the metaphorical process involved in *huang2jin1* and (2) what are the principles that influence the metaphorical interpretations of *huang2jin1*?

Three linguistic phenomena are observed. First, "metaphor allows us to understand a relatively abstract or inherently unstructured subject matter in terms of a more concrete or at least a more highly structured subject matter" (Lakoff 1993: 39). That is, a more concrete subject matter is employed to explain other concepts (Lakoff and Johnson 1980; Lakoff 1993; Goddard 1998; Charteris-Black 2000; Charteris-Black and Ennis 2001; Charteris-Black and Musolff 2003; Ungerer and Schmid 2006; McGlone 2007). Since *huang2jin1* is a concrete object with concrete characteristics, *huang2jin1* is the SD, exemplifying eight concepts: (I) Chinese emperor, (II) solidity, (III) eternity, (IV) word, (V) literary work, (VI) excellence, (VII) perfection and (VIII) opportunity as shown in Figure 3.1.

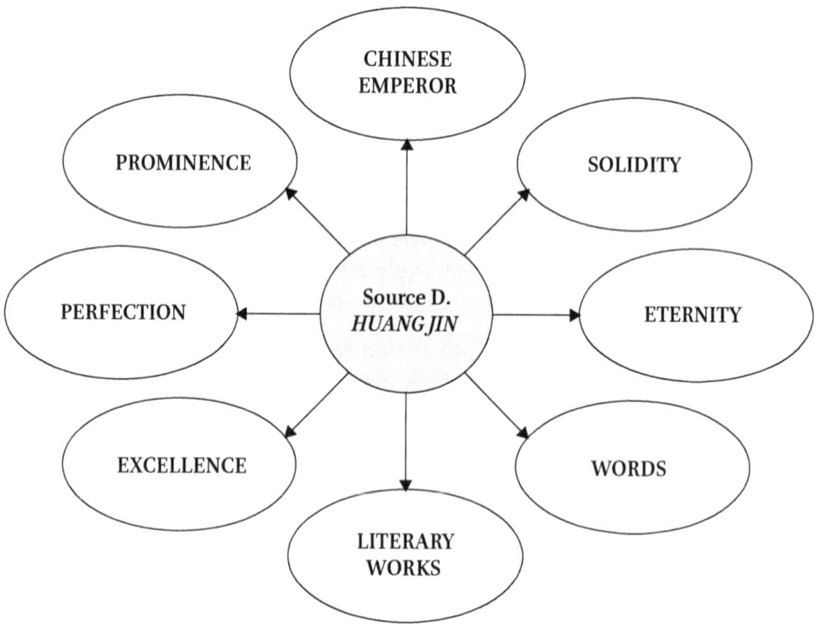

Figure 3.1. The metaphorical process between *huang2jin1* and other concepts.

Second, the use of metaphor has a cognitive basis—to ease understanding. Tsao, Tsai and Liu (2001: 110) suggest that human beings' conceptualizations conform to economic principles. Thus, we expect the mapping between the abstract and the concrete to conform to cognitive economy, which by definition refers to "the linguistic phenomena in which a certain item with a great amount of information is digested with the least cognitive efforts" (Ungerer and Schmid 2006: 71). From this standpoint, people naturally select the most prevalent or the easiest substances for their metaphorical interpretations. In this way, the borrowing of *huang2jin1*'s salient properties for abstract reasoning conforms to cognitive economy.

For example, *huang2jin1* is a noble metal, which is extracted to account for the CHINESE EMPEROR IS *HUANG2JIN1*. Likewise, *huang2jin1* is a stable chemical element, which is connected with SOLIDITY IS *HUANG2JIN1*. Here, the metaphorical expressions of *huang2jin1* manifest what Grundy (2000: 120) identifies as the important role of the principle of economy: a facilitator that allows people to understand the assumptions about the background of utterances.

Third, the SD-TD pairing of *huang2jin1* is quality-based. It is achieved by investigating the conceptual correspondences between *huang2jin1* and its SDs in terms of the three categories of the CMM approach: entities, qualities and functions (Ahrens 2002). Since the three categories focus on a very basic level of schematic knowledge about how metaphor is utilized, observing which criteria are employed with greater frequency in structuring *huang2jin1* might lead to a better understanding.

Table 3.2. The tokens and percentage of the entity, quality, and function of *huang2jin1*.

FLE	Entity		Quality		Function		
	N	%	N	%	N	%	Total
huang2jin1	0	0%	94	100%	0	0%	94

Table 3.2 presents the metaphorical tokens together with their percentages, classified into the entities, functions, and qualities that correspond between the SD-TD pairings. “N” in Table 3.2 refers to the total number of each pairing. All of the 94 metaphorical tokens of *huang2jin1* are classied into the quality category, indicating the SD-TD pairings of *huang2jin1* are 100 percent quality-based.

“Metaphor is at the nexus of mind and language” (Tendahl and Gibbs 2008: 1823). That is, how we think and the linguistic forms that our expressions take are intimately related. *Huang2jin1* is a precious, stable metal with quality. It is also natural that its salient attributes become the most relevant constituents of schematic knowledge that contribute to the SD-TD mapping.

Above all, the metaphorical extensions of *huang2jin1* have cultural factors that are crucial to metaphorical interpretations. When the attributes of *huang2jin1* are extracted to interpret other concepts, those concepts that are explained via metaphor are enhanced with positive cultural implications. For instance, only the monarch can be thought of as *huang2jin1* as pointed out in 3.1.1 (CHINESE EMPEROR IS *HUANG2JIN1*). Furthermore, LITERARY WORK IS *HUANG2JIN1* suggests that literary works are intrinsically excellent, as demonstrated by *dian3 shi2 cheng2 jin1* 點石成金 'point-stone-become-gold = make the poor written pieces into beautiful ones.' Finally, WORD IS *HUANG2JIN1*, as shown in the word formations of *xin4* 信 'trustworthiness' and *jin1 nuo4* 金諾 'gold-promise = solemn promise' indicates that one's statement is precious because it has to be truthful.

Different folk conventions influence language users' perception (Gibbs 1999; Su 2000; Charteris-Black and Ennis 2001; Charteris-Black and Musolff 2003; Chung, Ahrens and Sung 2003; Chung, Ahrens and Huang 2003; Deignan and Potter 2004; Ungerer and Schmid 2006). According to Ungerer and Schmid (2006: 51), cultural models are "the models shared by people belonging to a social group or subgroups." This implies culture is integrated with metaphorical extensions and influences the minds of the language users (Gibbs 1999). Our mind is partially structured by metaphors, both of which are grounded in our experiences and reflected in our literal language (Lakoff and Johnson 1980: 47–61). During the metaphorical construction and conceptualization of everyday life, culture is crucial because "we experience our world in such a way that culture is already present in the very experience itself" (Lakoff and Johnson 1980: 57). Moreover, Tsao, Tsai and Liu (2001: 72) state that one's metaphorical thinking develops within the constraints of their specific cultural background. Thus, Mandarin speakers' metaphorical perception and interpretations are inevitably influenced by cultural models specific to Mandarin.

3.3. Conclusion

Metaphors may imply people's underlying expectations (Charteris-Black 2000: 160–164). In other words, a set of metaphorical set expression uncover people's interpretation of a specific notion. With the metaphorical applications of *huang2jin1*, Mandarin speakers' perceptions were observed. Metaphor refers to the process by which an abstract concept is understood in terms of a concrete object. *huang2jin1* is the SD which attributes other TDs: (1) Chinese emperor, (2) solidity, (3) eternity, (4) word, (5) literary work, (6) excellence, (7) perfection and (8) opportunity. Since *huang2jin1* is a concrete object with concrete features, it is applied as the SD, further explaining or unveiling the cognitive or cultural significance of other abstract ideas.

Moreover, people's conceptualizations will be attracted to more relevant information (Tendahl and Gibbs 2008: 1831). In other words, metaphorical mappings are inclined to people's background knowledge. For instance, the mappings between *huang2jin1* and its TDs are quality-based and are therefore applied in metaphorical use because its value or chemical attributes are salient and significant in people's perception.

Furthermore, our linguistic assimilations have a basis in cognitive efficiency. In other words, they conform to the notion of cognitive economy ensuring that most information is perceived with the least effort or within the least amount of time (Ungerer and Schmid 2006: 71). The metaphorical extensions of *huang2jin1* abide by the principle of economy, and the most salient attributes of *huang2jin1* exemplify its TDs. For instance, *huang2jin1* is a precious metal, which exemplifies excellence, as in '*jin1 tou2 nao3* 金頭腦 'gold-head-brain = brilliant people' or *jin1 pai2 zhi4 zuo4 ren2* 金牌製作人 'gold-medal-produce-make-person = excellent producer.' Moreover, *huang2jin1*, as a stable chemical element on earth, is compared to solidity, as in *xin1 ru2 jin1 shi2* 心如金石 'heart-like-gold-stone = faithful will' or eternity, as in *jin1 lan2 zhi1 jiao1* 金蘭之交 'gold-orchid-POSS.-relationship = close and intimate friendship.'

Above all, cultural values are observed in the metaphorical use of *huang2jin1* as the Chinese emperor, literary works, and statements are precious and highly valued. Su (2000: 415) states that metaphorical understanding is dependent on cultural knowledge for mapping is a complicated cognitive process as metaphorical operations are involved in multi-level conceptual knowledge. By identifying sets of related metaphors as being shown in *huang2jin1* in Mandarin, we observe both cognitive and cultural operations of metaphorical application. In the next chapter, we will have another FLE, *jin1qian2*.

CHAPTER FOUR

MANDARIN SPEAKERS' PERCEPTION OF *JIN1QIAN2* 'MONEY'

May Hsin-Mei Huang & Shelley Ching-yu Hsieh*

4.0. Introduction

This chapter investigates the metaphorical expressions of the FLE *jin1-qian2* 金錢 'money.' We address three research questions: (a) What are the SDs that Mandarin native speakers utilize in interpreting *jin1qian2*? (b) What are the principles that guide people's interpretations of *jin1-qian2*? (c) How is *jin1qian2* evaluated? This chapter is divided into three sections. First, we apply Ahrens' (2002) CMM and Lakoff and Turner's (1989) GCB Metaphor as the research framework to categorize the data collected from *Academia Sinica Balanced Corpus Mandarin Chinese*. The metaphorical categorizations of *jin1qian2* along with an MP for each metaphorical pairing are presented. In 4.2, the strategies which construe *jin1-qian2* and the underlying expectation, perception and expectation behind linguistic use are presented. At last, we have a discussion in 4.3.

4.1. The Metaphorical Categorizations of *Jin1qian2*

After investigating expressions of *huang2jin1*, the present chapter goes further to investigate what rhetoric strategies are used in *jin1qian2* metaphor clusters. In total, the clusters interprets nine categories: (1) supernatural power, (2) humans, (3) prey, (4) plants, (5) water, (6) machines, (7) commodities, (8) medicine and (9) dirty objects.

4.1.1. JIN1QIAN2 *IS SUPERNATURAL POWER*

The first SD to exemplify *jin1qian2* is supernatural power. Examples (1)–(3) are the metaphorical expressions of *JIN1QIAN2* IS SUPERNATURAL POWER. First, there is *jin1qian2 jiu4shi4 ta1mende jiu4shi4zhu3* 金錢就

---

* The original version of the present chapter was published in the *Tamkang Journal of Humanities and Social Sciences*, 38: 51–70.

是他們的救世主 'money is their Savior,' (1) in which *Jiu4shi4zhu3* 救世主 'Savior' is the lexical correspondence which is defined as the function corresponding between the SD and TD. Another example is (2), *ta1 shi2zu2de bai4jin1* 她十足的拜金 'she is a material girl,' in which *bai4* 拜 'worship' is the lexical correspondence that is categorized as the function corresponding between the SD and TD.

(1) *jiu4 shi4 zhu3* 救世主 'Savior': Function

jin1 qian2	*jiu4 shi4*	*ta1mende*	*jiu4shi4zhu3*[1]
金 錢	就 是	他們的	救世主
money	just	their	Savior

'Money is their Savior.'

(2) *bai4* 拜 'worship': Function

ta1	*shi2*	*zu2*	*de*	*bai4*	*jin1*
她	十	足	的	拜	金
she	completely			worship	money

'She is a material girl.'

(3) *mo2 li4* 魔力 'magic power': Entity

jin1qian2	*de*	*mo2 li4*
金 錢	的	魔 力
money	POSS.	magic power

'The magic power of money.'

Though supernatural power can be positive, for example benevolent deities, as in (1)–(2), or negative, for example devils, as in (3). The majority of *jin1qian2*, 11 instances, are exemplified positively by deities. A minor 2 instances are exemplified negatively by devils. Overall, the emphasis on the notion of the positive magic power of *jin1qian2*, which is either worshiped or respected, allows us to postulate the MP.

(I) MP for *JIN1QIAN2* IS SUPERNATURAL POWER: *Jin1qian2*, like supernatural power, is worshiped and respected for it has inescapable magic power.

4.1.2. JIN1QIAN2 *IS HUMAN*

Human is the second SD exemplifying *jin1qian2*. Examples (4)–(6) are the metaphorical expressions of *JIN1QIAN2* IS HUMAN. In (4), *ren2jian1de*

[1] The presentation and translations of examples (1)–(59) were phrased when semantic segments or units were recognized. For example, *jin1 qian2* was phrased in (1) as *jin1qian2* because it constitutes the semantic unit 'money.'

shi4 quan2 you2 jin1qian2 kong4zhi4 人間的事全由金錢控制 'money controls everything in the world,' *kong4zhi4* 控制 'control' is the lexical correspondence that is defined as the function corresponding between the SD and TD. In (5), *cheng2wei2 jin1qian2 de nu2li4* 成為金錢的奴隸 'to become a slave to money,' *nu2li4* 奴隸 'slave' is the function that corresponds between the SD and TD.

(4) *kong4 zhi4* 控制 'control': Function
ren2 jian1 *de* *shi4 quan2* *you2*
人 間 的 事 全 由
man's world POSS. thing completely passive
jin1qian2 *kong4 zhi4*
金 錢 控 制
money control
'Money controls everything in the world.'

(5) *nu2 li4* 奴隸 'slave': Function
cheng2wei2 *jin1qian2* *de* *nu2li4*
成 為 金 錢 的 奴隸
become money POSS. slave
'To become a slave to money.'

(6) *xiao4 li4* 效力 'take efforts': Function
gu3 shi4 *yu3* *jin1qian2* *jiao1hu4* *xiao4li4*
股 市 與 金 錢 交 互 效 力
stock market and money mutually take efforts
'Stock market and money mutually take efforts.'

The emphasis on both the social interaction and the power or influence of *jin1qian2* allows us to postulate the MP.

(II) MP for *JIN1QIAN2* IS HUMAN: *Jin1qian2*, like humans, has life, social interaction, and the controlling power to influence social interaction.

4.1.3. JIN1QIAN2 *IS PREY*

Jin1qian2 is characterized as prey in examples (7)–(9). All of them depict the functions of being preyed upon, dealing with notions of being hunted or fished. For example, in (7), *shang3jin1 lie4ren2* 賞金獵人 'reward hunter,' *lie4ren2* 獵人 'hunter' is the lexical correspondence. Though *lie4ren2* is not prey; however, *lie4ren2* has prey as their target. In other words, *lie4ren2* hunts prey. In this standpoint, *lie4ren2* is the lexical correspondence that is the function corresponding between the SD and TD. In (8), *ni3 diao4dao4 qian2 le ma1* 你釣到錢了嗎 'Did you catch money yet?,' *diao4* 釣 'fish' is the function that corresponds between the SD and TD.

(7) *lie4 ren2* 獵人 'hunter': Function
shang3jin1 lie4ren2
賞 金 獵 人
reward hunter
'reward hunter'

(8) *diao4* 釣 'fish': Function
ni3 diao4 dao4 qian2 le ma1
你 釣 到 錢 了 嗎
you fished money ASP INT.
'Did you catch money yet?'

(9) *lao1* 撈 'to net': Function
zhun3 bei4 da4 lao1 yi4 bi3 (qian2)
準 備 大 撈 一 筆 (錢)
prepare big net an amount of money
'To be ready to net a great amount of money.'

The emphasis on the notion of fishing allows us to postulate the MP.

(III) MP for *JIN1QIAN2* IS PREY: *Jin1qian2*, like prey, is hunted, fished and sought after.

4.1.4. JIN1QIAN2 *IS PLANT*

Jin1qian2 is characterized as plants in examples (10)–(12). In (10), *jin1-qian2 gua1ge3* 金錢瓜葛 'money entanglement,' *gua1* 瓜 'melon' and *ge3* 葛 'kudzu vine' are the lexical correspondences that are the entities corresponding between the SD and TD. In (11), *deng3dai4 tou2zi1 de jin1qian2 kai1hua1jie2guo3* 等待投資的金錢開花結果 'when the money we invest yields positive returns,' *hua1* 花 'flower' and *guo3* 果 'fruit' are the entities corresponding between the SD and TD.

(10) *gua1* 瓜 'melon': Entity, *ge3* 葛 'kudzu vine': Entity
jin1 qian2 gua1 ge3
金 錢 瓜 葛
money melon kudzu vine
'money entanglement'

(11) *hua1* 花 'flower': Entity, *guo3* 果 'fruit': Entity
deng3 dai4 tou2 zi1 de jin1 qian2 kai1 hua1
等 待 投 資 的 金 錢 開 花
wait invest POSS. money blossom
jie2 guo3
結 果
bear fruit
'When the money we invest yields positive returns.'

(12) *meng2 ya2* 萌芽 'sprout': Function
jing1 ji4 po4 mie4 de jie2guo3 qi3 yin1 yu2
經 濟 破 滅 的 結果 起 因 於
economy extinction POSS. result originate from
qi1 nian2 qian2 meng2 ya2 de jin1 qian2 you2 xi4
七 年 前 萌芽 的 金 錢 遊戲
seven years ago sprout POSS. money game
'The extinction of the economy resulted from the money game sprouting seven years ago.'

The emphasis on the notion of the vitality of plants, which sprout, blossom and bear fruits allows us to postulate the MP.

(IV) MP for *JIN1QIAN2* IS PLANT: *Jin1qian2*, like plants, sprouts, blossoms, and bears fruit.

4.1.5. JIN1QIAN2 *IS WATER*

Jin1qian2 is conceptualized as water in examples (13)–(15). In (13), *ren2chao2 jiu4shi4 qian2chao2* 人潮就是錢潮 'people are business,' *chao2* 潮 'tide' is the lexical correspondence that is the entity corresponding between the SD and TD. In (14), *tou2ru4 jin1qian2 de xuan2wo1* 投入金錢的旋渦 'to invest in the money whirlpool,' *xuan2wo1* 漩渦 'whirlpool' is the entity corresponding between the SD and TD. Though *chao2* 潮 'tide' and *xuan2wo1* 漩渦 'whirlpool' are natural phenomena, which are evoked by some other natural forces besides water, they both involve water.

(13) *chao2* 潮 'tide': Entity
ren2 chao2 jiu4 shi4 qian2 chao2
人 潮 就 是 錢 潮
people tide just money tide (business tide)
'People are business.'

(14) *xuan2 wo1* 漩渦 'whirlpool': Entity
tou2 ru4 jin1qian2 de xuan2 wo1
投 入 金錢 的 漩 渦
throw money POSS. whirlpool
'To invest in the money whirlpool.'

(15) *zhang3 chao2* 漲潮 'the rising tide': Function
zu3 zhi3 jin1qian2 da4 shi4 de zhang3
阻 止 金錢 大 勢 的 漲
stop money big situation POSS. rising
chao2 man4 yan2
潮 蔓 延
tide spread
'To stop the violent spread of the money.'

The emphasis on the notion of the water's flow, which rises as a tide or floods, allows us to postulate the MP.

(V) MP for *JIN1QIAN2* IS WATER: *Jin1qian2*, like water, flows, rises in tides, or floods.

4.1.6. JIN1QIAN2 *IS MACHINE*

Jin1qian2 is conceptualized as machines in examples (16)–(17). In (16a), *ti2sheng1 jin1qian2 xiao4neng2* 提升金錢效能 'promote the efficiency of money,' *xiao4neng2* 效能 'efficiency' is the lexical correspondence that is the entity corresponding between the SD and TD. In (17), *zheng4dang3 cao1zuo4 jin1qian2 ji1qi4* 政黨操作金錢機器 'the political party operates the money machine,' *cao1zuo4* 操作 'to operate' is the function corresponding between the SD and TD.

(16) *xiao4 neng2* 效能 'efficiency': Entity

a.

ti2 sheng1	*jin1 qian2*	*xiao4neng2*
提 升	金 錢	效 能
promote	money	efficiency

'To promote the efficiency of money.'

b.

zeng1 jia1	*jin1 qian2*	*de*	*xiao4 neng2*
增 加	金 錢	的	效 能
gain	money	POSS.	efficiency

'To take actions to promote the efficiency of money.'

(17) *cao1 zuo4* 操作 'to operate': Function

zheng4 dang3	*cao1 zuo4*	*jin1qian2*	*ji1qi4*
政 黨	操 作	金 錢	機器
party	operate	money	machine

'The political parties operate the money machine.'

The emphasis on the function of a machine allows us to postulate the MP.

(VI) MP for *JIN1QIAN2* IS MACHINE: *Jin1qian2*, like machines, is efficiency-related because it is expected operate efficiently, as well as promote efficiency.

4.1.7. JIN1QIAN2 *IS COMMODITY*

Jin1qian2 is conceptualized as commodities in examples (18)–(20). In (18), *jin1qian2 jiao1 yi4* 金錢交易 'money transactions,' *jiao1yi4* 交易 'transaction' is the lexical correspondence that is the function corresponding between the SD and TD. In (19), *jin1qian2 shang1ji1* 金錢商機 'the business of money,' *shang1ji1*商機 'business' is the entity corresponding between the SD and TD.

(18) *jiao1 yi4* 交易 'transactions': Function
jin1qian2 *jiao1yi4*
金 錢 交 易
money transactions;
'Money transactions'

(19) *shang1 ji1* 商機 'business': Entity
jin1 qian2 *shang1ji1*
金 錢 商 機
money business
'The business of money'

(20) *shi4 chang3 hang2 qing2*
市場行情 'quotations': Entity
jin1qian2 *bing4fei1* *wan4 ling2* *dan1* *zhi3* *yao4*
金 錢 並 非 萬 靈 丹 只 要
money not panacea only
fu2 he2 *shi4chang3hang2qing2*
符 合 市場行情
confirm to quotations
'Money works as long as it conforms to the market requirements.'

The emphasis on the market value of commodities allows us to postulate the MP.

(VII) MP for *JIN1QIAN2* IS COMMODITY: *Jin1qian2*, like commodities, is exchanged and has its market value.

4.1.8. JIN1QIAN2 *IS MEDICINE*

Jin1qian2 is conceptualized as medicine in examples (21)–(23). In (21), *zhe4bi3(qian2) shi4 wo3de jiu4ming4 qian2* 這筆(錢)是我的救命錢, *jiu4ming4* 救命 'saving lives' is the lexical correspondence that is the function corresponding between the SD and TD. In (22), *jin1qian2 shi4 yi4tie3 wan4ling2dan1 yi4 fu2 jian4 xiao4* 金錢是一帖萬靈丹一服見效 'money is a panacea once you take it,' *fu2* 服 'take' is the function corresponding between the SD and TD.

(21) *jiu4 ming4* 救命 'to save life': Function
zhe4 bi3(qian2) shi4 wo3de jiu4 ming4 qian2
這 筆(錢) 是 我的 救命 錢
this (money) be my save money
'This amount of money saves my life.'

(22) *fu2* 服 'take': Function
jin1 qian2 shi4 yi4 tie3 wan4ling2dan1 yi4 fu2
金錢 是 一 帖 萬靈丹 一 服
money be one panacea once take
jian4 xiao4
見 效
see effect
'Money is a panacea once you take it.'

(23) *ma2 bi4* 痲痺 'paralyze': Function
jin1qian2 jiu4 xiang4 ma3 fei1 ma2 bi4 ren2
金 錢 就 像 嗎 啡 痲 痺 人
Money PART like morphine paralyze people
xin1
心
heart
'Money is morphine which paralyzes people's hearts.'

The emphasis on the curative effects of medicine allows us to postulate the MP.

(VIII) MP for *JIN1QIAN2* IS MEDICINE: *Jin1qian2*, like medicine, has curing effects and is able to save people's lives.

4.1.9. JIN1QIAN2 *IS DIRTY OBJECT*

Jin1qian2 is conceptualized as dirty objects in examples (24)–(26). In (24), *ni3 cai2 zhuan4 ji3ge4 chou4 qian2 jiu4 xiao1zhang1* 你才賺幾個臭錢就囂張 'such a small amount of stinky money you have earned can make you so arrogant,' *chou4* 臭 'stinky' is the lexical correspondence that is the quality corresponding between the SD and TD. In (25), *xi3qian2* 洗錢 'money laundering,' *xi3* 洗 'to wash' is the function corresponding between the SD and TD.

(24) *chou4* 臭 'stinky': Quality
ni3 cai2 zhuan4 ji3 ge4 chou4 qian2
你 才 賺 幾個 臭 錢
you only earn several stinky money

jiu4 *xiao1 zhang1*
就 囂張
PART arrogant
'Such a small amount of stinky money you have earned can make you so arrogant.'

(25) *xi3* 洗 'to wash': Function
xi3 *qian2*
洗 錢
wash money
'money laundering'

(26) *fu3 hua4* 腐化 'rot': Function
jin1qian2 *fu3hua4* *ren2* *xin1*
金錢 腐化 人 心
money rot people heart
'Money rots human beings' hearts.'

The emphasis on the pollution caused by the dirty objects allows us to postulate the MP.

(IX) MP for *JIN1QIAN2* IS DIRTY OBJECT: *Jin1qian2*, like dirty objects, pollutes, rots, and stinks.

The TD *jin1qian2* is interpreted in terms of nine different SDs: (1) supernatural power, (2) humans, (3) prey, (4) plants, (5) water, (6) machines, (7) commodities, (8) medicine and (9) dirty objects. *Jin1qian2* is the TD construed in terms of other concrete objects as shown in Figure 4.1.

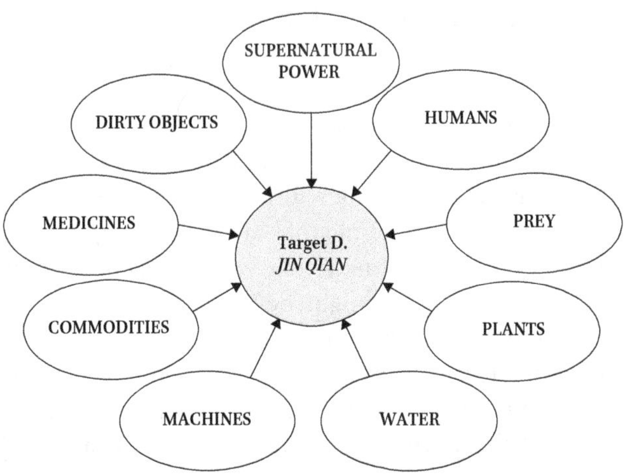

Figure 4.1. The conceptual mapping between *jin1qian2* and other SDs.

Thinking and communicating metaphorically affords humans the ability "to understand a relatively abstract or inherently unstructured subject matter in terms of a more concrete or at least a more highly structured subject matter" (Lakoff 1993: 39). This is achieved by employing a more concrete subject matter to explain other concepts (e.g., Lakoff and Johnson 1980; Lakoff 1993; McGlone 2007). In this way, *jiin1qian2* operates as the abstract idea revealed by metaphorical assimilation thus staying flexible in the minds of people so it can be employed for further description and elaboration of ideas.

In addition, we further examined the lexical correspondences employed in conceptualizing *jin1qian2* in terms of the CMM (Ahrens 2002): the three categories—entities, qualities and functions. Because these three categories focus on a very basic level of schematic knowledge about how metaphor contributes, we intend to explore which categories are employed with greater frequency in conceptualizing *jin1qian2*. Table 4.1 presents the metaphorical tokens with their percentages classified into the entities, functions, and qualities that correspond between the SD-TD pairings.

Table 4.1. The tokens and percentage of the entity, quality, and function.

FLE	Entity		Quality		Function		
	N	%	N	%	N	%	Total[2]
jin1qian2	23	22%	5	5%	76	73%	104

"N" in Table 4.1 refers to the total number of each pairing. Among the 104 identified tokens of *jin1qian2*, 23 of them (22%) are entities, 5 of them (5%) are qualities, and the other 76 of them (73%) are functions. The attributes mapped onto the TD *jin1qian2* suggest that the perception of *jin1qian2* is primarily function-based.

"Metaphor is at the nexus of mind and language" (Tendahl and Gibbs 2008: 1823). That is, how we think and how we express our thoughts are intimately related. As an economic tool in the market, *jin1qian2* is necessarily function-oriented in nature. Thus, when conceptualizing *jin1qian2*, its functions are naturally highlighted. Here we see that metaphorical operations develop in our experiences.

In addition, the present study also attempts to unravel which linguistic strategy is preferred by Mandarin speakers when interpreting *jin1qian2* expressions. With this purpose in mind, we further examine the tokens and percentage each SD contributes to the abstract reasoning of *jin1qian2* as shown in Table 4.2.

Table 4.2. The percentage of the SDs that attributes *jin1qian2*.

SDs	N	(%)
SUPERNATURAL POWER	13	13%
HUMAN	37	37%
PREY	5	5%
PLANT	5	5%
WATER	14	14%
COMMODITY	8	8%
MACHINE	5	5%
MEDICINE	7	7%
DIRTY OBJECT	7	7%
Total	101	100%

"N", in Table 4.2, refers to the total number of tokens in which *jin1qian2* is conceptualized. There are in total 101 metaphorical instances of *jin1-qian2*. When conceptualizing, 13 of them, which is 13%, are comprehended in terms of supernatural power, 37 of them, which is 37%, are conceptualized in terms of human, and so on. Based on the analysis in Table 4.2, human (37%) is the preferred SD.

4.2. Discussion

The investigations into the metaphorical extensions of *jin1qian2* reveal four assumptions. First, *jin1qian2* is the TD of the metaphorical interpretations because it is often interpreted by other concrete objects. Second, the SD-TD pairing of *jin1qian2* is function-oriented. This linguistic phenomenon is rightly accorded because *jin1qian2* is used in the market as currency, which confirms that our metaphorical interpretations are developed rationally.

Third, personification is the most preferred cognitive strategy in the application of *jin1qian2*. The prevalence of personification results from a combination of people's egocentricity and the principle of cognitive economy. Egocentricity is defined as "people's tendency to use egocentric reference systems to code information about their environment" (Waller, Lippa and Richardson 2007: 3). That people use themselves as the center to interpret other objects in the world can not be more natural. Such cognitive behavior is revealed by their use of language when conceptualizing *jin1qian2*. Moreover, cognitive economy by definition refers to "the linguistic phenomena in which a certain item with a great amount of information is digested with the least cognitive efforts" (Ungerer and Schmid 2006: 71). According to Tsao, Tsai and Liu (2001: 110), human beings' conceptualizations should conform to economic principles. Furthermore, Grundy (2000: 120) mentions that the principle of cognitive economy enables people to understand the assumptions about the background of utterances. From this standpoint, people would prefer to select the most prevalent and basic substances for their metaphorical interpretations. This way, it meets our cognitive needs and eases our cognitive burden.

Human is chosen as the most prevalent SD in conceptualization of *jin1qian2* for it eases cognitive effort by saving the amount of information processing required. For example, a Chinese saying construes this cognitive tendency: *jin4 qu3 zhu1 shen1 yuan3 qu3 zhu1 wu4* 近取諸身遠取諸物 'near-take-from-body-far-take-from-object = for things near and close, we depict them in terms of ourselves = for things far away, we designate them by means of the attributes of the creature.' That is, people easily and naturally use themselves to exemplify others for it is, in terms of cognitive efforts, the most effort-saving.

Ungerer and Schmid (2006: 126) also point out that personification is a common cognitive strategy found in everyday life as non-human creatures or objects are attributed with the ability to talk, walk, or think like human beings. Furthermore, Lakoff and Johnson (1980: 33–34) mention that personification can be "the most obvious ontological metaphors." Similarly, Chung, Ahrens and Huang (2005: 560) state that "human conceptualizations are the more concrete concepts which humans can easily recall when describing an abstract idea." Above all, personification is the easiest for human cognition as Henderson (1994: 348) points out that "personification is a device for us to talk about abstract forces or processes that make us feel more at home in a hostile world."

Most significantly, the present study discovers that *jin1qian2* is conceptualized as being positive and powerful in Chinese culture. Take *JIN1QIAN2* IS SUPERNATURAL POWER for example. *Jin1qian2* is upgraded to be respected and admired for its magical power. That supernatural power is highly respected or revered is rooted in their culture as can be observed in the saying *jing4 tian1 fa3 zu3* 敬天法祖 'respect-heaven-follow-ancestor = respect the gods and your ancestors' and in *zun1 tian1 di4 jing4 gui3 shen2* 尊天地敬鬼神 'respect-heaven-land-respect-ghost-deity = respect the gods, the ghosts, and the earth.' Thus, when conceived of as supernatural, the concept of *jin1qian2* is empowered and *jin1qian2* is imbued with irresistible, even unavoidable power.

Further, *JIN1QIAN2* IS PLANT indicates *jin1qian2* bears fruit, blossoms, or sprouts. Similarly, *JIN1QIAN2* IS WATER indicates *jin1qian2* is able to evoke big trends like *jin1qian2 da4shi4 de zhang3chao2 man4yan2* 金錢大勢的漲潮蔓延 'the violent spread of money,' or has destructive power as in *jin1qian2 you2xi4 fan4lan4* 金錢遊戲氾濫 'Money games flood.' *JIN1QIAN2* IS MEDICINE reinforces the effective and crucial image of *jin1qian2* since medicine cures disease, benefiting the world. Nevertheless, even though *JIN1QIAN2* IS DIRTY OBJECT is negative, the power of *jin1qian2* is still evident. For example, example (24) *ni3 cai2 zhuan4 ji3ge chou4 qian2 jiu4 xiao1zhang1 de bu4de2liao3* 你才賺幾個臭錢就囂張的不得了 'such a small amount of stinky money you have earned can make you so arrogant' suggests that money is dirty, but it enables people to feel proud, thereby corrupting their humility.

The positive attitude toward money in Mandarin is manifested when *jin1qian2* is analyzed in terms of the GCB Metaphor (Lakoff and Turner 1989). In this present chapter, the metaphorical extensions of *jin1qian2* involve the extended GCB Metaphor, which specifies the relationship between humans and the universe, including supernatural power as shown in Figure 4.2 on p. 58.[2]

The extended GCB Metaphor in this chapter is a six-level hierarchy. At the highest level above humans, supernatural power is superior to humans for supernatural power has magic attributes and behaviors which humans do not. In the extended GCB Metaphor, humans are at level 2, animals at level 3, and so on.

Figure 4.3 (see p. 58) presents *jin1qian2*'s pairing in the extended GCB Metaphor in which the correspondences and percentage between the SDs and *jin1-qian2* are demonstrated.

As an economic tool used as currency in the market, *jin1qian2* is in the complex objects at level 5. *JIN1QIAN2* IS SUPERNATURAL POWER is at level one, which is 13% of all the metaphorical expressions. *JIN1QIAN2* IS HUMAN (36%) is at level 2, *JIN1QIAN2* IS PREY (5%) is at level three, and so on. Overall, 60% of the metaphorical expressions are mapped from the upper levels of the hierarchy, consisting of supernatural power (13%),

2 Figure 4.2 is different from that presented in Figure 2.2. in 2.2.3. (The hierarchy of GCB Metaphor), for the figure here is simplified and only the categories demonstrated are included.

Extended Great Chain of Being Metaphor

Supernatural power

↓

Humans

↓

Animals

↓

Plants

↓

Complex objects

↓

Natural physical things

Figure 4.2. Extended Great Chain of Being Metaphor.

humans (36%), animals (5%), and plants (6%); 26% is from commodities, machines, medicine, and dirty objects, which belong to the same level, and only 15% are from water at the lowest level.

According to Sun (2009: 31–32; 119–120), it is a degradation if the beings are interpreted in terms of those at the lower levels. On the contrary, if the beings at the lower level are attributed in terms of those at the higher level, they are upgraded or complimented. That sixty percent of the SDs come from the upper levels above the complex objects level indicates that *jin1qian2* is considered to be positive in people's perceptions.

Metaphors reveal how we evaluate subject matter (Young 2001). Lea and Webley (2006: 163–164) indicate that the strong interest in money is biological. The strong interest here suggests people's positive stance towards *jin1qian2*. In the light, the tendency evaluating *jin1qian2* as being positive is predictable for metaphorical interpretations are developed, operated, and elaborated in our life. The present chapter once again reinforces the very power of *jin1qian2* to compel people's attention, especially in an industrialized society.

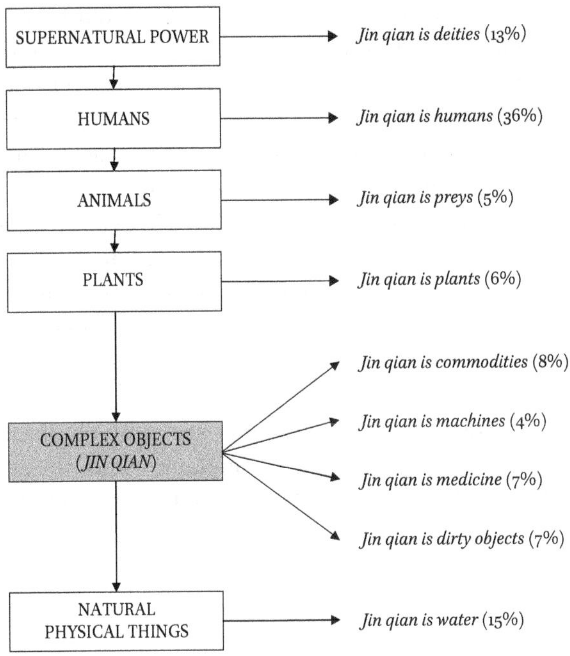

Figure 4.3. *Jin1qian2*'s pairings in extended Great Chain of Being Metaphor.

4.3. Conclusion

"Metaphor leads to new ways of understanding" (Charteris-Black 2000: 154). By investigating how people interpret *jin1qian2,* their perceptions were observed. Metaphor refers to the process whereby an abstract concept is understood in terms of a concrete object. *Jin1qian2* is the TD which is represented by means of other SDs: specifically, (1) supernatural power, (2) humans, (3) prey, (4) plants, (5) water, (6) machines, (7) commodities, (8) medicine and (9) dirty objects.

Moreover, metaphorical mappings conform to people's perceptions. *Jin1qian2* is mostly function-based because it is the tool in the market exchange; that is, their functions are their most salient characteristics and are therefore applied in their metaphorical use.

Furthermore, based on the GCB Metaphor (Lakoff and Turner 1989), we found that *jin1qian2* is conceptualized as having the power to control, as 60 percent of its metaphorical uses are interpreted by supernatural power, humans, plants, which are at the highest levels in the GCB Metaphor (Figure 4.3).

Above all, our linguistic assimilations are motivated by cognitive factors. In other words, it conforms to the principle of cognitive economy, by which the most amount of information is perceived with the least effort or within the least amount of time (Ungerer and Schmid 2006: 71; Grundy 2000: 120). For example, humans are the most common SD for metaphorical interpretations involving *jin1qian2* because it eases our cognitive process and saves more cognitive efforts. This strategy is crucial in linguistic comprehension, as indicated by the notion of personification, because people interpret information with egocentric reference systems (Waller, Lippa and Richardson 2007: 3) and because people are inclined to simplify information (Ungerer and Schmid 2006; Tsao, Tsai and Liu 2001; Grundy 2000).

Ultimately, the ideas behind metaphors are mutually interdependent as Charteris-Black (2000: 154) note that "metaphors do not exist in isolation from each other." As has been observed in this study of Mandarin, the underlying conceptualizations can be found by identifying sets of related metaphors such as the FLE *jin1qian2*.

CHAPTER FIVE

THE METAPHORICAL EXPRESSIONS OF *YIN2* 'SILVER'

Lydia Yu-ling Chang & Shelley Ching-yu Hsieh

5.0. Introduction

This chapter focuses on the metaphorical extensions of *yin2* 銀 'silver' in Mandarin in terms of the approach of Fauconnier and Turner (1998) CIN. The following research questions will be answered: (1) How is *yin2* 銀 categorized in fixed expressions? (2) How is *yin2* categorized in metaphor clusters? (3) Are the categorizations of *yin2* in fixed expressions and metaphor clusters similar to each other or mutually exclusive? The data are taken from the *Chinese Mandarin Online Dictionary, Great Dictionary*, and the database *Newspapers in Taiwan*.

This chapter has three divisions. First, we present the fixed expressions and metaphorical clusters of *yin2* along with their linguistic coding in 5.1. Then the metaphor clusters of *yin2* and their categorizations are further manifested in 5.2. Finally, there is a discussion and conclusion in 5.3.

5.1. The Conceptualizations of *Yin2* and Their Linguistic Coding

In this chapter, the cognitive observations of *yin2* in both fixed expressions (e.g., *bin4 fa3 ru2 yin2* 鬢髮如銀 'moustache-hair-like-silver; the elders') and metaphor clusters (e.g., *hu2gua1 nü3er2 ta4shang4 yin2se4lu4* 胡瓜女兒踏上銀色路 'Mr. Hu's daughter is going into show business') are demonstrated. *Yin2*, referred to as Argentum in chemistry, is a bright white metal and this physical feature makes *yin2* useable as currency. Furthermore, its use as a currency gives it an economic function. From a linguistic viewpoint, *yin2* is a polysemy carrying various meanings. There are two basic meanings of the Chinese character *yin2*: "metal" and "white" (see Table 5.1 on p. 62 for examples). In sections 5.1 and 5.2, we detail the five main categories for *yin2*'s fixed expressions and metaphor clusters, respectively. Section 5.2.6 demonstrates the application of Fauconnier and Turner's CIN (1998) on *yin2*'s metaphor clusters. We summarize this chapter in section 5.3.

Table 5.1. *Yin2* and its basic meanings.

Basic meanings	*Yin2* expressions
Metal	*yin2 pai2* 銀牌 'silver-plate = second position' *yin2 jian4* 銀劍 'silver-sword = silver sword' *yin2 gui4* 銀櫃 'silver-closet = a safe deposit'
Color white	*yin2 he2* 銀河 'silver-river = galaxy' *yin2 fa3* 銀髮 'silver-hair = elderly' *yin2 bai2 shi4 jie4* 銀白世界 'silver-white-age-boundary = snow'

Five basic categories are filtered out based on the classifications of the 266 instantiations of *yin2* fixed expressions in terms of its collocations. The categorization permits us to elaborate and examine *yin2* in different ways. In this section, we will examine *yin2*'s expressions from a conceptual viewpoint and look at the way they are interpreted.

5.1.1. YIN2 *AS PERSON*

In fixed expressions, *yin2* is shown as a person as presented in Table 5.2.

Table 5.2. *Yin2* fixed expression of human category.

Category	*Yin2* fixed expressions	Characteristics/ Features
HUMAN	(1) *bai2 fa4 yin2 bin4* 白髮銀鬢 'white-hair-silver-moustache = elderly people' (2) *jin1 tou2 yin2 mian4* 金頭銀面 'gold-head-silver-face = well dressed' (3) *Yi1 zi3 yao1 yin2* 衣紫腰銀 'clothes-purple-waist-silver = officer'	human body parts
	(4) *jin1 nu2 yin2 bi4* 金奴銀婢 'gold-slave-silver-servant = well dressed slaves' (5) *yin2 hun1* 銀婚 'silver-marriage = the 25th wedding anniversary'	social status
	(6) *chuan1 jin1 dai4 yin2* 穿金戴銀 'wear-gold-wear-silver = rich people.'	human behavior

Yin2 is used to portray a person in three aspects (body parts, social status, and behavior) presented in Mandarin as category human. Looking at *yin2* collocations from a body part perspective, we find that *yin2* is often used to describe the color of a person's hair, even describing the graying facial hair as (1) *bai2 fa3 yin2 bin4* 白髮銀鬢 'elderly' showing the nature of old age in human beings. Relevant descriptions for implementing the basic meaning of the color white of *yin2* to represent aged people are *bin4 fa3 ru2 yin2* 鬢髮如銀 'moustache-hair-like-silver,' and *bin4 ru2 yin2 si1* 鬢如銀絲 'moustache-like-silver-silk.' This fixed expression *yin2fa3zu2* 銀髮族[1] 'silver-hair-clan' is made to portray elderly people as a specific group.

After looking at how the change of hair color is described, the study goes further to look at body parts above the neck and then to portions that are below the neck. The fixed expression (2) *jin1 tou2 yin2 mian4* 金頭銀面 'well dressed' uses *jin1* 金 'gold' and *yin2* combined with a human's head and face to imply how wealthy a person is. Both FLEs *jin1* and *yin2* usually give us images of luxury, therefore the combination of *jin1* and *yin2* represents the wealth of people. In (3) *yi1 zi3 yao1 yin2* 衣紫腰銀 'officer,' the beautiful clothes and expensive accessories are attributes of an officer.

Jin1 nu2 yin2 bi4 金奴銀婢 'well dressed slaves' in (4) is a good example of an *yin2* fixed expression, referring to social status. Both *nu2* 奴 and *bi4* 婢 symbolize people of low status. Behavior also makes *yin2* categorized as a person. Behaviors, like (5) *yin2hun1* 銀婚 'the 25th wedding anniversary,' and (6) *chuan1 jin1 dai4 yin2* 穿金戴銀 'rich people,' only occur with human beings, as no animals or plants will have a twenty-fifth wedding anniversary and wear beautiful clothes or silver accessories. *Yin2* is used to describe a person from the three perspectives of body parts, social status, and human behaviors.

5.1.2. YIN2 *AS ANIMAL*

Yin2 is used to describe another kind of living being, animals, as presented in Table 5.3.

---

[1] In People's Republic of China, the elders are described as *xi4yang2hong2* 夕陽紅 'sunset-sun-red.' That is, the natural phenomonon *xi4yang2* 夕陽 'sunset-sun = sunset,' implying the elders coming into the last stage of their lives is applied in People's Republic of China, while the color of the hair (gray) is applied in Mandarin in Taiwan as in *yin2fa3zu2* 銀髮族 'silver-hair-clan.'

Table 5.3. *Yin2* fixed expression of animal category.

Category	*Yin2* fixed expressions	Characteristics/Features
ANIMAL	(7) *yin2 hu2* 銀狐 'silver-fox = a silver fox' (8) *yin2 shu3* 銀鼠 'silver-mouse = a snow weasel'	land animal
	(9) *yin2 jiao1* 銀鮫 'silver-shark = Chimaera phantasma'	sea animal

Collocations of *yin2* in the animal realm start by depicting animals that live on the ground. *Yin2* is used to depict land animals like (7) *yin2 hu2* 銀狐 'silver fox' and (8) *yin2 shu3* 銀鼠 'snow weasel.' The reason why they both carry the FLE *yin2* is because a portion of both of their bodies is silver in color. Color is one of the basic meanings of *yin2*.

Besides the animals on the ground, *yin2* signifies those in the sea. For instance, (9) *yin2 jiao1* 銀鮫 'Chimaera phantasma' is a kind of soft-bone fish, whose color is silver and which usually lives in areas where cold and warm waters meet in the sea. Here, the fish is included in the *yin2* category also due to the color of its body being silver.

5.1.3. YIN2 *AS PLANT*

Yin2 銀 fixed expressions refer not only to animate creatures according to their living environment, but also to plants. Table 5.4 gives some examples.

Table 5.4. *Yin2* fixed expression of plant category.

Category	*Yin2* fixed expressions	Characteristics/ Features
PLANT	(10) *yin2 bai2 yang2* 銀白楊 'silver-white-poplar = Abele'	poplar
	(11) *pu2 tao2 ye4 yin2 lian2 hua1* 葡萄葉銀蓮花 'grape-grapes-leaf-silver-lotus-flower = Anemone Vitifolia Buch'	fruit leaf flower
	(12) *huo3 shu4 yin2 hua1* 火樹銀花 'fire-tree-silver-flower = bright fireworks'	tree

In line with 5.1.3 *YIN2* AS PLANT, the FLE *yin2* 銀 depicts plants because of its white color shown in (10) *yin2 bai2 yang2* 銀白楊 'Abele.' That is a tree whose cortex is a grayish-white color. In (11) the whiteness of the flower *yin2 lian2 hua1* 銀蓮花 is described with *yin2*. This fixed expression has fruit, leaf, and flower in one expression. Moreover, the color white tends to stand for brightness. (12) *Huo3shu4 yin2hua1* 火樹銀花 'bright fireworks' literally describes trees, but figuratively indicates the brightness of a street.

5.1.4. YIN2 *AS OBJECT*

The section shifts from the category of living beings to non-living things, as shown in Table 5.5.

Table 5.5. *Yin2* fixed expression of object category.

Category	*Yin2* fixed expressions	Characteristics/ Features
	(13) *jin1 wo1 yin2 wo1* 金窩銀窩 'gold-nest-silver-nest = luxury house'	nest
	(14) *Qing1 yin2 guan4* 傾銀罐 'lean-silver-jar = a glass made container'	jar
OBJECT	(15) *yin2 bei1* 銀杯 'silver glass = a silver made glass'	glass or cup
	(16) *yin2 dan4* 銀彈[2] 'silver-bullet = money'	bullet
	(17) *yin2 bi4* 銀幣 'silver-currency = money'	money

Going further to the category object, we notice some characteristics of Chinese *yin2*'s fixed expressions as *yin2* portrays containers. When people want to fill or empty something, they need containers. For example, in *yin2* there are various kinds of containers: *wo1* 窩 'house,' *ping2* 瓶 'bottle,' *guan4* 罐 'jar,' *pen2* 盆 'basin,' *bei1* 杯 'glass,' *gui4* 櫃 'cabinet,' and *ku4* 庫 'garage.' Here, we can find that *yin2* fixed expressions are container-based, but sized differently. *Wo1* 窩 'nest' is a type of confine suitable for people to live in and it is larger than other containers in the expressions in terms of their size. The order, in terms of capacity/size, for *yin2* fixed expressions is: (13) *yin2wo1* 銀窩 'expensive house' > *yin2ku4* 銀庫 'a place for money' > *yin2gui4* 銀櫃 'a safe deposit' > *yin2ping2* 銀瓶 'a wine bottle' > (14) *qing1yin2guan4* 傾銀罐 'a glass container.' It is possible to observe that some containers are more hermitically sealed, which may have a lid, while some are more plate style.

Another phenomenon that we observed is *YIN2* AS TOOLS FOR WAR. When wars happen, people usually need a lot of tools. The two most important characteristics for a "tool" on the battlefield are for it to be sharp enough to hurt an enemy and hard enough to protect ourselves. *Dao1* 刀 'knife,' *dan4* 彈 'bullet,' and *jian4* 劍 'sword' are weapons for attacking rivals and we can say *yin2dao1* 銀刀 'silver knife,' *yin2dan4* 銀彈 'silver bullet,' and *yin2jian4* 銀劍 'silver sword.' While *dun4* 盾 'shield' and *qiao4* 鞘 'sheath' are tools used for both protecting ourselves and as weapons. The physical nature of *yin2* being a metal makes these weapons available.

5.1.5. YIN2 *AS NATURAL PHYSICAL THING*

This last section about *yin2* fixed expressions analyzes how people understand *yin2* as natural physical things (see Table 5.6). Natural physical things are things that are from the cosmos or found in ecology.

Example (18) *yin2he2* 銀河 'galaxy' describes a cluster of stars just like the stream of a river. The color of *yin2* fits with the white color of a shimmering river as we mentioned earlier that the color white tends to stand for brightness. Example (19) *yin2he2 dao4xie4* 銀河倒瀉 'plenty of speedy water' uses the color of *yin2* and the motion of a river to describe the way a river runs.

Table 5.6. *Yin2* fixed expression of natural physical thing category.

Category	*Yin2* fixed expressions	Characteristics/ Features
NATURAL PHYSICAL THING	(18) <u>*yin2*</u> *he2* 銀河 '<u>silver</u>-river = galaxy'	river
	(19) <u>*yin2*</u> *he2 dao4 xie4* 銀河倒瀉 '<u>silver</u>-river-reverse-flow = plenty of speedy water'	to flow rapidly

5.2. Metaphor Clusters of *Yin2* and Their Categorization

After analyzing *yin2* fixed expressions, the study goes further to explore how *yin2* is used in metaphor clusters in daily conversation. A metaphor is a rhetoric strategy used to say one thing to imply another. Metaphors can also be used as a symbol to stand for beings or objects in different fields. A common instance is when people use the features of a tiger to imply the bad temper of a person by uttering *she is a tiger*. So, after examining *yin2* fixed expressions, we start investigating *yin2* in a more elaborate way by exploring its metaphorical extensions. Our analysis presents *yin2* in *yin2* metaphorical clusters interprets 5 categories: a farmer, a bird, fruit and flowers, a bullet, and a star.

5.2.1. YIN2 *AS FARMER*

Integrating the basic meanings of *yin2* into daily conversation, we find that *YIN2* IS A FARMER occurs in the following examples:

(20) *fu4 yue4 tou2zi1 yin2hang2 zai4 duo1nian2*
赴 越 投資 銀行 在 多年
Go Viet invest bank in many years
geng1yun2 xia4 mai4ru4 shou1ge1 jie1duan4
耕耘 下 邁入 收割 階段
cultivate down step into to reap stage
'After many years of investment in Vietnam, the bank starts to earn some profit.'

(21) *zhong1hua2kai1fa1yin2hang2 duo1nian2 xin1ku3*
中華開發銀行 多年 辛苦
CDI bank many years hardworking
bo4zhong3 zhong1 dao4 shou1huo4qi2
播種 終 到 收穫期
sowing finally to harvest season
'After investing for many years, CDI bank finally earns some profits.'

(22) *tou2zi1 yin2hang2 nao3jin1 zhuan3dekuai4*
投資 銀行 腦筋 轉得快
Invest bank brain turning quickly
shou1huo4feng1
收穫豐
harvest
'The investment bank reacts so fast that it has a good turnover.'

Yin2hang2 銀行 'bank' is a place for lending, saving, and investing money. Still, *yin2hang2* 銀行 is not only a financial institution, but may also be compared with a hard working farmer by pointing out their resemblances and highlighting their characteristics as shown in (20) *shou1ge1* 收割 'to reap,' (21) *bo4zhong3* 播種 'sowing,' and (22) *shou1huo4* 收穫 'harvest.'

5.2.2. YIN2 *AS BIRD*

Yin2 is seen as another kind of living creature, animals. As an animal, it might be able to walk, climb or fly. The characteristic of flight, as shown in (23)–(24) *fei1* 飛 'to fly' is a specific feature that distinguishes birds from human beings. We will further elaborate this characteristic of flight.

(23) *fei1chang2nan2* *5566* *yin2zi* *fei1 le*
緋常男 5566 銀子 飛了
Scandal boy 5566 money fly ASP
'Due to the scandal of the idol group 5566, they lost the chance to earn money.'

(24) *yin2zi* *man3tian1* *fei1* *qiu2yuan2* *xiao4* *kai1huai2*
銀子 滿天 飛 球員 笑 開懷
Money full sky fly player laugh happily
'Baseball players are so happy due to earning a lot of money.'

5.2.3. YIN2 *AS FRUIT AND FLOWERS*

YIN2 IS A PLANT and also includes parts of a tree. As a result, *yin2* is the fruit of a tree or a beautiful flower.

(25) *zheng4fu3* *ji1 jin1* *shi1fei2* *san1shang1yin2*
政府 基金 施肥, 三商銀
Government bound fertilize COTA
duo3duo3 *hong2* *fu2e2* *qing1xi3*
朵朵 紅 浮額 清洗
quantifier red low amount clean
'Government bound invests on COTA commercial bank and it gets rid of its debt.'

(26) *jing1guo4* *duo1nian2* *tou2 zi1* *tai2yin2*
經過 多年 投資, 台銀
Pass many year invest Taiwan Bank
hua1kai1 *bing4di4*
花開 並蒂
blossom stalk
'After many years of investment, Taiwan bank has good outcome.'

(27)

da4jia1	*pan4*	*jing1ji4*	*yin2hang2*	*suo1*
大家	拚	經濟	銀行	縮
Everybody	fight	economy	bank	shrink
yin2	*gen1*			
銀	根			
silver	root			

'Everyone tries hard to make money, but banks don't lend money to the public.'

From the expressions in (25) *shi1fei2* 施肥 'fertilize,' (26) *hua1kai1 bing4di4* 花開並蒂 'blossom and stalk' and (27) *gen1* 根 'root,' we see that banks act as trees with flowers being the successful result of investment and roots being money. No matter what contours *yin2* has, it falls under the concept of "money" and "preciousness" in this category.

5.2.4. YIN2 *AS BULLET*

Taking into account that the fixed expressions and metaphorical clusters of *yin2* transit from animate beings to inanimate substances, now we focus on how *yin2* is conceptualized as bullets of a gun. The examples are as shown in (28) *si4ji1fa1dong4* 伺機發動 'wait for launching,' (29) *miao2zhun3* 瞄準 'target,' and (30) *shang4tang2* 上膛 'upload.' In the examples below, a soldier's rapid shooting is compared to money spreading to everyone.

(28)

tou2xin4	350*yi4*	*yin2dan4,*	*si4ji1*	*fa1dong4*
投信	350 億	銀彈,	伺機	發動
bank	35 billion	money	wait	launch

'The money, 35 billion in the investment, is getting ready to work.'

(29)

da4liang4	*yin2dan4*	*xuan3hou4*	*miao2zhun3*
大量	銀彈,	選後	瞄準
Big amount	money	after election	target
tai2gu3			
台股			
Taiwan stock			

'A large amount of money targets Taiwanese stock market after election.'

(30)

yin2dan4	*shang4tang2*	*ti2zhen4*	*gu3shi4*	*ai4*
銀彈	上膛	提振	股市	愛
Money	upload	lift	stock market	love
tai2	*ye3yao4*	*pan4*	*shou1yi4*	
台	也要	拚	收益	
Taiwan	also	fight	profit	

'Government is preparing money for investment, both earning profit and loving Taiwan are important to this country.'

5.2.5. YIN2 *AS STAR*

Finally, when we refer to *yin2* in *yin2he2* 銀河, two meanings exist. First, *yin2he2* may mean 'galaxy' by using the color of *yin2* to describe the luminance of stars. Second, *yin2he2* may have the meaning of 'show business' as in examples (31)–(33):

(31)	*xiao3bei4*	*hang2xiang4*	*yin2he2*	*xing2cheng2*
	小貝	航向	銀河	行程
	Beckham	sail to	galaxy	schedule
	man3dang3			
	滿檔[3]			
	full file			

'Beckham starts his show business and his schedule is packed.'

(32)	*ai4nü3*	*jia1ru4*	*yin2he2*	*hu2gua1*	*hu4hang2*
	愛女	加入	銀河	胡瓜	護航[4]
	Beloved daughter	*join*	galaxy	Hu Gua	convoy

'Beloved daughter enters show business and Mr. Hu protects her.'

(33)	*ri4*	*qian2shou3xiang4*	*zi3*	*chuang3*	*yin2he2*
	日	前首相	子	闖	銀河
	Japan	former Premier	son	go	galaxy
	mei2	*tian2tou2*			
	沒	甜頭[5]			
	no	benefit			

'Japanese former Premier's son goes into show business but no support.'

We have placed *yin2* metaphorical expressions into categories according to their characteristics and features. Section 5.2.6 will use the CIN to verify these findings.

5.2.6. *Application of Conceptual Integration Network on Metaphorical Clusters* Yin2

According to Fauconnier and Turner's (1998) CIN, there are at least two mental spaces (see Table 5.7) and these two mental spaces are extracted and gathered together to integrat or blend. This operation comes out a new blended space which contains the information projected from two

[2] It is *xing2cheng2hen3jin3* 行程很緊 'walk-schedule-very-tight' in People's Republic of China.

[3] It is *bao3jia4hu4hang2* 保駕護航 'protect-drive-protect-sail' in People's Republic of China.

[4] It is *mei2shou1huo4* 沒收穫 'no-receive-gain' in People's Republic of China.

original input spaces. Moreover, Fauconnier and Turner (2002) explain that the new blended space does not only contain the information from the two original input spaces, but also possesses its own established information apart from the original two input spaces. Fauconnier and Turner (2002:48–49) further propose that "projection from the input spaces into the blended space involves three processes: composition, completion, and elaboration."

Ungerer and Schmid give examples below and show how composition is involved when two or more input spaces are merged in the blended space. The examples given by Ungerer and Schmid (2006: 259–260) are as following: (a). When a company will hire a director, she will post an advertisement which says ADMINSTERING AN INJECTION. (b) When a firm is raising profits, it shows on the newspaper as IMPROVING HEALTH. The explanation given is that,

> The process of completion is also required to understand the blend in the above example if the newspaper states *Volkswagen obviously NEEDS A SHOT IN THE ARM* because the phrase underspecifies the situation: neither the person giving the injection (i.e. the agent) nor the instrument needed for the injection space is mentioned in this sentence (Ungerer and Schmid 2006: 259–260).

Ungerer and Schmid (2006: 260) also draw out the important point for that "the depth (and presumably also the duration) of this process of elaboration is in principle open-ended and will vary among readers." Going back to their example *Volkswagen obviously NEEDS A SHOT IN THE ARM*, Ungerer and Schmid (2006) explain that some readers may be satisfied with the fused information (the blended space). People may think that the new director will improve the company's economic situation. On the other hand, others may actually imagine that the "director will give an injection to the (personified) company." The decoding processes of the CIN are demonstrated in Table 5.7.

Table 5.7. Blending processes of Conceptual Integration Network.

Step 1	Ingredients
Composition or Completion or Elaboration	Input space 1 Input space 2
Step 2	**Outcome**
Compression	Blended space

To understand the analysis more easily, the utterances are shown by using figures. In Figure 5.1 we see that there are three spaces for a complete blending process: a daily talk space (Input space 1), a *yin2* related space (Input space 2), and a compressed blending space. The daily talk space builds up primary background knowledge for readers and then the *yin2* related space comes in and compresses the two messages into a new blended space. For example, in (20) *fu4 yue4 tou2 zi1yin2 hang2 zai4 duo1 nian2 geng1 yun2 xia4 mai4 ru4 shou1 ge1 jie1 duan4* 赴越投資銀行在多年耕耘下邁入收割階段 'After many years of investment in Vietnam, the bank starts to earn some profit,' there is a process of farming and cultivation that continues for many years. The news reporters' intention is to create a merger that encapsulates the result of the bank's investment in Vietnam and the improved growth. The exercise in (20) *duo1nian2geng1yun2* 多年耕耘 'many years of cultivation' suggests that it had had a tough time in the beginning when the bank first invested in Vietnam. However, the message in (20) *mai4ru4shou1ge1jie1duan4* 邁入收割階段 'going into harvest step,' which is associated with the previous phrase, entails that there is a positive result for the banking investment.

Another instance of *YIN2* IS HUMAN BEING is shown in (22). Here we use the expression *nao3jin1 zhuan3dekuai4* 腦筋轉得快 'always have new idea' to describe the dramatic change of an investing decision. This novel expression in (22) *tou2 zi1 yin2 hang2 nao3 jin1 zhuan3 de kuai4 shou1 huo4 feng1* 投資銀行腦筋轉得快收穫豐 'The investment bank reacts so fast that it has a good turnover' is under a basic metaphorical understanding: *YIN2* IS HUMAN BEING. A human has a remarkable brain that can solve problems. For example, when people face a problem at school or in the workplace, they usually try to tackle the problem. The brainstorming and problem solving procedures that a human does are similar to the processes of banks implementing good policies to make money. Moreover, the result of making money from investments is like cultivating grain from farming, just as the above example (21) shows. In (21) *zhong1 hua2 kai1 fa1 yin2 hang2 duo1 nian2 xin1 ku3 bo4 zhong3 zhong1 dao4 shou1 huo4 qi2* 中華開發銀行多年辛苦播種終到收穫期 'After investing for many years, CDI bank finally earns some profits,' after we blend the concept of SD (farming event) and TD (banking event), we perceive this extraordinary metaphorical expression without any difficulties. As Huang, Ahrens and Chung (2003: 102) showed, ECONOMY IS A PERSON; only humans can do certain specific actions, like *bo4zhong3* 播種 'sowing' as the example (21) shows. The blending process of example (21) is easier to achieve as Figure 5.1 demonstrates.

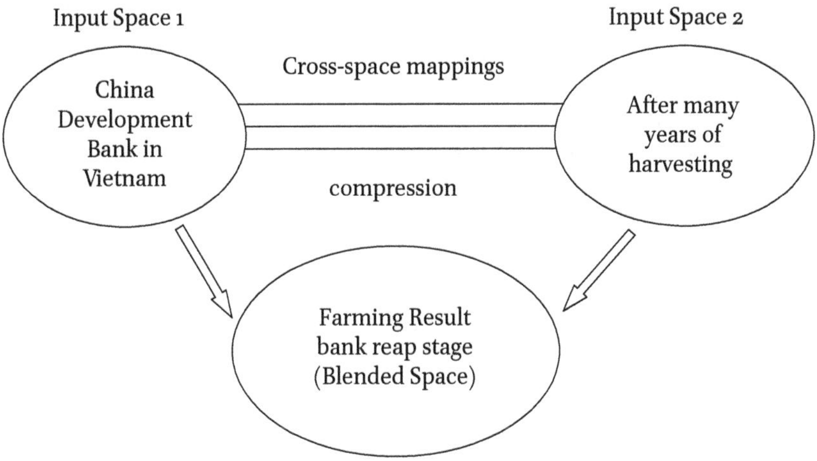

Figure 5.1. Network representation of bank investment blend.

Next, the study examines the result in section 5.2.2 (*YIN2* AS BIRD). In (23), *yin2zifeille* 銀子飛了 'money has flown,' *yin2zi* 銀子 'money' is understood as a bird because it flies by itself as indicated by *fei1* 飛 'to fly.' The negative scope about a member of an idol group having relationships with females scarifies their supporters. Afterwards, their sponsorship chose not to finance the idol group anymore. The money was instantly gone like a bird flying away by itself. Instance (24) *yin2ziman3tian1fei1* 銀子滿天飛 'the money is flying all over sky,' suggests that the cash flows into a basketball player's pocket like birds flying across the sky. We categorized *yin2zi* 銀子 'money' as a bird but not an airplane because an airplane should be flown by a pilot, but a bird can fly itself.

Besides, both examples (23) and (24) compose their input space 1 and 2 first (i.e. idol group 5566 is the input space 1, and money is gone is the input space 2 for (23)), readers then compress the two pieces of information and reach the conclusion that money is like a bird. When money flies away, it means that people lose the chance of earning it. The same implementation is also applicable to (24), as people need to go through two stages when they blend. For a better understanding of how the brain works, another figure of the CIN is demonstrated in Figure 5.2 on p. 74.

Third, the study inspects the result in section 5.2.3 (*YIN2* AS FRUIT AND FLOWERS). In (25), *san1shang1yin2duo3duo3 hong2* 三商銀朵朵紅 'COTA bank is making profit,' the *san1shang1yin2* 三商銀 'COTA banks' is understood as flowers and therefore followed by the measure word *duo3* 朵 'quantifier; quantifier of flower' to portray the thriving phenomenon in

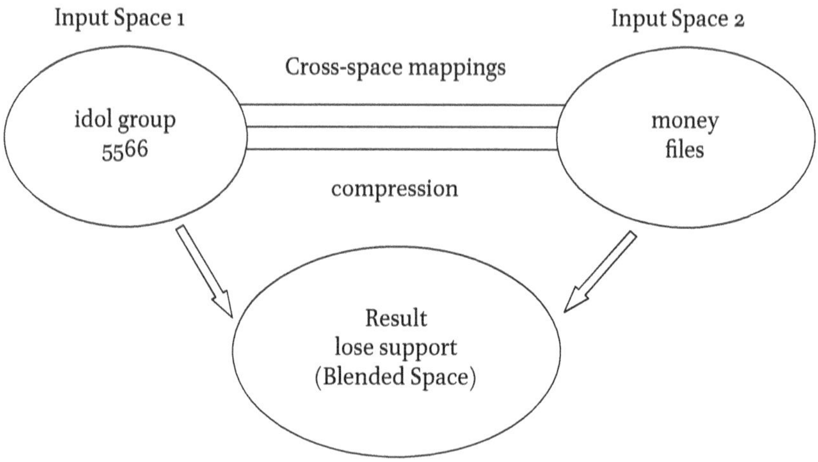

Figure 5.2. Network representation of idol group blend.

the stock market. In (26), *tai2yin2 hua1kai1bing4di4* 台銀花開並蒂 'Taiwan Bank is making profit,' it illustrates that the Bank of Taiwan is a kind of flower which blooms and bears fruit. The proliferating process of a flower is similar to the growing stage of a bank. The bank will first invest and wait for a certain period of time for the profit, just as the farmer will first water the flowers and then wait for them to blossom and produce fruit.

In (27) *da4jia1pan4jing1ji4, yin2hang2suo1yin2gen1* 大家拚經濟, 銀行縮銀根 'Everyone works hard for the economy, but bank shrinks their support,' it depicts a bank as a tree, and the bad economy consequently causes the cash flow of the bank to shrink. Due to the background of the bad economy, banks try not to raise the interest rate thereby leading to the dwindling of the banks' profits, which is like a tree shrinking due to insufficient nutrients.

Screening from the CIN, the blending process for these four examples is composed of both a composition and elaboration operation in stage one for the two domains. In stage two, we compress what we have in input space 1 and input space 2 to derive our result. Here, the profitable investment is like the blossoming flower, and the less successful bank is like the root of the shrinking tree. The integrating procedures of the expressions in 5.2.3 (*YIN2* AS FRUIT AND FLOWERS) are demonstrated as Figure 5.3.

From the expressions in (25) *shi1fei2* 施肥 'fertilize,' (26) *hua1kai1 bing4di4* 花開並蒂 'blossom and stalk' and (27) *gen1* 根 'root,' we see that banks act as trees with flowers being the successful result of investment and roots being money. No matter what contours *yin2* has, it falls under the concept of "money" in this category.

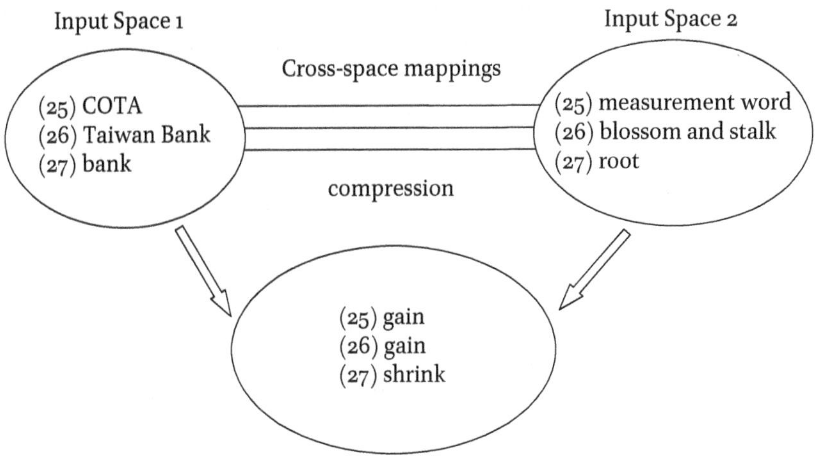

Figure 5.3. Network representation of bank blend.

Table 5.8. Blending processes of the CIN on *yin2*.

Step 1:	Ingredients
Composition or Completion or Elaboration	*YIN2* IS BULLET: *yin2 dan4* 銀彈 'silver-bullet; money' *gu3 shi4* 股市 'stock-market; stock market' *YIN2* IS STAR: *yin2 he2* 銀河 'silver-river; galaxy' *man3 dang*3 滿檔 'full-file; busy'
Step 2:	**Outcome**
Compression	*YIN2* IS BULLET: Profit *YIN2* IS STAR: Good start in show business

Let's now turn to investigate *yin2* metaphor clusters and look at their collocations. In the above, *yin2* is also seen as inanimate things: *YIN2* IS BULLET AND STARS. Instead of using figures to demonstrate the blending processes, now we implement a different approach to show the mapping procedure (see Table 5.8).

In (28)–(30), *yin2* is collocated with *dan4* 彈 'bullet' as in *yin2dan4* 銀彈 'money' and is understood as the bullet of a weapon. The *yin2dan4* can be used to help the stock market as in (29) *da4liang4yin2dan4, xuan3hou4-miao2zhun3tai2gu3* 大量銀彈, 選後瞄準台股 'a large amount of money targets Taiwanese stock market after election.' or in (30) *yin2 dan4 shang4 tang2 ti2 zhen4 gu3 shi4* 銀彈上膛提振股市 'money is ready to help stock market.' The shooting of bullets is like the distributing of money to the financial market, which can either hurt or save people, and in these cases, saves the market.

Yin2 can be understood as natural physical things: e.g., stars in the universe or galaxy. People nowadays even use the expression *yin2he2* 銀河 'galaxy' to describe the path to show business. Examples (31)–(33) are good instances of this kind of expression. The reason why we use *yin2he2* to illustrate show business is because people in this walk of life need to appear in movies or on television. The screen that is used in the film exhibitions is originally black and white. However, silver has a very reflective quality, which helps the light shine back with particular luminosity. Black and white films, which relied heavily on the reflective quality of light, thus benefited from being screened on a silver surface. As a result, a silver surface is called *yin2guang1mu4* 銀光幕[5] 'silver-light-curtain = screen.' Couples whose lives are tied to show business are called *yin2se-4qing2lü3* 銀色情侶 'silver-color-love-couple = idol couple.' And, people who start their lives in show business are like explorers who begin their adventure in the universe, as suggested in (31) *xiao3 bei4 hang2 xiang4 yin2 he2 xing2 cheng2 man3dang3* 小貝航向銀河行程滿檔 'Beckham starts his show business and his schedule is packed.'

5.3. Conclusion

The chapter examined *yin2* fixed expressions and *yin2* metaphorical clusters by applying Fauconnier and Turner's (1998) CIN. In *yin2* fixed expressions, YIN IS A HUMAN, YIN IS AN ANIMAL, YIN IS A PLANT, YIN IS AN OBJECT and YIN IS A NATURAL PHYSICAL THING. Probing thoroughly into *yin2* fixed expressions in the human category; we find that *yin2* is usually used to describe a person on three aspects: body parts, social status and behaviors. For example, (3) y*i1 zi3 yao1 yin2* 衣紫腰銀 'clothes-purple-waist-silver' meaning purple clothes and expensive (silver) accessories is usually used to depict people in a high social status in the past.

Examining *yin2* fixed expressions in animal and plant categories, we find that white color feature of *yin2* is often used to describe the skin color of animals or leaves. As a result, we have fixed expressions as (7) *yin2 hu2* 銀狐 'silver fox' and (10) *yin2 bai2 yang2* 銀白楊 'Abele.' Next, *yin2* is

[5] It is *ping2mu4* 屏幕 'shield-curtain' and *ying2mu4* 螢幕 'light-curtain' in People's Republic of China.

used to depict objects in relation to their physical features. *Yin2* is a kind of metal and often used as materials for making containers. In object category of *yin2*, the fixed expression (13) *jin1 wo1 yin2 wo1* 金窩銀窩 'luxury house,' 銀 gives us an impression of luxuriousness. Last, *yin2* is also in the natural physical thing category because the color of *yin2* is similar to the color of stars. Therefore, we have fixed expressions as (18) *yin2 he2* 銀河 'galaxy' to describe how we see and interpret a constellation of stars. When the white stars gather together, they are like a stream of clean river. As a result, *yin2* is also used to portray the way we see our sky.

In addition, the second portion of this chapter examined *yin2* metaphor clusters and looked at their collocations. With Fauconnier and Turner's (1998) CIN, the analysis undergoes three stages; by composing, completing or elaborating the two mental spaces and blending the spaces together to derive the result. The outcome shows that there are five basic categories. *Yin2* is understood as a farmer, bird, tree or flower, bullet, and star. For instance, the metaphorical expression (20) *fu4 yue4 tou2 zi1 yin2 hang2 zai4 duo1 nian2 geng1 yun2 xia4 mai4 ru4 shou1 ge1jie1 duan4* 赴越投資銀行在多年耕耘下邁入收割階段 'After many years of investment in Vietnam, the bank starts to earn some profit,' is understood as a farmer by first composing the input space (major space) *duo1 nian2 geng1 yun2* 多年耕耘 'many years of cultivation' (background space) *mai4 ru4 shou1 ge1 jie1 duan4* 邁入收割階段 'going into harvest step.' After the cross-mapping process, we blend the two spaces together and get the result that the bank is profiting from its investments. The bank is understood as a farmer here because the action *geng1 yun2* 耕耘 'cultivate' and *shou1 ge1* 收割 'harvest' is done only by a farmer. A bank originally is only a financial institution, but it is seen as a farmer in the metaphorical expression.

Incorporating the above, we probe that *yin2* fixed expressions and its metaphor clusters are similar to each other. *Yin2* is seen as a human, an animal, a plant, an object and a natural physical thing in the fixed expressions while *yin2* is understood as a farmer, a bird, a tree, a bullet and a star in the metaphor clusters.

CHAPTER SIX

THE CONCEPTUALIZATION OF 'POVERTY' IN MANDARIN

Sophia Chen-Ying Wu & Shelley Ching-yu Hsieh

6.0. Introduction

This chapter involves a corpus-based approach focused on exploring how Mandarin users conceptualize the notion of impoverishment FLEs *pin2qiong2* 貧窮 'poor,' *pin2* 貧 'poor' and *qiong2* 窮 'poor' by means of Emergent Grammar (Hopper 1987) and SUMO (Niles and Pease 2001). The goals of investigating are: (1) how Mandarin users evaluate the FLE *pin2-qiong2*, and the quasi-synonyms *pin2* 貧 'poor' and *qiong2* 窮 'poor' from an emergent perspective, and (2) the cognitive and linguistic realizations that occur in the realizations and interpretations of *pin2qiong2, pin2* and *qiong2*. The study is organized as follows. Section 6.1 verifies the emergent conceptualization of 'poverty.' Section 6.2 further probes 'poverty' by means of SUMO. Section 6.3 is a conclusion.

6.1. The Emergent Conceptualization of 'Poverty'

Pin2, qiong2 and *pin2qiong2* are derived from the same concept of 'poverty.' The usages of the target lexical items in the dictionary and in the corpus are compared to consider how language users influence the lexical terms. According to Tao (2003), various linguistic expressions show their distinct preferences for a set of words. Quasi-synonyms sharing the same concept combine in different patterns to emerge subtle dissimilarities because of texts and interactions between people. The conceptual process can be observed by means of the semantic changes.

6.1.1. *The Semantic Changes*

Emergent Grammar (Hopper 1987) is the actual use of language re-arranged in different ways (Hopper 1987). In other words, grammar does not mean a system of fixed structure, but a record of emergent usages by human beings. Semantic changes of lexical items can prove this. The original and usually fixed usage of one lexical term is what is shown in dictionaries.

However, language develops. Innovations can be investigated in corpora. Here we go a step further to construe the difference between dictionary entries and corpus data of the quasi-synonyms of poverty.

In 6.1.1, we focus on the semantic changes of *pin2*, *qiong2* and *pin2-qiong2*. The definitions of the three quasi-synonyms in the on-line dictionary are in 6.1.1.1; the expressions found in the on-line corpus are in 6.1.1.2. The comparison between the on-line dictionary and corpus is in 6.1.1.3.

6.1.1.1. *The Definitions in the Chinese Dictionary*

The entry of *pin2qiong2* in the *Revised Mandarin Chinese Dictionary* is an adjective compound meaning that a person lacks money and his life is difficult. In Mandarin, the words we use to express '*poverty*' are not only the compound adjective, '*pin2qiong2*,' but also the two simple FLEs, '*pin2*' and '*qiong2*.'

Pin2 (as shown in Table 6.1) can be classified into three grammatical categories. The grammatical functions are: an adjective, a verb and a noun.

Pin2 as an adjective is a modifier, which can be applied to combine with three kinds of nouns to delineate various situations. It describes that someone's life condition is in poverty and distress, like *pin2 min2* in (1), the poverty or poor condition of blood, like *pin2 xie3* in (2) and someone is too talkative, like *pin2 zui3* in (3). Another is that *pin2* is a verb which means to impoverish people, like *pin2* in (4). The other is in the category of a noun representing destitute surroundings for which *pin2* in (5) is evidence.

Table 6.1. The syntactical functions of *pin2* in the dictionary.

Syntactical functions of *pin2*	Examples
Adjective	(1) *pin2 min2*貧民 'poor people = the poor' (2) *pin2 xie3* 貧血 'poor blood = anemia' (3) *pin2 zui3* 貧嘴 'poor mouth = garrulous'
Verb	(4) *qiang2 ben3 er2 jie2 yong4, ze2 tian1 bu4 neng2 pin2* 彊本而節用則天不能貧 'strengthen the origin and save expense; therefore, God cannot impoverish us = if we not only improve the agricultural yields but also save the expense; there is no chance to become impoverished'
Noun	(5) *jun1 zi3 you1 dao4 bu4 you1 pin2* 君子憂道不憂貧 'a gentle man worries a doctrine not poverty = a person of nobility should focus on how to realize his dream instead of worrying about the disadvantaged living condition he has'

Table 6.2. The syntactical functions of *qiong2* in the dictionary.

Syntactical functions	Examples
Adjective	(7) *qu4 wei4 wu2 qiong2* 趣味無窮 'interest taste no poor = fascinating'
	(8) *qiong2 xiong1 ji2 e4* 窮凶極惡 'poor fierce very evil = very ferocious'
	(9) *qiong2 suan1* 窮酸 'poor sour = poor jealousy and pedantic'
	(10) *jun1 zi3 yi4 you3 qiong2 hu1* 君子亦有窮乎 'a gentle man is also poor = does a person of nobility suffer from poverty'
	(11) *qiong2 xiang1 pi4 rang3* 窮鄉僻壤 'poor country remote soil = an obscure village'
Verb	(12) *qiong2 li3 jin4 xing4, yi3 zhi4 yu2 ming4* 窮理盡性，以至於命 'investigate logic examine nature to achieve to life = examine principles thoroughly in order to understand human's nature'
Noun	(13) *yi4 qiong2 er4 bai2* 一窮二白 'one poverty two white = poor and blank'
Adverb	(14) *qiong2 jiu4* 窮究 'thoroughly probe = to make a thorough inquiry'

As for the other lexeme *qiong2*, based on the on-line *Revised Mandarin Chinese Dictionary*, *qiong2* like *pin2* can be an adjective that modifies a noun (See Table 6.2).

Qiong2 has more syntactical functions than *pin2* does as presented in Table 6.2. In addition to being a verb, a noun and an adjective, *qiong2* also has the syntactical function of an adverb. As Table 6.2 shows, there are four connotations of *qiong2* as an adjective. First of all, a description of an endless state can be realized by means of *qiong2* in (7). Then, an expression of an extreme state like *qiong2* in (8), a description of impoverishment like *qiong2* in (9) or an expression of being poverty-stricken and an unknown situation like *qiong2* in (10) are shown. Finally, describing a remote and desolate area like *qiong2* in (11) is also found in the dictionary. *Qiong2* is also a verb (12) and a noun (13). The last syntactical function of *qiong2* is an adverb, which means thoroughness as in (14)

On the basis of the definitions, both lexemes, *pin2* and *qiong2*, contain more than one concept. The idea of poverty is not only the concept both quasi-synonyms share to point out one's lack of money but also the financial concept we are trying to conceptualize. Unlike these two lexemes, the explanation of the compound adjective, *pin2qiong2*, is confined to the lack of money or a poor life people lead. The grammatical function of the compound is limited. Nevertheless, we find that *pin2* can function as an adjective, a noun and a verb while *qiong2* can serve as an adjective and noun regarding the idea of poverty.

6.1.1.2. *The Expressions in the On-Line Corpus*

We have presented the expressions of *pin2, qiong2* and *pin2qiong2* in the dictionary in order to see whether there is a discrepancy. Now let us turn to exemplify the data in the on-line corpus: *Newspapers in Taiwan*.[1] For the purpose of this study, among the 13 various newspapers, *jing1ji4ri4bao4* 經濟日報 'Economic Daily News' which covers much more news related to the economic aspect was chosen as the primary source of our data. The periods of data collection are limited to before and after the Economic Crisis, which happened during late 2008: February 16th to September 15th in 2008 and September 16th in 2008 to April 15th in 2009.

Table 6.3 displays the examples retrieved from the corpus, the lexeme *pin2* which is related to the meaning of poverty can be categorized into two grammatical groups, that is, adjectives and nouns.

Table 6.3 shows that *pin2* can be an adjective that precedes a noun, as in (15) or precedes other synonymous or antonymous adjectives to form

Table 6.3. The syntactical functions of *pin2* in the corpus.

Syntactical functions of *pin2*		Examples
Adjective	before a noun	(15) *pin2 tong2* 貧童 'poor child = poor child'
	before an adjective	(16) *pin2 kun4* 貧困 'poor besieged = poor' (17) *pin2 fu4* 貧富 'poor wealthy = poor and wealthy'
	after a noun	(18) *xin1 pin2* 心貧 'heart poor = being poor in spirit'
	after an adjective	(19) *chi4 pin2* 赤貧 'red poor = impoverished'
	after an adverb	(20) *yi4 pin2 ru2 xi3* 一貧如洗 'one poor like wash = penniless'
Noun		(21) *xiao4 pin2 bu2 xiao4 chang1* 笑貧不笑娼 'laugh poverty not laugh prostitute = poverty is more shameful than prostitution' (22) *fu2 pin2* 扶貧 'support poverty = help poor people'

[1] This database (http://newspaper.ntl.gov.tw) consists of 13 domestic newspapers in Taiwan, such as *lian2he2 bao4* 聯合報 'United Daily News,' *zhong1guo2shi2bao4* 中國時報 'China Times,' *shi4jie4 ri4bao4* 世界日報 'World Journal,' and so on. In total, the corpus covers 20, 529, 489 lexical items up to year 2010.

a coordinate compound as in (16) and (17). In addition, *ping2* can also follow a noun to form a subject-predicate compound in (18), follow a relevant adjective to form a coordinate compound in (19) or follow an adverb in (20). As for being a noun, *pin2* often follows a verb such as the example (21) and (22). In short, *pin2* can be a modifier and a noun.

Table 6.4. The syntactical functions of *qiong2* in the corpus.

Syntactical functions of *qiong2*		Examples
Adjective	before a noun	(23) *qiong2 ren2* 窮人 'poor people = the poor'
	before an adjective	(24) *qiong2 ku3* 窮苦 'poor bitter = poverty-stricken'
	after a linking verb	(25) *min2 zhong4 bian4 qiong2* 民眾變窮 'people crowd become poor = common people become poor'
	after an adverb	(26) *qiong2 shang4 jia1 qiong2* 窮上加窮 'poverty upon plus poor = poorer'
Verb	(27) *zai4 qiong2 yi2 ci4* 再窮一次 'again impoverish one time = become poor again'	
Noun	(28) *zhuang1 qiong2* 裝窮 'pretend poverty = rich people claim to be poor'	

As for *qiong2*, from the data collected in the on-line corpus, *qiong2* that is used to describe someone's economic status has three syntactical functions (see Table 6.4).

We see that the usage of *qiong2*, which means a poor condition, has three grammatical categories: adjectives, nouns and verbs. First of all, *qiong2* is an adjective and has four variations. It can be used before a noun in (23) and an adjective—whether a synonym or an antonym—in (24). Also, it can be used after a linking verb in (25) and after an adverb in (26). Additionally, *qiong2* is a verb in (27). Besides, *qiong2* can be a noun which is used after a verb, like (28) *zhuang1* 裝 'pretend.'

On the other hand, the compound *pin2qiong2* is displayed in Table 6.5. *Pin2qiong2* can be identified as an adjective modifying a noun, like (29) *pin2qiong2 xian4* or can be modified by an adverb, like (30) *zui4 pin2qiong2 de ren2*. Furthermore, it can be a noun that completes a verb phrase such as (31) *mian4 dui4 pin2qiong2*.

The above presentation of *pin2, qiong2* and *pin2qiong2* in the dictionary and in the newspaper shows that the data presented in the dictionary have seldom been revised or had new meanings added to them, so that

Table 6.5. The syntactical functions of *pin2qiong2* in the corpus.

Syntactical functions of *pin2qiong2*		Examples
Adjective	before a noun	(29) *pin2qiong2 xian4* 貧窮線 'poor line = the standard of poverty'
	after an adverb	(30) *zui4 pin2qiong2 de ren2* 最貧窮的人 'the most poor POSS. person = the most poor people'
Noun		(31) *mian4 dui4 pin2qiong2* 面對貧窮 'face to poverty = face poverty'

the items in dictionaries tend to be fixed. However, an on-line newspaper corpus is a naturally evolving system that records new information from newspapers and can easily gain emergent meanings. In other words, due to the continually changing data given in the newspaper corpus, the new meanings of the FLEs emerge.

6.1.1.3. *The Comparison between the Dictionary and Corpus*

This section investigates how the target concept of poverty is presented in the form of three quasi-synonyms in the dictionary and in the corpus. Hopper's (1987) viewpoint of Emergent Grammar is adopted for the analysis of the data. According to Hopper:

> The notion of Emergent Grammar is meant to suggest that structure, or regularity, comes out of discourse and is shaped by discourse as much as it shapes discourse in an on-going process (1987: 142).

That is to say, there exist no fixed structures as well as regular grammar because of the ever-changing discourse. The comparison of the target linguistic expressions derived from the dictionary as well as from the on-line updated corpus is thus necessary.

Based on what we have categorized, most usages of *pin2*, *qiong2* and *pin2qiong2* in the dictionary are consistent with the newspaper corpus. However, there are still some differences between these target terms' parts of speech. First of all, take *pin2* as an example. In the dictionary, *pin2* can be viewed as an adjective, a noun and a verb, but in the newspaper corpus, the usage of being a verb is not found. As to *qiong2* in the dictionary, it has four grammatical classifications because of its polysemous meanings. However, if we focus on the meaning related to poverty, *qiong2* belongs to two grammatical categories: nouns and adjectives. In the newspaper corpus, in addition to being a noun or an adjective, *qiong2* can also be a verb which is modified by an adverb. This phenomenon can be explained by means of Hopper's (1987) Emergent Grammar. "Grammar is what results when formulas are re-arranged, or dismantled and re-assembled, in different ways" (Hopper 1987: 145). In other words, with the prevalent acceptance of *qiong2* used as a verb to convey the action of being impoverished in the current corpus, *qiong2* emerges as a new part of speech that is not yet accounted for in the dictionary. Gradually, the syntactical functions of *qiong2* re-assemble.

Finally, the synonymous compound *pin2qiong2*, at first, is just an adjective in the dictionary, but in the newspaper corpus, it can also be a noun to denote a kind of situation of being poor. This is another example that should suffice to illustrate the argument of Emergent Grammar (Hopper 1987).

6.1.2. *The Semantic Prosody*

As discussed above, the three target FLEs, *pin2, qiong2* as well as *pin2-qiong2*, whether in the Chinese dictionary or in the newspaper corpus, combine with other linguistic expressions. However, due to the effect of Emergent Grammar (Hopper 1987), the juxtaposition of these collocates is different and is presented as follows.

To the left of semantic prosody of *pin2, qiong2* and *pin2qiong2* is presented in 6.2.2.1. The right semantic prosody of *pin2, qiong2* and *pin2-qiong2* is shown in 6.2.2.2. In 6.2.2.3, the comparison of semantic prosody of *pin2, qiong2* and *pin2qiong2* is displayed.

Tao (2003) argued that the investigation of semantic prosody serves as a method to illustrate Emergent Grammar (Hopper 1987). Semantic prosody, a juxtaposition of the target item together with other collocated words, varies from data source to data source. "Semantic prosody is a semantic quality that is acquired through language use" (Tao 2003: 846). It can be inferred that examining the semantic prosody of target linguistic expressions from people's daily novel communication may also shed light on Emergent Grammar. In the examined newspaper corpus, the compound *pin2qiong2* can serve as a noun which means an impoverished condition and can also serve as an adjective to describe something or somebody that is badly-off. Different parts of speech of *pin2qiong2* in the sentence will integrate with different words to meet its grammatical functions.

6.1.2.1. *To the Left*

Among various combinations of *pin2qiong2*, the form of the verb phrase to its left part is preferred. According to the data collected, the most left semantic prosody of *pin2qiong2* is inclined to form a verb phrase, that is, a verb precedes *pin2qiong2*, a compound noun, to show how to deal with one's unfavorable economic situation. The most frequent verb which combines with *pin2qiong2* is *tuo1 li2* 脫離 'shed-leave; come off' to mean that the subject hates the situation and tries to get rid of it. Other synonyms are *bai3 tuo1* 擺脫 'put-shed; get rid of' and *yuan3 li2* 遠離 'far-leave; far away.' Some of the verbs are related to war like *tiao3 zhan4* 挑戰 'raise-war; challenge,' *xiao1 mi3* 消弭 'eliminate; put an end' and so on. Based on the verbs to the left side of *pin2qiong2*, these words imply a negative attitude which people hold to deal with things they dislike, such as troubles or difficulties which are rather abstract to people. *Pin2-qiong2* can be inferred as an annoying thing people want to fight in order to make it disappear in front of them. As a result, various related verbs are employed in order to show how determined human beings are prepared to tackle this issue.

With the wider application of various verbs, the representation of *pin2-qiong2* becomes more and more vivid. Thus, *pin2qiong2* can be seen as a concrete substance that people can do something to when facing it, like *jian3 shao3* 減少 'minus-less; decrease' and *bi3 jiao4* 比較 'compare; compare.' *Pin2, qiong2* can also be referred as a substance people try to handle, like *chu3 li3* 處理 'manage-administer; cope with' and *gai3 shan4* 改善 'change-perfect; improve.' In addition to being a noun, *pin2qiong2* as an adjective can follow an adverb of degree to emphasize the condition, like *zui4* 最 'the most; the most' or the possessive marker *de* 的.

6.1.2.2. *To the Right*

Conveying differentiated concepts by means of communication results in the emergence of semantic prosody. The different juxtapositions of the target FLE reveal the implication (Tao 2003). Therefore, in addition to the left of semantic prosody of *pin2qiong2*, the right semantic prosody of *pin2-qiong2* is also of concern. The opposite way of combining with the target terms reveals different patterns. The frequent combinations to the right of *pin2qiong2* are adjective phrases. The preference of association with other words or phrases differs from the position the target FLE occupies. Unlike to the left of semantic prosody of *pin2qiong2*, the right semantic prosody shows that there are two kinds of adjective phrases that attach to *pin2qiong2*. One is that the possessive marker *de* 的 together with a noun following *pin2qiong2*, and the other is a noun following *pin2qiong2* directly. Basically, these nouns can be classified within several groups. One of these groups can be marked as human beings such as *ren2* 人 'people; people,' *zhe3* 者 'those-who; those who' and so on. *Pin2qiong2* combines with these words to describe the economic status of a person. *Pin2qiong2* can also describe a group's economic condition, like *guo2 jia1* 國家 'country-home; a country' and *xiang1 cun1* 鄉村 'country-village; a country' where people gather together. In addition, some words related to statistics often follow *pin2qiong2* such as *zhi3 biao1* 指標 'finger-mark; an index' and *lü4* 率 'rate; the ratio.' These two expressions are quantified expressions of their poverty. Expressions, such as *yin1 zi3* 因子 'cause-son; a factor' and *yin1 su4* 因素 'cause-plain; a factor' are modified by *pin2qiong2* when people want to denote the relationship between poverty and its related factors. For example, *pin2 qiong2 yin1 zi3* 貧窮因子 'poor-poor-cause-son; the factor of poverty' indicates the causes that lead to poverty.

6.1.2.3. *The Comparison before and after the Economic Crisis*

We have examined the left and the right parts which co-occur with *pin2-qiong2*. Based on the results, we have found that semantic prosody does help to depict how a word is evaluated as Tao (2003: 846) suggested, that "semantic prosody is usually realized as favorable (positive) neutral or non-favorable (negative) connotations." The data collected for the chapter shows that the semantic prosody between two spans, before and after the Economic Crisis, is slightly different as shown in Table 6.6.

Table 6.6 shows that although the neutral semantic prosody between two periods of time before or after the Economic Crisis has the highest percentage, the gap between the negative and positive is not the same. It shows that the difference between negative and positive semantic prosody after the Economic Crisis is bigger than it was before the Crisis. Therefore, it can be inferred that people living in the age of the Economic Crisis suffer more pressure than before and try to let off their feelings by expressing metaphorical sentences. '*Poverty*' combined with the negative prosody conveys a positive connotation. That is, people take actions to overcome the problem of 'poverty' instead of passively facing the problem. The difference between the negative prosody and positive connotations provides us with the communication need as Tao (2003) also suggested.

Table 6.6. Semantic prosody from two periods of time.

Time	Negative		Neutral		Positive		Total
	No.	%	No.	%	No.	%	
before the Economic Crisis	54	34.2	68	43.0	37	23.4	158
after the Economic Crisis	48	39.0	52	42.0	23	19.0	123

6.2. The Discussion of 'Poverty' by Means of SUMO

As mentioned above, in order to have an understanding of the metaphorical expressions, *pin2, qiong2* and *pin2qiong2*, based on Emergent Grammar (Hopper 1987), the comparison of the target expression in the dictionary together with the corpus, the semantic prosody and the categorical shift are presented to further understand the economic concept of 'poverty.' In addition, the comparison of *'poverty'* in different periods of time can be regarded as a practice of Emergent Grammar since the three target FLEs before and after the Economic Crisis have distinct representations. Lastly, the basic ontological knowledge is used to get the hidden essence of these related metaphorical linguistic expressions.

SUMO is an abbreviation of suggested upper merged ontology developed by the IEEE Standard Upper Ontology Working Group that helps understand the conceptualization of lexical items. "It consists of a set of general concepts, relations, and axioms and formalizes the description of structures of knowledge domain" (Gong 2009: 5). SUMO can be classified into eleven categories. They are base-ontology, graph-theory, mere topology, numeric-functions, objects, processes, qualities, set-class theory, structural-ontology, temporal-concepts and units of measurement. Each category including their sub-categories and examples to explain the relationships of concepts is listed in Table 6.7.

Table 6.7. The classification of ontology.

Sections of ontology	Examples of sub-categories	Definition
base-ontology	Agent	Something or someone that can act on its own and produce changes in the world
graph-theory	Tree	A Tree is a Directed Graph that has no Graph Loops
mere topology	Hole	A hole is an immaterial body located at the surface of an Object. Since every Hole is ontologically dependent on its host (i.e., the object in which it is a hole), being a Hole is defined as being a hole in something. Note that two Holes may occupy the same region, or part of the same region, without sharing any parts.

Table 6.7 *(cont.)*

Sections of ontology	Examples of sub-categories	Definition
numeric-functions	Number E	Number E is the Real Number that is the base for natural logarithms. It is approximately equal to 2.718282.
objects	Objects	One of the parts of speech. The Class of Words that conventionally denote Processes.
processes	Intentional process	A Process that is deliberately set in motion by a Cognitive Agent.
qualities	Psychological attribute	Attributes that characterize the mental or behavioral life of an Organism
set-class theory	Finite Set	A Set containing a finite number of elements.
Sections of ontology	Examples of sub-categories	Definition
structural-ontology	Domain	Provides a computationally and heuristically convenient mechanism for declaring the argument types of a given relation. The formula (domain real int class) means that the int'th element of each tuple in the relation rel must be an instance of class. Specifying argument types is very helpful in maintaining ontology. Representation systems can use these specifications to classify terms and check integrity constraints. If the restriction on the argument type of a Relation is not captured by a Set Or Class already defined in the ontology, one can specify a Set Or Class compositionally with the functions Union Fn, Intersection Fn, etc.
temporal-concepts	Year	The Class of all calendar Years.
units of measure	Currency Measure	Includes all standard measures of monetary value, including United States Dollar, United States Cent, Lire, Yen, etc.

Among eleven categories of ontology, the data we have collected for this study exist in four groups, processes, qualities, base and structure. As Figure 6.1 shows, it is interesting that the data, which are classified into different processes on the basis of Halliday's (1985) transitivity, belong to the same ontology.

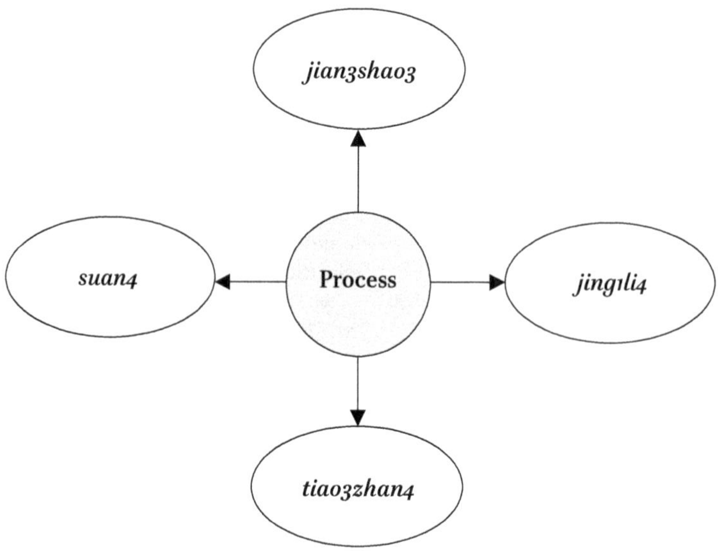

Figure 6.1. The ontology of the process of 'poverty'.

Figure 6.1 shows that the verb *jian3shao3* 減少 'minus-less; decrease' belongs to the material process, *jing1li4* 經歷 'go-experience; experience' belongs to the mental process, *suan4* 算 'count; might be considered as' belongs to the relational process and *tiao3zhan4* 挑戰 'raise-war; challenge' belongs to the verbal process. Nevertheless, they are classified into the same ontology.

To be more specific, the verb *jian3shao3* 減少 'minus-less; decrease' belongs to the material process because we see *pin2qiong2* as an entity when we decrease *pin2qiong2* as in *jian3 shao3 pin2qiong2* 減少貧窮 'minus-less-poverty; decrease poverty.' *Jing1li4* 經歷 'go-experience; experience' falls into the mental process for *pin2qiong2* is thought of a phenomenon because poverty can be experienced as in *jing1 li4 pin2qiong2* 經歷貧窮 'go-experience-poverty; experience poverty.' *Suan4* 算 'count; might be considered as' belongs to the relational process because we see *pin2-qiong2* as a countable noun when we say *suan4 shi4 pin2qiong2* 算是貧窮

'count-be-poverty; might be considered as poverty' and *tiao3zhan4* 挑戰 'raise-war; challenge' belongs to the verbal process because we challenge *pin2qiong2* as if *pin2qiong2* were a person to challenge as shown in *tiao3-zhan4 pin2qiong2* 挑戰貧窮 'raise-war-poverty; challenge poverty.' The four verbs above are classified into the ontology "processes" by following Halliday's definition. Namely, "processes" mentioned in Table 6.7 means a cognitive agent deliberately proceeds with something.

To sum up, the relationship between the transitivity and the ontology can be interpreted as the conceptual process of the idea of 'poverty' in Figure 6.2. The transitive process is dominated by the ontology to depict the metaphorical process of the idea of 'poverty.' As Huang (1995) says it is difficult to differentiate an ontological or factual question from a semantic one. The line between them is vague.

Therefore, it can be inferred that the ontology and the semantics are complementary and can be utilized as a tool to interpret each other. According to the data, most verbs which juxtapose with the idea of 'poverty' are assigned to the ontology of "process" and the ontology of "quality." Consequently, it is inferred that 'poverty' gives people a negative impression and is considered to be a negative mark.

"A semantic question often emerges from an apparently factual question, and the latter can be resolved often only by resolving the former" (Huang 1995: 133). That is, a further understanding of the ontological knowledge can be gained by exploring the semantic phenomenon. Take '*poverty*' as an example. People spare all their efforts to get rid of 'poverty' by a series of intentional and sometimes painstaking processes. These processes of

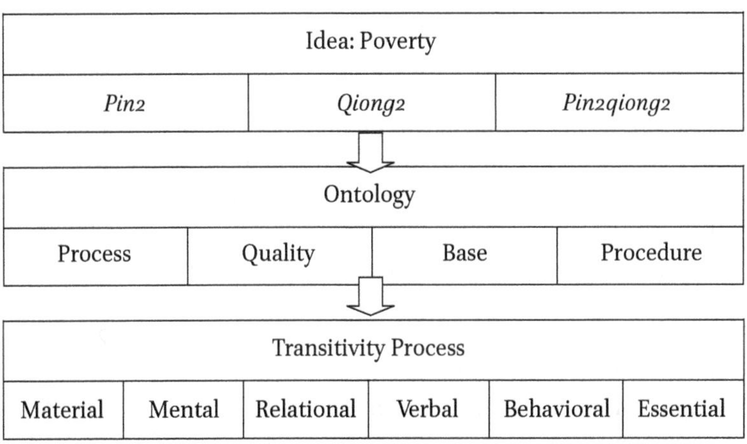

Figure 6.2. The conceptualization of 'poverty'.

dealing with 'poverty' are in accordance with some procedures which are characterized by qualities of positive effectiveness. Figure 6.2 on the previous page shows the process of conceptualizing the idea of 'poverty.'

In Figure 6.2, the concept of being poor is substantiated into three quasi-synonyms, *pin2, qiong2* and *pin2qiong2*. Although each quasi-synonym has a different distribution of transitivity, they share four similar ontological types: process, quality, base and procedure. That is, from the philosophy of ontology, these linguistic expressions that are derived from one economic notion denote the same meaning.

6.3. Conclusion

'Poverty' is a negative economic circumstance of economic activities and is highly pertinent to the economic field. Therefore, it can be inferred that '*poverty*,' which is seen to be relevant to economics, is not concrete. The purpose of this present chapter is to explore how people depict the complicated concept, which is used to describe one's disadvantaged economic status in the newspaper corpus. We asked two questions for this research: (1) How do Mandarin native speakers evaluate *pin2, qiong2* and *pin2-qiong2* from an emergent perspective? (2) What cognition or economic reactions occur in the realizations and interpretations of *pin2, qiong2* and *pin2qiong2*?

To answer the questions, we see that although the three quasi-synonyms, *pin2, qiong2* and *pin2qiong2* have the same concept of 'poverty,' it is assumed that each quasi-synonym itself does not always share the exact same distribution among the parts of speech in the dictionary and in the newspaper corpus. In other words, in the fixed dictionary or in the ever-changing corpus, each quasi-synonym in most cases has the same syntactical functions, such as being nouns or adjectives. However, there is a slight difference. As mentioned before, the parts of speech of *pin2* are an adjective, a verb and a noun in the dictionary while serving as adjectives and nouns in the on-line corpus. This phenomenon is in accordance with Emergent Grammar (Hopper 1987). The ongoing development of language leads to changes in the parts of the speech for the FLEs. In addition, in terms of Halliday's (1985) classification, comparing the collected data during two periods of time, before and after the Economic Crisis, the number of examples assigned to the material process drops while the number of examples in the remaining four processes rises. According to Emergent Grammar, it can be interpreted that after the influence of the Crisis, people tend to adopt a more conservative way to describe their financial status and hint that they are in a passive situation, which is out of control and unpredictable. That is, the presentation of 'poverty' is controlled by people and is related to how people interpret the world around them. For example, after the Economic Crisis, people tend to use more negative semantic prosody of *pin2qiong2* than before the Crisis. This highlights the determination of people to fight against the bad results of a bad economy.

In addition, though *pin2, qiong2* and *pin2qiong2* are extended from the same concept of 'poverty,' Mandarin speakers have different expectations and attitudes toward them. *Qiong2* is more widely accepted as an FLE to describe people's impoverished situation than *pin2*. Therefore, *qiong2* is substantiated into various linguistic forms to meet different grammatical functions. On the other hand, *pin2qiong2* has fewer variations in its part of speech because it is a fixed compound.

Finally, the cognitive realization of 'poverty' is manifested by observing the ontology. Despite different categorizations of each similar linguistic expression sharing the same concept of 'poverty,' the analysis of the ontology gives the philosophical perspective insights. No matter what different processes these quasi-synonyms have, in essence, they are the same because they are classified into the ontology of process, quality, base and procedure. This interpretation is consonant with Smith and Stone's viewpoint:

> Public opinions about specific socioeconomic matters typically reflect global beliefs that people hold about the causes of wealth and poverty. For most people, these beliefs emanate from a mental concoction of daily observations, experiences, and lay philosophies in other words, a metatheory about social inequalities (1989: 93).

In other words, people conceptualize the idea as a basic element which is attached with a negative quality. As a result, in order to get rid of this situation, people try to adopt different procedures to cope with being poor.

This chapter focuses on the conceptualization of economically disadvantaged conditions in the form of three quasi-synonyms, *pin2qiong2* 貧窮 'poor,' *pin2* 貧 'poor' and *qiong2* 窮 'poor' in the newspaper corpus from a cognitive-emergent perspective. To conclude, *pin2 qiong2, pin2* and *qiong2* are derived from the same economic concept of 'poverty,' but they have different metaphorical characteristics. In addition, the ontology behind *pin2 qiong2, pin2* and *qiong2* conveys how Mandarin Chinese native speakers' perception and economic reactions influences the interpretation of the idea of 'poverty.'

CHAPTER SEVEN

STOCK MARKET JARGONS IN MANDARIN: RELATED METAPHORS AND THEIR SOURCE DOMAINS

Carrie Hsin-wen Tseng & Shelley Ching-yu Hsieh

7.0. Introduction

This study aims to investigate stock market jargons as they are used in non-stock-market-related articles in newspapers in Taiwan. For instance, *nan2han2 ou3xiang4 shen1jia4 ge4ge4 zhang3ting2ban3* 南韓偶像身價個個漲停板 'Every South Korean idol's value rises' is used in an article to indicate that the idol group is extremely loved. This chapter focuses on (1) Is there any preferred syntactic category employed in the SD of stock market? (2) Does any cultural feature occur in the SD of stock market? (3) What are the attributes of the GCB Metaphor in the SD of stock market?

Five sections are organized in this chapter. First, we present the token distribution and MP postulation for each conceptual metaphor by means of the CMM framework (Ahrens, 2002) in 7.1. Then we verify each MP postulation by an individual expression that is highly frequent in 7.2. Section 7.3 further demonstrates the structure of the GCB Metaphor formed by the conceptual metaphors in the SD of stock market. In 7.4 the preferred syntactic category in the SD of stock market is discussed. Finally a conclusion is in 7.5.

7.1. The Categorization of Conceptual Metaphors

The categorization of conceptual metaphors is analyzed on the basis of the CMM, which examines metaphorical expressions in terms of entities (nouns), qualities (adjectives), and functions (verbs) that map between a SD and a TD. In order to define and delimit the SD, the present study has chosen to look at sentences appearing with stock market jargons gathered from non-stock-market-related articles in newspapers. The number of tokens is the criterion used to determine whether the conceptual metaphor is used or not. If the number of tokens of a conceptual metaphor is less than 10, it will not be listed in Table 7.1, nor discussed, as it is not significant: for example, POLICY AS STOCK MARKET with 4 tokens and

COUNTRY AS STOCK MARKET with 2 tokens. Table 7.1 shows the number of tokens for each conceptual metaphor. Eleven conceptual metaphors are found in the SD of stock market. The sequence of each conceptual metaphor is based on the significance of the token.

Table 7.1. The number of tokens for each conceptual metaphor.

Conceptual metaphors		Tokens
1	SPORTS CONTEST AS STOCK MARKET	339
2	PEOPLE'S VALUE AS STOCK MARKET	254
3	SHOW BUSINESS AS STOCK MARKET	159
4	MARRIAGE AS STOCK MARKET	139
5	POLITICS AS STOCK MARKET	132
6	SUPERIOR FORCE AS STOCK MARKET	66
7	FORTUNE TELLING AS STOCK MARKET	54
8	TEMPERATURE AS STOCK MARKET	49
9	EMOTION AS STOCK MARKET	46
10	AGE AS STOCK MARKET	38
11	OUTLOOK ON LIFE AS STOCK MARKET	27
Total		1303

In what follows, the categorization of conceptual metaphors and an MP are discussed. The number of tokens for each conceptual metaphor is discussed in section 7.2, further analyzed in terms of the GCB Metaphor in 7.3, and categorized into entities, qualities, and functions in 7.4.

7.1.1. *HUMAN ACTIVITY IS STOCK MARKET*

The TD human activity is divided into five types: SPORTS CONTEST AS STOCK MARKET, SHOW BUSINESS AS STOCK MARKET, MARRIAGE AS STOCK MARKET, POLITICS AS STOCK MARKET, and FORTUNE TELLING AS STOCK MARKET. Human activity represents a series of specific exercises that only belong to mankind and that other creatures are incapable of achieving.

7.1.1.1. *SPORTS CONTEST IS STOCK MARKET*

Sport is a popular activity in human society. Its fierce competition is like the rapidly rising and falling indices of a stock market. Sports contest is conceptualized in terms of a stock market. That is, a stock market as the SD gets mapped onto sports contest as the TD. Examples (1) and (2), *wei3pan2* 尾盤 'final session' and *zhu3li4* 主力 'main force' are the metaphorical expressions which are identified as the entities that correspond between the SDs and TDs. Here, nouns are assigned to name the entities.

In (1), *wei3pan2* 尾盤 'final session' refers to the session before the stock market closes and can be conceptualized as the player's final shot that wins the competition by a narrow margin before the ball game ends. *Wei3pan2* 尾盤 'final session' is always the crucial moment that turns defeat into victory or turns victory into defeat. In (2), *zhu3li4* 主力 'main force' refers to individuals or groups with sufficient capital and power to influence stock values and is conceptualized as players making a great contribution to their team.

(1) *wei3pan2* 尾盤 'final session'; Entity
Bu4 lai2 en1 la1 wei3 pan2 hu2 ren2 shou1 hong2
布 萊 恩 拉 尾盤 湖 人 收 紅
Brian pull final session Lakers receive red
qiang1 xiang3 qian2 tiao4 tou2 jin4 wang3
槍 響 前 跳 投 進 網
firearm sound before jump shot enter net
'Brian's final jump shot wins the ball game for the Lakers.'

(2) *zhu3li4* 主力 'main force'; Entity
Da4 zhan4 qian2 xi4 kai1 mu4 zhan4 zhu3 li4 yi4 dui1
大 戰 前 夕 開 幕 戰 主力 一 堆
Great war eve opening battle main force a crowd
shang1 bing1
傷 兵
wounded soldier
'The main players got hurt before the start of the competition.'

In (3a) to (4b), *gao1dang3* 高檔 'good status' and *di1dang3* 低檔 'bad status' are the metaphorical expressions which are identified as the qualities that correspond between the SDs and TDs. Here, adjectives are assigned to name the qualities. In (3a) and (3b), *gao1dang3* 高檔 'good status' refers to stock value in good condition and is conceptualized as great strength in competition. In (4a) and (4b), *di1dang3* 低檔 'bad status' refers to stock value in bad condition and is conceptualized as poor strength or low ranking in competition.

(3) *gao1dang3* 高檔 'good status'; Quality
a. *Hui1lang2 er4 xian4 kang2 da4 xi4 hua4 jie3 shang1*
灰 狼 二 線 扛 大 戲 化 解 傷
Timberwolves two line carry big play reconcile wounded
bing1 wei2 ji1 zhan4 li4 bao3 chi2 gao1 dang3
兵 危 機 戰 力 保 持 高 檔
soldier crisis power keep good status
'The Timberwolves took the responsibility to solve the crisis of their injury problems, and their strength still remains in good condition.'

b. *Chen2 huai2 shan1 da3 ji2 wei2 chi2 gao1dang3*
陳 懷 山 打 擊 維 持 高檔
Chen Huai-shan strike keep high file
'Chenhuaishan's strike remains in good condition.'

(4) *di1dang3* 低檔 'bad status'; Quality

a. *Qiu2ji4 yi4 kai1 sai4 jiu4 xian4ru4 di1*
球季 一 開 賽 就 陷入 低
Ball season one open competition PART sink into low
chao2 da3 ji2 lü4 di1 dang3 pai2 huai2
潮 打 擊 率 低檔 徘 徊
tide strike rate bad status hover
'When the ball season starts, the batting average is poor.'

b. *Shang4 ban4 ji4 pai2 ming2 yi4 zhi2 zai4 di1*
上 半 季 排 名 一 直 在 低
The first half season rank all the time in low
dang3 pai2 huai2 de di4 yi1 jin1 gang1 dui4
檔 徘 徊 的 第 一 金剛隊
status hover the first AGAN team
qian2 tian1 yan3chu1 an1 da3
前 天 演出 安 打
the day before yesterday perform base hit
he2 de2 fen1
和 得 分
and get points
'The AGAN team, with a poor ranking in the first half of the season, put in a great batting performance and posted a big score the day before yesterday.'

Examples (5)–(7), *kai1di1zou3gao1* 開低走高 'going from bad to good status,' *die2shen1fan3tan2* 跌深反彈 'fall deeply before gaining' and *ni4shi4-shang4yang2* 逆勢上揚 'rising in bad conditions' are the metaphorical expressions which are identified as the functions that correspond between the SDs and TDs. Here, verbs are assigned to name the functions. In (5), *kai1di1zou3gao1* 開低走高 'going from bad to good status' refers to an index or stock value going from high to low and is conceptualized as a player with a low status winning the championship. In (6), *die2shen1fan3tan2* 跌深反彈 'fall deeply before gaining' refers to an index or stock value falling then gaining and is conceptualized as the team with the worst status winning the baseball game. In (7), *ni4shi4shang4yang2* 逆勢上揚 'rising in bad conditions' refers to a stock value that keeps rising despite the bad status of the market and is understood metaphorically as the team's performance getting better in bad conditions.

(5) *kai1di1zou3gao1* 開低走高 'going from bad to good status'; Function
Fa4 guo2 wang3 qiu2 gong1 kai1 sai4 *kai1 di1 zou3 gao1*
法國網球公開賽 開 低 走 高
French Open start low go high
yi4 lai2 yi4 wang3 jue2 zhan4 guo4 cheng2 xi4ju4hua4
一 來 一 往 決 戰 過程 戲劇化
one come one go decide fight process dramatic
ke1rui4er3 hou4lai2 ju1 shang4 qiang3zou3 guan4 jun1
柯瑞爾 後來 居 上 搶走 冠軍
Courier later situate up rob champion
'In the French Open, the progress of the decisive battle was dramatic, and Courier came from behind to win the championship.'

(6) *die2shen1fan3tan2* 跌深反彈 'fall deeply before gaining'; Function
Ben3 zhou1 dui4 shi1 lian2 zhan4 san1 chang3
本 周 對 獅 連 戰 三 場
This week facing Lions recessive fight three period
you1 guan1 neng2 fou3 die2 shen1 fan3 tan2
攸 關 能 否 跌 深 反 彈
vital can no fall deep contrary bounce
'The results of the three games against the Lions will influence the rankings this week.'

(7) *ni4shi4shang4yang2* 逆勢上揚 'rising in bad conditions'; Function
Zhi3 you3 xiong2 dui4 ni4 shi4 shang4 yang2
只 有 熊 隊 逆 勢 上 揚
Only have Bears against trend raise
'Only the Bear's team performance is getting better in these bad conditions.'

In SPORTS CONTEST AS STOCK MARKET, stock market jargons used as metaphorical expressions can be classified into entities, qualities, and functions. From the examples examined above, we arrive at some conclusions. The stock market jargons identified as functions tend to be conceptualized as the fierce process of competition in sport by dynamic descriptions, whereas stock market jargons identified as qualities tend to be conceptualized as good or bad performances of players and/or teams. However, the major mapping relation between the stock market jargons identified as entities cannot be found because their mapping attributes are not so concentrated.

(I) An MP for SPORTS CONTEST AS STOCK MARKET can be postulated: sports contest is understood as a stock market because the activity of trading in a stock market is like the fierce competition of a sports contest.

7.1.1.2. *SHOW BUSINESS IS STOCK MARKET*

Show business entertains people. Related news in the newspaper always draws the attention of readers. Show business is conceptualized in terms of a stock market. That is, a stock market as the SD gets mapped onto show business as the TD. In (8) and (9), *ting2sun3dian3* 停損點 'stop-loss point' and *niu2shi4* 牛市 'bull market' are metaphorical expressions which are identified as the entities that correspond between the SDs and TDs. In (8), *ting2sun3dian3* 停損點 'stop-loss point' refers to a loss limit that investors can bear and is understood metaphorically as an artist using a press conference to explain her affair, which is regarded as the stop-loss point for smoothing over following activities. In (9), *niu2shi4* 牛市 'bull market' refers to a stock value rising or being expected to rise and is associated with a show gaining in popularity over many years.

(8) *ting2sun3dian3* 停損點 'stop-loss point'; Entity
Ci3 ju3 xing2 tong2 jiang1 men1 shao1 zhong1 de fei1wen2
此 舉 形 同 將 悶燒 中 的 緋聞
This action like use smolder in POSS. affair
yi2ci4 li4 kong1 dai4 yan2 ji4 zhe3 hui4
一次 利 空 代 言 記 者 會
once profit hollow endorsement press conference
jiu4 ru2 tong2 ting2 sun3 dian3 jie1 xia4 lai2 cai2 neng2
就 如 同 停 損 點 接 下 來 才 能
PART like stop loss point then can
zheng4chang2 de xuan1chuan2 Ella de xin1 xi4
正 常 地 宣 傳 Ella 的 新 戲
normally promote Ella POSS. new play
dian4 shi4 yuan2 sheng1dai4 shen4 zhi4 yan3 chang4 hui4
電 視 原 聲 帶 甚 至 演 唱 會
TV original sound track even concert
'Ella's endorsement press conference, the stop-loss point, was used as a vehicle to explain all the rumors surrounding her about various affairs so that Ella could promote her new TV play, TV original sound track, and concert.'

(9) *niu2shi4* 牛市 'bull market'; Entity
Ju4 bao4 dao3 xiang1 jiao4 mei3 guo2 ou3 xiang4
據 報 導 相 較 《美 國 偶 像》
According to news report compare America idol
deng3 guo2 wai4 zhen ren2 xiu4 jie2 mu4 chuang4 ban4
等 國外 真 人 秀 節 目 創辦
etc. abroad reality show program found
duo1 nian2 zhi4jin1 yi1ran2 niu2shi4 bu2 tui4
多 年 至今 依然 牛市 不 退
many years so far still bull market not recede
'According to the report, the reality show 'American Idol,' which has been running for many years, is still popular.'

In (10) to (12), *jie3pan2* 解盤 'analyze the stock status,' *kai1pan2* 開盤 'market opening,' and *kai1gao1zou3gao1* 開高走高 'high from beginning to end' are the metaphorical expressions which are identified as the functions that correspond between the SDs and TDs. In (10), *jie3pan2* 解盤 'analyze the stock status' refers to stock trends being analyzed and predicted and is understood metaphorically as the nominated singers' strengths being analyzed. In (11), *kai1pan2* 開盤 'market opening' refers to the opening of the stock market and is associated with the beginning of a show. In (12), *kai1gao1zou3gao1* 開高走高 'high from beginning to end' refers to a stock value being high from beginning to end and is conceptualized as the movie being popular from beginning to end.

(10) *jie3pan2* 解盤 'analyze the stock status'; Function

Quan2 min2 zhi2 xuan3 ge3 lai2 mei3 tai2 wan1 pin3 wei4
全 民 直 選 葛 萊 美 台 灣 品 味
All people direct choose Grammy Taiwan taste
yue4 mi2 shi4li4 quan2 mian4 gan1 rao3 ge3 lai2 mei3
樂 迷 勢力 全 面 干 擾 葛 萊 美
Music fan power overall interference Grammy
ru4 wei2 ge1 shou3 shi2 li4 jie3 pan2
入 圍 歌 手 實 力 解 盤
nominate singer actual strengths explain tray
'People in Taiwan are involved in and interfere in the Grammy Awards with their tastes and powers. The nominees' actual strengths are analyzed.'

(11) *kai1pan2* 開盤 'market opening'; Function

Jin1 ma3 shou1shi4 kai1 pan2 ying2
金 馬 收視 開 盤 贏
Golden Horse Awards TV rating open tray win
ya3 tai4
亞 太
Asia Pacific Awards
'When the two shows started, the Golden Horse Awards was beating the Asia Pacific Awards in the TV ratings.'

(12) *kai1gao1zou3gao1* 開高走高 'high from beginning to end'; Function

007 *kai1 gao1 zou3 gao1 cheng1ba4 bei3 shi4 piao4 fang2*
007 開 高 走 高 稱 霸 北 市 票 房
007 start high go high dominate Taipei box office
'007 dominates the Taipei box office from start to finish.'

In SHOW BUSINESS AS STOCK MARKET, the stock market jargons used in metaphorical expressions are only classified into entities and functions. Qualities do not contribute to the conceptual correspondences between the SDs and TDs.

(II) MP for SHOW BUSINESS AS STOCK MARKET can be postulated: show business is understood as a stock market because a stock market needs a bullish market to prosper; likewise, show business also needs a prosperous environment.

7.1.1.3. *MARRIAGE IS STOCK MARKET*

Husband and wife are partners involved in managing the marriage relationship. A marriage might be good or bad, successful or failing, depending on the couple's efforts in terms of management and negotiation. However, good personality definitely helps in such negotiation, and management, too, requires some compatibility of the spouse in the marriage. That is, marriage can be seen as a business investment. Marriage is therefore sometimes conceptualized in terms of a stock market. A stock market as the SD gets mapped onto marriage as the TD. In (13) and (14), *beng1pan2* 崩盤 'a stock market collapse' and *die2ting2ban3* 跌停板 'the falling of stock value' are the metaphorical expressions which are identified as the entities that correspond between the SDs and TDs. In (13), *beng1pan2* 崩盤 'a stock market collapse' refers to a collapse of the stock market and is associated with the end of the marriage relationship. In (14), *die2ting2ban3*跌停板 'the falling of stock value' refers to a stock value continuously falling and is conceptualized as the marriage relationship not being in a good condition.

(13) *beng1pan2* 崩盤 'a stock market collapse'; Entity

Hun1 yin1	*che4 di3*	*po4 lie4*	*bu4*	*ke3*	*wan3hui2*	*jiao4*
婚 姻	徹 底	破 裂	不	可	挽 回	叫
Marriage	completely	break	not able		save	call

beng1	*pan2*
崩	盤
collapsing	tray

'A broken marriage which can't be rebuilt is called a stock market collapse.'

(14) *die2ting2ban3* 跌停板 'the falling of stock value'; Entity

Shuang1 shi2 guo2 qing4	*quan2 qiu2*	*gu3 shi4*	*beng1*
雙 十 國 慶	全 球	股 市	崩
Double Tenth Day	worldwide	stock market	collapse

pan2	*wang2 jing4 ying2*	*yu3*	*chen2 wei1 tao2*	*de*
盤	王 靜 瑩	與	陳 威 陶	的
tray	Wang Jing-ying	and	Chen Wei-tao	POSS.

hun1 yin1	*ye3*	*gen1*	*zhe*	*die2*	*ting2*	*ban3*
婚 姻	也	跟	著	跌	停	板
marriage	also	follow		fall	stop	board

'On double tenth day, the worldwide stock markets collapsed and the marriage of Wang Jing-ying and Chen Wei-tao went from bad to worse.'

In (15) and (16), *gao1dang3* 高檔 'good status' and *di1dang3* 低檔 'bad status' are the metaphorical expressions which are identified as the qualities that correspond between the SDs and TDs. In (15), *gao1dang3* 高檔 'good status' refers to a stock value in good condition and is associated with someone's spouse having high economic social status. In (16), *di1dang3* 低檔 refers to a stock value in bad condition and is conceptualized as someone marrying an old man of wealth. In this case, *di1dang3* 低檔 'bad status' is mapped onto the old man instead of his wealth.

(15) *gao1dang3* 高檔 'good status'; Quality

Sui1	*ta1*	*san1 duan4*	*hun1 yin1 quan2*	*shi4*	*gao1 dang3*
雖	她	三 段	婚 姻 全	是	高 檔
Though	her	three section	marriage all		good status

huo4	*dan4 zui4 hou4 hai2 shi4*	*li2*	*le*
貨	但 最 後 還 是	離	了
goods	but finally still	divorce	ASP

'In spite of her three ex-husbands each having high status, she still ultimately divorced them.'

(16) *di1dang3* 低檔 'bad status'; Quality

Jia4	*nian2 mai4*	*fu4 weng1*	*jiao4*	*di1 dang3*	*cheng2 jie1*
嫁	年 邁	富 翁	叫	低 檔	承 接
Marry	age old	wealthy man	call	low file	receive

'To marry an old man of wealth is called getting a low-status husband.'

In (17) and (18), *tao4lao2* 套牢 'tie up' and *jie3tao4* 解套 'recovering from bad status' are the metaphorical expressions which are identified as the functions that correspond between the SDs and TDs. These two expressions are antonyms. *Tao4lao2* 套牢 'tie up' means that the stock cannot be sold to get profits in a bearish market. But, *jie3tao4* 解套 'recovering from bad status' means that the stock can be sold to get profits after a bearish market. In (17), *tao4lao2* 套牢 'tie up' is associated with someone, a Taiwanese singer, Big S, being trapped in a marriage. In (18), *jie3tao4* 解套 'recovering from bad status' is conceptualized as someone leaving the marriage.

(17) *tao4lao2* 套牢 'tie up'; Function

Da4 S	*zhi3*	*yao4*	*zi4you2*	*bu4 xiang3*	*bei4*	*tao4 lao2*
大 S	只	要	自由	不 想	被	套 牢
Big S	only	want	freedom	not think	passive	tie up

'Big S only wants freedom, so she doesn't want to get married.'

(18) *jie3tao4* 解套 'recovering from bad status'; Function

Cong2	*hun1 yin1*	*guan1 xi4*	*zhong1*	*jie3 tao4*
從	婚 姻	關 係	中	解 套
From	marriage	relationship	in	untie cover

'Get freedom from the marriage relationship.'

In MARRIAGE AS STOCK MARKET, the marriage descriptions appearing with stock market jargons may generate negative concepts as indicated in the above examples. From this viewpoint, it is revealed that Mandarin speakers' attitudes towards marriage are pessimistic by using the conceptual notion of the stock market being full of risks, such as economic recession, inflation, or financial risk. Therefore, in the mapped sense, marriage is also full of many kinds of risks, such as unpredictability, complications, and/or infidelity.

(III) MP for MARRIAGE AS STOCK MARKET can be postulated: marriage is understood as a stock market because investors need to take all the risks in a stock market; likewise, married couples need to take all the risks in their marriage relationship.

7.1.1.4. *POLITICS IS STOCK MARKET*

Politics plays a prominent role in Taiwan society. Many people are interested in all kinds of political issues, especially election issues. Politics is conceptualized in terms of a stock market. That is, a stock market as the SD gets mapped onto politics as the TD. In (19) to (21), *ji1ben3mian4* 基本面 'fundamental,' *beng1pan2* 崩盤 'a stock market collapse' and *pan2zheng3* 盤整 'market correction' are the metaphorical expressions which are identified as the entities that correspond between the SDs and TDs. In (19), *ji1ben3mian4* 基本面 'fundamental' refers to the fundamental profits of a listed company and is conceptualized as fundamental issues between Taiwan and China. In (20), *beng1pan2* 崩盤 'a stock market collapse' refers to a collapse of a stock market and is conceptualized as the people's weak confidence in government. *Pan2zheng3* 盤整 'market correction' refers to a leading stock falling in value after an index has risen a lot in a short term. It is a kind of circulation in a stock market. In (21), *pan2zheng3* 盤整 'market correction' is conceptualized as the political party's successor being reappointed after losing the election.

(19) *ji1ben3mian4* 基本面 'fundamental'; Entity

Liang3	*an4*	*hui2gui1*	*zheng4*	*leng3*	*jing1*	*re4*
兩	岸	回歸	政	冷	經	熱
Two	shore	return	politics	cold	economy	hot

<u>*ji1 ben3 mian4*</u>
<u>基 本 面</u>
<u>fundamental</u>

'Taiwan and China should go back to focusing on the fundamental issue of the economy rather than on politics.'

(20) *beng1pan2* 崩盤 'a stock market collapse'; Entity
Ren2 min2 dui4 zheng4 fu3 de xin4 xin1 zheng4
人 民 對 政 府 的 信 心 正
People face government POSS. confidence right
mian4 lin2 beng1 pan2 wei2 ji1
面 臨 崩 盤 危 機
face collapse tray crisis
'People lose their confidence in the government.'

(21) *pan2zheng3* 盤整 'market correction'; Entity
Min2 jin4 dang3 bai4 xuan3 jie1 ban1 mian4 lin2
民 進 黨 敗 選 接 班 面 臨
DPP lose election succeed face
pan2 zheng3
盤 整
tray mend
'DPP loses the election, and the party's successor needs to be reappointed.'

In (22) and (23), *zhi3die2hui2sheng1* 止跌回升 'bounce back from a slump' and *tan4di3* 探底 'dip into bottom' are the metaphorical expressions which are identified as the functions that correspond between the SDs and TDs. In (22), *zhi3die2hui2sheng1* 止跌回升 'bounce back from a slump' refers to a stock value that stops falling, then rises, and is conceptualized as the political party recovering its morale. In (23), *tan4di3* 探底[1] 'dip into the bottom' refers to a stock value that keeps going down to the bottom and is conceptualized as the dropping of the party's approval ratings.

(22) *zhi3die2hui2sheng1* 止跌回升 'bounce back from a slump'; Function
Bei3 gao1 ping2 pan2 min2 jin4 dang3 shi4 qi4
北 高 平 盤 民 進 黨 士 氣
Taipei Kaohsiung equal tray DPP morale
zhi3 die2 hui2 sheng1
止 跌 回 升
stop fall back raise
'The party's approval ratings between Taipei and Kaohsiung are even; the DPP's morale is coming back.'

(23) *tan4di3* 探底 'dip into the bottom'; Function
You3 mei2 ti3 ren2 jing3 gao4 zhi3 wu3 yue4 dang3
有 媒 體 人 警 告 指 五月 黨
Have media people warn point May party

[1] In Taiwan Mandarin, people say *tan4di3* 探底 'detect-bottom,' while it is *xian1lao3di3* 掀老底 'lift-old-bottom' in the Mandarin speaking in People's Republic of China.

zhu3 xi2 gai3 xuan3 ru2 ji4 xu4 *nei4 dou4 min2 jin4 dang3*
主 席 改 選 如 繼 續 內 鬥 民 進 黨
chairman reelect if continue internal conflict DPP
hui4 ji4 xu4 *tan4 di3*
會 繼 續 探 底
can continue detect bottom
'Media people warn that if in May there is still internal conflict over the re-election of the party chairman, the DPP will reach its lowest approval ratings.'

In POLITICS AS STOCK MARKET, stock market jargons as qualities do not contribute to the conceptual correspondences between the SDs and TDs. Furthermore, the choice of stock market jargons as functions tend to be mapped with the Orientational Metaphors proposed by Lakoff and Johnson (1980) that give us the concepts that good and more are oriented up, whereas bad and less are oriented down, for example, *Things are looking up*. So it is up and down, such as *die2* 跌 'fall' and *sheng1* 升 'rise' in (22), and *tan4di3* 探底 'dip into bottom' in (23), which makes POLITICS AS STOCK MARKET.

(IV) MP for POLITICS AS STOCK MARKET can be postulated: politics is understood as a stock market because investors need to take all the risks in the stock market, and governments and political parties need to take all the risks in what they do.

7.1.1.5. *FORTUNE TELLING IS STOCK MARKET*

Most human beings are curious about their unknown destiny. Through fortune-telling, they can seek advice relating to their lives. Fortune-telling is conceptualized in terms of the stock market. That is, a stock market as the SD gets mapped onto fortune telling as the TD. In (24) to (26), *jie3pan2* 解盤 'analyze the stock status,' *kai1di1zou3gao1* 開低走高 'going from bad to good status,' and *zhi3die2hui2sheng1* 止跌回升 'bounce back from a slump' are the metaphorical expressions which are identified as the functions that correspond between the SDs and TDs. In (24), *jie3pan2* 解盤 'analyze the stock status' refers to stock trends being analyzed and predicted and is conceptualized as the fortune of a particular star sign being analyzed and predicted. In (25), *kai1di1zou3gao1* 開低走高 'going from bad to good status' refers to an index or stock value going from low to high and is conceptualized as a particular star sign's luck in increasing the making of money. In (26), *zhi3die2hui2sheng1* 止跌回升 'bounce back from a slump' refers to a stock value stopping a fall then rising and is understood metaphorically as luck in making money goes from down to up.

(24) *jie3pan2* 解盤 'analyze the stock status'; Function
2003 xing1 zuo4 jie3 pan2 jin1 niu2
2003 星 座 解 盤 金 牛
2003 constellations explain tray gold cattle
piao1 yao2
飄 搖
sway
'Taurus' fortune will be unstable in 2003.'

(25) *kai1di1zou3gao1* 開低走高 'going from bad to good status'; Function
Bai2 yang2 zuo4 cai2 yun4 kai1 di1 zou3 gao1 jian4
白 羊 座 財 運 開 低 走 高 漸
Aries money fate start low go high gradually
ru4 jia1 jing4
入 佳 境
enter good circumstance
'Aries' luck in making money will go from bad to good.'

(26) *zhi3die2hui2sheng1* 止跌回升 'bounce back from a slump'; Function
Guo4 le ben3 zhou1 cai2 yun4 ji2 ke3
過 了 本 週 財 運 即 可
Pass ASP this week money fate can
zhi3 die2 hui2 sheng1
止 跌 回 升
stop fall back raise
'The luck in making money in the coming week is going from bad to good.'

In FORTUNE TELLING AS STOCK MARKET, the syntactic categories mapped between the SDs and TDs are only functions. Furthermore, the stock market jargons applied to the mapping of the correspondences between fortune telling and stock market tend to describe the concept of MORE IS UP as in (25) and (26). From this viewpoint, it is revealed that in modern Chinese culture, fortune tellers tend to make positive predictions and offer positive counsel.

(V) MP for FORTUNE AS STOCK MARKET can be postulated: fortune is understood as a stock market because stock markets have trends which need to be analyzed and predicted so that investors can make good investments, while horoscopes need to be analyzed and predicted for people to be careful.

7.1.2. *HUMAN TRAIT IS STOCK MARKET*

Human traits as the TD are categorized into three types: emotion, age and people's value. Human traits represent human beings' specific characteristics.

7.1.2.1. *EMOTION IS STOCK MARKET*

Emotion is one of the human's unique psychological states. The mind's moods are like the rising and falling indices of a stock market. Emotion is thus conceptualized in terms of a stock market. That is, a stock market as the SD gets mapped onto the TD of emotion. In (27), *zhang3ting2ban3* 漲停板 'limit up' is the metaphorical expression which is identified as the entity that corresponds between the SD and TD. It refers to a stock value that keeps rising to its maximum amount in one trading day and is conceptualized as a single mother being with great happiness.

(27) *zhang3ting2ban3* 漲停板 'limit up'; Entity
Wei4 hun1 ma1 ma jia3 jing4 wen2 xing4 fu2
未 婚 媽 媽 賈 靜 雯 幸 福
Unmarried mother Jia Jing-wen happiness
zhang3 ting2 ban3 nü3 er2 shuang1 man3 yue4 jiu3 quan2 jia1
漲 停 板 女 兒 雙 滿 月 酒 全 家
limit up daughter two-month-old celebration family
tian2mi4 chu1xi2
甜蜜 出席
sweet attend
'The happiness of unmarried mother, Jia Jing-wen, increased when all the family attended her daughter's two-month-old celebration.'

In (28), *zhi3die2hui2sheng1* 止跌回升 'bounce back from a slump' is the metaphorical expression which is identified as the function that corresponds between the SDs and TDs. It refers to a stock value that stops falling then rises and is conceptualized as people's moods being in a good state after having been in a bad state.

(28) *zhi3die2hui2sheng1* 止跌回升 'bounce back from a slump'; Function
A1 xin4 shuo1 mei3 dang1 xin1 qing2 bu4 hao3 ting1 dao4
阿 信 說 每 當 心 情 不 好 聽 到
A-xin say whenever mood not good hear
pi1 tou2 si4 de ge1 xin1 qing2 li4 ke4 zhi3 die2 hui2 sheng1
披 頭 四 的 歌 心 情 立刻 止 跌 回 升
Beatles POSS. song mood immediately stop fall back raise
'By listening to Beatles's songs, A-xin's mood can go from bad to good.'

In EMOTION AS STOCK MARKET, the stock market jargons used to conceptualize emotion are limited to *zhang3ting2ban3* 漲停板 'limit up' and *zhi3die2hui2sheng1* 止跌回升 'bounce back from a slump' in Orientational Metaphors. Therefore, we can say that emotion is characterized by the orientation concepts of upward and downward and that HAPPY IS UP and SAD IS DOWN.

(VI) MP for EMOTION AS STOCK MARKET can be postulated: emotion is understood as a stock market because the indices of the stock market rise and fall, and human emotion too has its ups and downs.

7.1.2.2. *AGE IS STOCK MARKET*

Age reflects what a human being's ability should be. Age is conceptualized in terms of a stock market. That is, a stock market as the SD gets mapped onto the TD of age. In (29) and (30), *tan4di3* 探底 'dip into the bottom' and *xia4tan4* 下探[2] 'dip' are the metaphorical expressions which are identified as the functions that correspond between the SDs and TDs. In examples (29) and (30), *tan4di3* 探底 'dip into the bottom' and *xia4tan4* 下探 'dip' refer to a stock value that keeps falling and are conceptualized as a decrease in the average age of the individuals being referred to.

(29) *tan4di3* 探底 'dip into the bottom'; Function

Ou3 xiang4 nian2 ling2 tan4 di3 shen3 jian4 hong2 jiu3
偶 像 年 齡 探 底 沈 建 宏 9
Idol age detect bottom Shen Jian-hong nine
sui4 jiu4 bei4 jing1 ji4 ren2 qian1 xia4
歲 就 被 經 紀 人 簽 下
year PART passive agent sign down
'The age of idols is getting younger and younger, and Shen Jian-Hong at the age of nine has a contract with his promoter.'

(30) *xia4tan4* 下探 'dip'; Function

Xiao1 fei4 nian2 ling2 xia4 tan4 tai2 wan1 LV
消 費 年 齡 下 探 台 灣 LV
Consumption age down detect Taiwan LV
xiao1 fei4 li4 shi4 ya4 zhou1 NO.2
消 費 力 是 亞 洲 NO.2
consumption power is Asia NO.2
'The age of consumers is getting younger and younger, and Taiwan is ranked number 2 in Asia for the consumption of LV products.'

(VII) MP for AGE AS STOCK MARKET can be postulated: age is understood as stock market because stock prices are down, while human age decreases.

---

2 It is *zou4jiang4* 驟降 'sudden-drop' in People's Republic of China.

7.1.2.3. *PEOPLE'S VALUE IS STOCK MARKET*

Stock markets have various types of stocks with their own functions and values. Our society also has different kinds of individuals with their own functions and values. The different values are associated with the individuals' different social statuses. That is, how other people view them. One's value can be conceptualized in terms of the amount of profit one makes, or if one is considered desirable. Such standards can easily be related to the act of selling and buying on the stock market. That is, a stock market as the SD gets mapped onto people's value as the TD. In (31) to (33), *hang2qing2* 行情 'worth,' *ji1you1gu3* 績優股 'blue chip,' and *re4men2gu3* 熱門股 'active stock' are the metaphorical expressions which are identified as the entities that correspond between the SDs and TDs. In (31), *hang2qing2* 行情 'worth' refers to a stock's current price in the stock market and is associated with the buying and selling prices of the celebrity, Wu Zong-xian, as a TV host. In (32), *ji1you1gu3* 績優股 'blue chip' refers to a good stock and can be conceptualized as the unmarried man being an eligible bachelor. In (33), *re4men2gu3* 熱門股 'active stock' refers to a popular stock and can be conceptualized as the famous Japanese baseball player, Matsuzaka Daisuke, being popular.

(31) *hang2qing2* 行情 'worth'; Entity

Wu2 zong1 xian4	*zai4 da4 lu4*	*shi4*	*you3*	*zhe4 ge*	*hang2 qing2*
吳 宗 憲	在 大 陸	是	有	這 個	行 情
Wu Zong-xian	in China	is	have	this	worth

'In China, Wu Zong-xian is worth this price.'

(32) *ji1you1gu3* 績優股 'blue chip'; Entity

Jiang3 you3 bo2	*zan4*	*you3 chang2*	*wei4 hun1*	*ji1 you1 gu3*
蔣 友 柏	讚	友 常	未 婚	績 優 股
Jiang You-bo	praise	You-chang	unmarried	blue chip

'Jiang You-bo praises You-chang as an eligible bachelor.'

(33) *re4men2gu3* 熱門股 'active stock'; Entity

Song1 ban3 da4 fu3	*shi4*	*re4 men2 gu3*
松 坂 大 輔	是	熱 門 股
Matsuzaka Daisuke	is	active stock

'Matsuzaka is a popular player.'

In (34), *gao1dang3* 高檔 'good status' is the metaphorical expression which is identified as the quality that corresponds between the SDs and TDs.

It refers to a stock value in good condition and can be conceptualized as a person's value being high, such as the successful TV hosts, Zhang Fei, Zhang Xiao-yan and Hu Gua.

(34) *gao1dang3* 高檔 'good status'; Quality
Zhang1 fei1 zhang1 xiao3 yan4 hu2 gua1 yi2 yang4
張 菲 張 小 燕 胡 瓜 一 樣
Zhang Fei Zhang Xiao-yan Hu Gua alike
shen1 jia4 dou1 shi4 gao1 dang3
身 價 都 是 高 檔
worth all good status
'The values of Zhang Fei, Zhang Xiao-yan and Hu Gua are all high.'

In (35) to (37), *ni4shi4shang4yang2* 逆勢上揚 'rising in bad conditions,' *kai1di1zou3gao1* 開低走高 'going from bad to good status,' and *kan4zhang3* 看漲 'bullish' are the metaphorical expressions which are identified as the functions that correspond between the SDs and TDs. In (35), *ni4shi4shang4yang2* 逆勢上揚 'rising in bad conditions' refers to a stock value rising despite bad conditions and can be conceptualized as a man's value going up with increasing age. In (36), *kai1di1zou3gao1* 開低走高 'going from bad to good status' refers to an index or stock value going from low to high and can be conceptualized as buying and selling prices of the Korean actress, Yoon Eun-hye, going from low to high. In (37), *kan4zhang3* 看漲 'bullish' refers to a stock value being expected to rise and can be conceptualized as men with an Oedipus complex being predicted to be popular.

(35) *ni4shi4shang4yang2* 逆勢上揚 'rising in the bad status'; Function
Yi3 hun1 fu4 nü3 de hang2 qing2 sui2 zhe sui4 yue4
已 婚 婦 女 的 行 情 隨 著 歲 月
Married woman POSS. worth follow years
zou3 xia4 po1 er2 nan2 ren2 wang3 wang3
走 下 坡 而 男 人 往 往
go downhill but man often
ni4 shi4 shang4 yang2
逆 勢 上 揚
against trend up raise
'The values of married women go down with increasing age, whereas the values of men go up.'

(36) *kai1di1zou3gao1* 開低走高 'going from bad to good status'; Function
Yin3 en1hui4 kai1 di1 zou3 gao1 shen1 jia4 biao1 zhang3
尹 恩惠 開 低 走 高 身 價 飆 漲
Yoon Eun-hye start low go high worth whirl rise

132 *bei4*
132 倍
132 times
'Yoon Eun-hye's value increases 132 times, going from bad to good.'

(37) *kan4zhang3* 看漲 'bullish'; Function
Lian4 mu3 qing2 jie2 *nan2 ren2* *hang2 qing2* *kan4 zhang3*
戀 母 情 結 男 人 行 情 看 漲
Oedipus complex man worth bullish
'The value of men with an Oedipus complex is expected to rise.'

In PEOPLE'S VALUE AS STOCK MARKET, the stock market jargons used to conceptualize people's value tend to be positive. It demonstrates that people in Taiwan tend to evaluate one's positive value by using stock market jargon in non-financial discourse.

(VIII) MP for PEOPLE'S VALUE AS STOCK MARKET can be postulated: people's value is understood as a stock market because a stock market has its performance value; similarly, people are desirably wanted, indicating their value.

7.1.3. *SUPERIOR FORCE IS STOCK MARKET*

Superior force stands for power and capability. A human being with a force title means that they have the ability to handle the assigned mission. Superior force is conceptualized in terms of a stock market. That is, a stock market as the SD gets mapped onto the TD of superior force. In (38a) to (38b), *cao1pan2* 操盤 'stock operating' is the metaphorical expression which is identified as the function that corresponds between the SDs and TDs. It refers to the action of buying and selling stocks on the stock market. Usually, the one who is invited to conduct the action *cao1pan2* 操盤 'stock operating' is more capable, experienced, or powerful. On the stance, *cao1pan2* 操盤 'stock operating' can be conceptualized as human activities being operated by experienced people.

(38) *cao1pan2* 操盤 'stock operating'; Function
a. *Huo3 jian4* *huan4* *jiao4 lian4 zhao3* *ai4 de2 man4*
火 箭 換 教 練 找 艾 德 曼
Rockets change coach find Adelman
cao1 pan2
操 盤
operate stock
'Rockets find a new coach, Adelman, to train the players.'

b. *Hu2 gua1: mu4 hou4 you3 hei1 shou3 cao1 pan2*
胡 瓜：幕 後 有 黑 手 操 盤
Hu gua curtain behind have black hand operate stock
'Hugua expresses that there is an evil backstage manipulator executing the plan.'

(VIII) MP for SUPERIOR FORCE AS STOCK MARKET can be postulated: superior force is understood as related to a stock market because stock investors need superior force to help them make profits, and human activities need superior force to make them work.

7.1.4. *TEMPERATURE IS STOCK MARKET*

Temperature is closely related to human daily life. High and low temperatures are like the rising and falling indices of the stock market. Temperature is conceptualized in terms of the stock market. That is, stock market as the SD gets mapped onto temperature as the TD. In (39) *tan4di3* 探底 'dip into the bottom' and in (40) *xia4tan4*下探 'dip' are the metaphorical expressions which are identified as the functions that correspond between the SDs and TDs. These two fixed expressions refer to a stock value continuously falling and can be conceptualized as the temperature dropping as it is referred to of the cold flow in (39) or the northern area in (40).

(39) *tan4di3* 探底 'dip into the bottom'; Function
Han2 liu2 bao4 dao4 di1 wen1 zai4 xiang4 xia4
寒 流 報 到 低 溫 再 向 下
Cold front arrive low temperature again downward
tan4 di3
探 底
detect bottom
'The cold front arrives, and the temperatures are going down again.'

(40) *xia4tan4* 下探 'dip'; Function
Jin1 ming2 di1 wen1 bei3 bu4 di4 qu1
今 明 低 溫 北 部 地 區
Today tomorrow low temperature the northern area
xia4 tan4 jiu3 du4
下 探 九 度
down detect nine degree
'The temperature in the northern area will drop to nine degrees today and tomorrow.'

(IX) MP for TEMPERATURE AS STOCK MARKET can be postulated: temperature is understood as stock market because the stock index falls and temperatures drop.

7.1.5. *OUTLOOK ON LIFE IS STOCK MARKET*

Outlook on life reflects how human beings regard their lives. Outlook on life is conceptualized in terms of a stock market. That is, a stock market as the SD gets mapped onto the TD of outlook on life. Examples (41) to (43), *shui3jiao3gu3* 水餃股 'penny stock,' *ji1ben3mian4* 基本面 'fundamental,' and *li4duo1chu1jin4* 利多出盡 'short-lived gains' are the metaphorical expressions which are identified as the entities that correspond between the SDs and TDs. In (41), *shui3jiao3gu3* 水餃股 'penny stock' refers to a valueless stock and is conceptualized as the outlook on life being valueless. In (42), *ji1ben3mian4* 基本面 'fundamental' refers to the fundamental profits of a listed company and is conceptualized as a man's thinking going back to the fundamentals. *Li4duo1chu1jin4* 利多出盡 'short-lived gains' refers to a stock value falling when things are finally looking up and people are selling their stocks. In (43), this expression can be conceptualized as extreme pleasure being followed by sorrow.

(41) *shui3jiao3gu3* 水餃股 'penny stock'; Entity
Gu3 piao4 die2 cheng2 shui3 jiao3 gu3 hen3 ke3 bei1 dan4
股 票 跌 成 水 餃 股 很 可 悲 但
Stock fall become penny stock very sad but
bei1 ai1 de ying1 gai1 shi4 ren2 sheng1 jia4 zhi2
悲 哀 的 應 該 是 人 生 價 值
sorrowful should life value
bian4 cheng2 shui3 jiao3 gu3 de wen4 ti2 ba
變 成 水 餃 股 的 問 題 吧
become penny stock POSS. question PART
'Stocks becoming penny stocks is sad, but even sadder is life becoming valueless.'

(42) *ji1ben3mian4* 基本面 'fundamental'; Entity
Wo3 hui2 gui1 ji1ben3mian4 fang4 kong1 nao3zi
我 回 歸 基 本 面 放 空 腦子
I return foundamental idle mind
quan2 xin1 quan2 yi4 da3 qiu2 zhe4 gan3 jue2 zhen1 bang4
全 心 全 意 打 球 這 感 覺 真 棒
wholeheartedly play ball this feeling really great
'I feel great that I have gone back to fundamentals, desire nothing, and can concentrate on playing ball.'

(43) *li4duo1chu1jin4* 利多出盡 'short-lived gains'; Entity
Li4 duo1 chu1 jin4 shi4 gu3 shi4 tong1 lu4 de
利 多 出 盡 是 股 市 通 路 的
Profit many exit finish is stock market route POSS.
hang2 hua4 yi4 si dou1 cha4 bu4 duo1 dai4 biao3
行 話 意 思 都 差 不 多 代 表
jargon meaning all similar represent
tai4 duo1 hao3 shi4 zhi1 hou4 yi2 ding4 you3 huai4 shi4
太 多 好 事 之 後 一 定 有 壞 事
too many good work after sure have bad thing
chu1 xian4 kuang2 xi3 zhi1 hou4 bi4 you3 da4 bei1
出 現 狂 喜 之 後 必 有 大 悲
appear ecstasy after must have big sadness
mian4 dui4 hao3 shi4 yi2 ding4 yao4 xiao3 xin1
面 對 好 事 一 定 要 小 心
face good thing sure need careful
'Short-lived gain is a stock jargon. It means that bad things come after good things. When our luck is good, we must be careful.'

(X) MP for OUTLOOK ON LIFE AS STOCK MARKET can be postulated: outlook on life is understood as a stock market based on the following comparison: a stock price reflects a company's basic profitability, while outlook on life reflects a person's basic attitude toward life.

To sum up, metaphor is a set of conceptual correspondences between a SD and a TD (Lakoff and Johnson 1980; Kövecses 2002; Kövecses 2005). The present study investigates the metaphorical expressions of the stock market jargons and finds that the SD of stock market maps onto eleven TDs: sports contest, show business, marriage, politics, fortune telling, emotion, age, people's value, superior force, temperature and outlook on life.

7.2. The Verification of Mapping Principles

In this section, we attempt to verify the MPs between the SD and TD pairings of conceptual mappings. The criterion is based on the frequency of fixed expressions as Ahrens, Chung and Huang (2004) propose. If the lexical expression with the highest frequency of mapping conforms to the suggested MP, then the postulation of that MP is verified.

Section 7.2.1 will discuss the frequency distribution of fixed expressions for each conceptual mapping mentioned in 7.1. Section 7.2.2 will be integrated with the results of 7.2.1.

7.2.1. *The Frequency for Each Conceptual Metaphor*

Tables 7.2 to 7.5 demonstrate the frequency distributions of fixed expressions for each conceptual mapping. Each conceptual metaphor is used with various fixed expressions. In order to make the table more concise, a maximum of three fixed expressions, those with the highest frequencies in terms of entity, quality and function, are listed. It will not be listed in the table if the frequency of the lexical expression is less than 3. The sequence of the following tables will follow the significance of the tokens, that is, with the most tokens to the least. Moreover, the most frequent metaphorical expression for each conceptual metaphor in the table is in boldface.

7.2.1.1. *SPORTS CONTEST AND PEOPLE'S VALUE IS STOCK MARKET*

Table 7.2 presents the metaphors of SPORTS CONTEST and PEOPLE'S VALUE AS STOCK MARKET. In SPORTS CONTEST AS STOCK MARKET, the most frequent metaphorical expression is *kai1di1zou3gao1* 開低走高 'going from bad to good status' with 102 tokens. *Kai1di1zou3gao1* 開低走高 'bad to good status' has the underlying concept of unexpected progress. The MP is postulated to be related to progress in competition or in sport. The most frequent expression verifies the postulation of the MP: sports contest is understood

Table 7.2. SPORTS CONTEST and PEOPLE'S VALUE.

SPORTS CONTEST AS STOCK MARKET (339 tokens)		
Fixed expressions	E/Q/F	Freq.
hang2qing2 行情 'worth'	Entity	30
zhu3li4 主力 'main force'	Entity	23
wei3pan2 尾盤 'final session'	Entity	11
gao1dang3 高檔 'good status'	Quality	21
di1dang3 低檔 'bad status'	Quality	37
kai1di1zou3gao1 開低走高 'going from bad to good status'	Function	102
ni4shi4shang4yang2 逆勢上揚 'rising in the bad status'	Function	46
die2shen1fan3tan2 跌深反彈 'fall deeply before gaining'	Function	32
PEOPLE'S VALUE AS STOCK MARKET (254 tokens)		
Fixed expressions	E/Q/F	Freq.
hang2qing2 行情 'worth'	Entity	78
ji1you1gu3 績優股 'blue chip'	Entity	21
qian3li4gu3 潛力股 'potential stock'	Entity	19
gao1dang3 高檔 'good status'	Quality	8
kan4zhang3 看漲 'bullish'	Function	40
ni4shi4shang4yang2 逆勢上揚 'rising in bad conditions'	Function	16
kai1di1zou3gao1 開低走高 'going from bad to good status'	Function	12

as stock market because the activity of trading on the stock market is like a fierce competition, and a sports contest is also like a fierce competition. The most frequent metaphorical expression in PEOPLE'S VALUE AS STOCK MARKET is *hang2qing2* 行情 'worth' with 78 tokens and the underlying concept of value. In this case, the MP is postulated to associate with the values of people. The most frequent fixed expression verifies the postulation of the MP: people's value is understood as a stock market because a stock market has its performance value, and similarly, people have their own value which represents their social status.

7.2.1.2. *SHOW BUSINESS, MARRIAGE AND POLITICS IS STOCK MARKET*

In SHOW BUSINESS AS STOCK MARKET, Table 7.3 shows that the most frequent metaphorical expression is *hong2pan2* 紅盤 'rising stock market' with 48 tokens. *Hong2pan2* 紅盤 'rising stock market' has the underlying concept of good status. In this case, the MP is postulated as having to do with good status in show business. The most frequent fixed expression verifies the postulation of the MP: show business is understood as a stock market because a stock market needs a bullish market to prosper, and show business also needs prosperity.

In MARRIAGE AS STOCK MARKET, the most frequent metaphorical expression is *beng1pan2* 崩盤 'a stock market collapse.' The expression, collapse, is associated with risk. Therefore, the MP is postulated as having to do with risks in marriage. The most frequent lexical expression verifies the postulation of the MP: marriage is understood as stock market because investors need to take all the risks in the stock market, and married couples need to take all the risks in their marriage relationship.

In POLITICS AS STOCK MARKET, *beng1pan2* 崩盤 'a stock market collapse' is the most frequent metaphorical expression. In line with the above, the MP is postulated to associate with the risks in politics. The most frequent lexical expression verifies the postulation of the MP: politics is understood as a stock market because investors need to take all the risks in the stock market, and governments and political parties need to take all the risks in what they do.

Table 7.3. SHOW BUSINESS, MARRIAGE and POLITICS.

SHOW BUSINESS AS STOCK MARKET (159 tokens)		
Fixed expressions	E/Q/F	Freq.
hong2pan2 紅盤 'rising stock market'	Entity	48
niu2shi4 牛市 'bull market'	Entity	10
jie3pan2 解盤 'analyze the stock status'	Function	11

Table 7.3. (*cont.*)

kai1pan2 開盤 'market opening'	Function	11
kai1gao1zou3gao1 開高走高 'going high from beginning to end'	Function	6
MARRIAGE AS STOCK MARKET (139 tokens)		
Fixed expressions	E/Q/F	Freq.
beng1pan2 崩盤 'a stock market collapse'	Entity	48
die2ting2ban3 跌停板 'the falling of stock value'	Entity	3
gao1dang3 高檔 'good status'	Quality	4
di1dang3 低檔 'bad status'	Quality	4
tao4lao2 套牢 'tie up'	Function	12
jie3tao4 解套 'going out from bad status'	Function	6
zhi3die2hui2sheng1 止跌回升 'bounce back from a slump'	Function	4
POLITICS AS STOCK MARKET (132 tokens)		
Fixed expressions	E/Q/F	Freq.
beng1pan2 崩盤 'a stock market collapse'	Entity	41
ji1ben3mian4 基本面 'fundamental'	Entity	3
pan2zheng3 盤整 'market correction'	Entity	3
tan4di3 探底 'dip into the bottom'	Function	9
zhi3die2hui2sheng1 止跌回升 'bounce back from a slump'	Function	8

7.2.1.3. *SUPERIOR FORCE, FORTUNE TELLING AND TEMPERATURE IS STOCK MARKET*

In SUPERIOR FORCE AS STOCK MARKET, the most frequent metaphorical expression, *cao1pan2* 操盤 'stock operating' with 66 tokens, has the underlying concept of ability and experience. Therefore, the MP is postulated as having to do with the ability of humans in their activities. The most frequent lexical expression verifies the postulation of the MP: superior force is understood as relating to the stock market because stock investors need superior force to help them make profits, and a person may need superior force to help him/her.

In FORTUNE TELLING AS STOCK MARKET, Table 7.4 shows that the most frequent metaphorical expression is *jie3pan2* 解盤 'analyze the stock status' with 17 tokens. *Jie3pan2* 解盤 'analyze the stock status' has the underlying concept of analyzing. In this case, the MP is postulated to associate with analyzing fortune. The most frequent lexical expression verifies the postulation of the MP: fortune is understood as a stock market because stock trends need to be analyzed and predicted so that investors can make good investments, while horoscopes need to be analyzed and predicted for people to be careful.

In TEMPERATURE AS STOCK MARKET, the most frequent metaphorical expression is *xia4tan4* 下探 'dip' with the underlying concept of falling. Therefore, the MP is postulated to associate with the falling of temperature. The most frequent lexical expression verifies the postulation of the MP: temperature is understood as a stock market because the stock index falls just like temperatures drop.

Table 7.4. SUPERIOR FORCE, FORTUNE TELLING and TEMPERATURE.

SUPERIOR FORCE AS STOCK MARKET (66 tokens)		
Fixed expressions	E/Q/F	Freq.
cao1pan2 操盤 'stock operating'	Function	66
FORTUNE TELLING AS STOCK MARKET (54 tokens)		
Fixed expressions	E/Q/F	Freq.
jie3pan2 解盤 'analyze the stock status'	Function	17
kai1di1zou3gao1 開低走高 'going from bad to good status'	Function	8
zhi3die2hui2sheng1 止跌回升 'bounce back from a slump'	Function	6
TEMPERATURE AS STOCK MARKET (49 tokens)		
Fixed expressions	E/Q/F	Freq.
xia4tan4 下探 'dip'	Function	39
tan4di3 探底 'dip into the bottom'	Function	10

7.2.1.4. *EMOTION, AGE, AND OUTLOOK ON LIFE IS STOCK MARKET*

In EMOTION AS STOCK MARKET, Table 7.5 shows that the most frequent metaphorical expression is *zhi3die2hui2sheng1* 止跌回升 'bounce back from a slump' with 14 tokens. *Zhi3die2hui2sheng1* 止跌回升 'bounce back from a slump' has the underlying concept of up and down. Therefore, the MP is postulated as having to do with the upward and downward expression of emotion. The most frequent lexical expression verifies the postulation of the MP: emotion is understood as a stock market because the indices of stock markets rise and fall, and human emotion too has its ups and downs.

In AGE AS STOCK MARKET, the most frequent metaphorical expression, *xia4tan4* 下探 'dip,' has the underlying concept of reaching low point. In this case, the MP is postulated to associate with young age. The most frequent lexical expression verifies the postulation of the MP: age is understood as a stock market because as stock prices go down, so too does the age at which a given human activity is possible (see examples 29–30).

In OUTLOOK ON LIFE AS STOCK MARKET, *ji1ben3mian4* 基本面 'fundamental' with 9 tokens has the underlying concept of foundation. In this case, the MP is postulated as being related to fundamental attitudes. The most frequent lexical expression verifies the postulation of the MP: outlook on life is understood as a stock market based on the following comparison: stock price reflects a company's basic profitability, while outlook on life reflects a person's basic attitude toward life.

Table 7.5. EMOTION, AGE and OUTLOOK ON LIFE.

EMOTION AS STOCK MARKET (46 tokens)		
Fixed expressions	E/Q/F	Freq.
zhang3ting2ban3 漲停板 'limit up'	Entity	8
zhi3die2hui2sheng1 止跌回升 'bounce back from a slump'	Function	14
jie3tao4 解套 'recovering from bad status'	Function	6
AGE AS STOCK MARKET (38 tokens)		
Fixed expressions	E/Q/F	Freq.
xia4tan4 下探 'dip'	Function	32
tan4di3 探底 'dip into the bottom'	Function	6
OUTLOOK ON LIFE AS STOCK MARKET (27 tokens)		
Fixed expressions	E/Q/F	Freq.
ji1ben3mian4 基本面 'fundamental'	Entity	9
shui3jiao3gu3 水餃股 'penny stock'	Entity	4
li4duo1chu1jin4 利多出盡 'short-lived gains'	Function	5

In the next section, we will further examine the results presented above with the criteria of concept principle verification in terms of SUMO and WordNet.

7.2.2. *The Criteria of Mapping Principle Verification*

Suggested upper merged ontology (SUMO) and WordNet are the superior ontological knowledge which are used for linguistic research as foundational ontological knowledge to help define linguistic items. The goal of this section is to further integrate the results of 7.2.1 (The frequency of fixed expressions for each conceptual metaphor) with the ratio of the most frequent fixed expressions in the total tokens for each conceptual metaphor. Two criteria proposed by Ahrens, Chung and Huang (2004: 101) are used in verifying the MP. First, the total number of tokens for each conceptual metaphor is more than 10. Second, the percentage of the most frequent lexical expression in the total tokens for each conceptual metaphor is more than 30%. However, when the MP postulation is not clear, that is, if the examples and percentage of the most frequent lexical expression in the total tokens are less than 10 and 30% respectively, its lexical expression needs to be examined by WordNet and SUMO for verification of the salience of the conceptual metaphor.

We can look at Table 7.6 to examine whether the data conform to the two criteria. Column 2 in Table 7.6 lists the total number of tokens per metaphor found in the TD of each conceptual metaphor. Column 3 lists the number of instances in which the key lexical expression was found. Column 4 is the percentage of the most frequent lexical expression in the total tokens for each conceptual metaphor. Take SPORTS CONTEST AS STOCK MARKET for example: *kai1di1zou3gao1* 開低走高 'going from bad to good status' is found a total of 102 times in 339 tokens relating to that particular conceptual metaphor, a frequency of 30.09%. Take PEOPLE'S VALUE AS STOCK MARKET as another example: *hang2qing2*行情 'worth' is found 78 times in 254 tokens with people's value as the TD, a frequency of 30.71%. In these two cases, we find that the conceptual metaphors of SPORTS CONTEST and PEOPLE'S VALUE AS STOCK MARKET conform to the two criteria: total tokens per instance and percentage are more than 10 and 30%, respectively.

Table 7.6. Total number for each conceptual metaphor.

Conceptual metaphors	Total tokens	Most frequent	Percentage (%)	MP match
SPORTS CONTEST AS STOCK MARKET	339	102	30.09	Yes
PEOPLE'S VALUE AS STOCK MARKET	254	78	30.71	Yes
SHOW BUSINESS AS STOCK MARKET	159	48	30.19	Yes
MARRIAGE AS STOCK MARKET	139	48	34.53	Yes
POLITICS AS STOCK MARKET	132	41	31.06	Yes
SUPERIOR FORCE AS STOCK MARKET	66	66	100.00	Yes
FORTUNE TELLING AS STOCK MARKET	54	17	31.48	Yes
TEMPERATURE AS STOCK MARKET	49	39	79.59	Yes
EMOTION AS STOCK MARKET	46	14	30.43	Yes
AGE AS STOCK MARKET	38	32	84.21	Yes
OUTLOOK ON LIFE AS STOCK MARKET	27	9	33.33	Yes

According to the data in Table 7.6, SHOW BUSINESS, MARRIAGE, POLITICS, and all the other proposed TDs of conceptual metaphors conform to the two basic requirements, over 30% / 10 examples; therefore, the final column of MP which matches for each conceptual metaphor is marked "Yes." That is, the relationship between the most frequent lexical expression and the MP is straightforward. For example, as stated in 7.2.1 (The frequency of fixed expressions for each conceptual metaphor), in PEOPLE'S VALUE AS STOCK MARKET, *hang2qing2* 行情 'worth' is the most frequent metaphorical expression with the underlying concept of value. Therefore, the MP postulation relates to the concept of value, and accordingly, people's value is understood as a stock value because any given stock has its performance value. Likewise, people have their own value that represents their social status. For another example, in EMOTION AS STOCK MARKET, *zhi3die2hui2sheng1* 止跌回升 'bounce back from a slump' is the most frequent metaphorical expression with the underlying concept of emotions going up and down. Therefore, the MP postulation relates to the concept of ups-and-downs, and emotion is understood as a stock market.

Different people may have different way to analyze the SDs and TDs of conceptual metaphors. The purpose of 7.2 (The verification of mapping principles) is to further strengthen the MP postulations in 7.1 (The categorization of conceptual metaphors). By using the two criteria mentioned above, the results also show that the MP postulation and the frequency of metaphorical expression have a strong connection with each other. That is, the MP postulation can be established on the basis of the frequency of metaphorical expressions (Ahrens, Chung and Huang 2004: 100).

7.3. The Hierarchy of Conceptual Metaphors

This section will show the hierarchy of conceptual metaphors by means of the GCB Metaphor proposed by Lakoff and Turner (1989). The GCB Metaphor has two models: basic and extended. The basic GCB Metaphor comprises the five corresponding concept hierarchies from top to bottom: humans, animals, plants, complex objects, and natural physical things. The extended GCB Metaphor spreads its metaphorical level from humans up to the relations of society, universe and god.

In section 7.1 (The categorization of conceptual metaphors), the result of the analysis shows that the SD of a stock market is structured by the following metaphors: SPORTS CONTEST AS STOCK MARKET, SHOW BUSINESS AS STOCK MARKET, MARRIAGE AS STOCK MARKET, POLITICS

AS STOCK MARKET, FORTUNE TELLING AS STOCK MARKET, EMOTION AS STOCK MARKET, AGE AS STOCK MARKET, PEOPLE'S VALUE AS STOCK MARKET, SUPERIOR FORCE AS STOCK MARKET, TEMPERATURE AS STOCK MARKET, and OUTLOOK ON LIFE AS STOCK MARKET. As shown in Figure 7.1, eleven conceptual metaphors in the SD of stock market apply to the GCB Metaphor and form a different hierarchy. Three aspects of the hierarchy of conceptual metaphors in the SD of stock market in the GCB Metaphor, will be discussed in turn.

7.3.1. *The Extended Great Chain of Being Metaphor*

In Figure 7.1, each conceptual metaphor as TD is arranged in its relevant concept hierarchy. As can be seen, the ten conceptual metaphors as TDs (sports contest, show business, emotion, age, and so on) overlap in the humans and society level respectively, but only one conceptual metaphor of temperature is found in the natural level of physical thing. This implies that the hierarchy of conceptual metaphors in the SD of stock market has a strong connection with the humans level and the society level, but has a weak connection with the natural physical thing level. As stated earlier, the extended GCB Metaphor emphasizes the relationships between the levels of humans, society, universe, and god. Consequently, the conceptualization of a stock market will be explained and analyzed in terms of the extended GCB Metaphor.

SOCIETY (Abstract Complex Systems)
(Sport Contest, Show Business, Marriage, Politics, Stock Market)

↓

HUMANS
(Fortune Telling, Emotion, Age, People's Value, Superior Force, Outlook on Life)

↓

NATURAL PHYSICAL THINGS
(Temperature)

Figure 7.1. The hierarchy of the conceptual metaphors of stock markets.

7.3.2. *Conceptualization Process*

Kövecses (2002: 126) mentions that the process of the GCB Metaphor can function in two directions: one goes from a lower SD to a higher TD, the other goes from a higher SD to a lower TD. As we see in Figure 7.1, stock market as SD in the society level can be used to conceptualize the eleven conceptual metaphors as TDs from the humans level to the natural physical thing level. For example, emotion and age in the humans level are comprehended metaphorically as stock market in the society level. Temperature in natural physical thing level gets mapped onto stock market in the society level. In this case, the conceptualization in the SD of stock market proceeds from a higher SD to a lower TD in the extended GCB Metaphor. Further, a particular level of the GCB Metaphor is used to conceptualize at another level (Kövecses 2002: 126). As Figure 7.1 shows, the different entities in the same level are conceptualized with each other. For example, in the same society level, the SD, stock market can be understood metaphorically as the TDs—sports contest, politics, marriage, and so on. However, occasionally, it can be hard to identify which entity is higher or lower when they are in the same level. For example, we have difficulty in identifying the most superior entity in the humans level because almost every entity means something to different human beings.

7.3.3. *Abstract Complex Systems*

The society level can be regarded as an abstract complex systems that includes human ideas, a variety of other abstract and concrete entities, and particular relationships among entities (Kövecses 2002: 127–128). In other words, as Figure 7.2 shows, the abstract complex systems comprise society, economic system, social organizations, worldview, political system, government, and relationship. The conceptual metaphors in the society level of the present study conform to the extended GCB Metaphor. For example, stock market and marriage are part of the economic system and social organizations respectively; hence, the society level can be represented with abstract complex systems as Figure 7.2 shows.

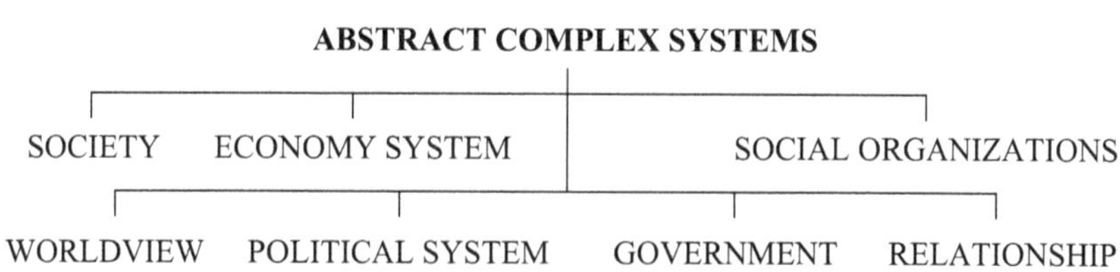

Figure 7.2. The entities in the abstract complex systems.

7.4. Entity, Quality and Function

The CMM helps analyze metaphorical expressions in terms of entity (noun), quality (adjective) and function (verb) (Ahrens 2002). By analyzing these three types, we can make predictions about different kinds of conceptual metaphors. This section discusses if any preferred syntactic category is chosen in the SD of stock market.

Table 7.7 presents the token and ratio of metaphorical expressions categorized into entity, quality, and function that correspond between the SD and TD in each TD. There are eleven conceptual metaphors in the TDs mapped onto the SD of stock market. N refers to the total number of each pairing in the three syntactic categories respectively. For example, there are 339 metaphorical pairings considered to be SPORTS CONTEST AS STOCK MARKET. Among the 339 metaphorical pairings, 74 of them (21.8%) are metaphorical expressions known as entities, 58 of them (17.1%) qualities, and 207 of them (61.1%) functions.

Table 7.7. The tokens and ratios of metaphorical expressions.

TDs	Entity		Quality		Function		Total
	N	%	N	%	N	%	
1. SPORTS CONTEST	74	21.8%	58	17.1%	207	61.1%	339
2. PEOPLE'S VALUE	150	59.1%	8	3.1%	96	37.8%	254
3. SHOW BUSINESS	69	43.4%	–	–	90	56.6%	159
4. MARRIAGE	60	43.2%	8	5.7%	71	51.1%	139
5. POLITICS	53	40.2%	–	–	79	59.8%	132
6. SUPERIOR FORCE	–	–	–	–	66	100%	66
7. FORTUNE TELLING	–	–	–	–	54	100%	54
8. TEMPERATURE	–	–	–	–	49	100%	49
9. EMOTION	8	17.4%	–	–	38	82.6%	46
10. AGE	–	–	–	–	38	100%	38
11. OUTLOOK ON LIFE	27	100%	–	–	–	–	27

'–' refers to 'no data presented'

As presented in Table 7.7, most conceptual metaphors in the TDs are function-based. They are sports contest, show business, marriage, politics, superior force, fortune telling, temperature, emotion, and age. The entity-based conceptual metaphors are People's value and outlook on life. In contrast, quality is not a prominent syntactic category in the SD of stock market, and it is only utilized in the TDs of sports contest (17.1%), people's value (3.1%) and marriage (5.7%). This result suggests that, in terms of stock market as a SD, function (verb) is the preferred syntactic category.

Why the conceptual metaphor has its own preferred syntactic category in terms of the SD of stock market? First, the metaphorical descriptions of the stock market tend to be dynamic, and therefore most mapped TDs tend to be described with dynamic descriptions. This explains why, of the syntactic categories mentioned above, functions (verbs) are chosen frequently to apply in the SD of stock market. Second, people's value and outlook on life are the two entity-based conceptual metaphors. Of these two TDs, the metaphorical descriptions that are used to judge people's value and reflect people's fundamental attitude toward life tend to be in a motionless state, such as example (33) *Song1ban3da4fu3shi4 re4men2gu3* 松坂大輔是熱門股 'Matsuzaka-is-active-stock = Matsuzaka is a popular player.' As mentioned above, this explains why the syntactic category entities (nouns) is attributed to metaphorical expressions in the TDs of people's value and outlook on life.

Lastly, let us turn to the syntactic category qualities (adjectives). Among one hundred and thirteen tokens of stock market jargon, *gao1dang3* 高檔 'good status' and *di1dang3* 低檔 'bad status' are the only two uses of stock market jargons known as qualities that are applied in the TDs of SPORTS CONTEST, PEOPLE'S VALUE, and MARRIAGE. Meanwhile, other stock market jargons known as entities and functions are not used to change their original syntactic categories to symbolize qualities for conceptual mappings. Mandarin speakers do not attempt to use the syntactic category qualities in the SD of stock market.

7.5. Conclusion

As Su (2000: 420) states, "language is part of culture, metaphor is one of the most important linguistic features in language that reflect cognitive vision and epitomize cultural context." That is to say, not only does the formulation of the conceptual mappings reflect human cognition but also the cultural background.

As having been indicated in this chapter, we are led to some implications regarding cultural features. First, when talking about marriage, Mandarin speakers tend to use stock market jargons to describe marriage negatively. Thus, it is notable that Mandarin speakers lack confidence in the marriage relationship, as they do in the bearish stock market. Second, the stock market jargons utilized to describe people's value tend to be positive; therefore, it reflects many Mandarin speakers' eager pursuit of profits in the stock market. Third, in FORTUNE TELLING AS STOCK MARKET, the orientational metaphorical concept of MORE IS UP is highlighted. It reveals that in Taiwanese culture, fortune telling tends to involve positive advice and guides people towards the brighter side of life.

When conceptualizing the SD of stock market, the concepts of GOOD IS UP, BAD IS DOWN, MORE IS UP and LESS IS DOWN are highlighted. On the other hand, when conceptualizing the TDs of the conceptual metaphors mapped onto the SD of stock market, the syntactic category, function, is frequently employed. We have more on stock market jargons in the next chapter.

CHAPTER EIGHT

STOCK MARKET JARGONS IN MANDARIN: RELATED COLLOCATIONS AND THE COGNITIVE STRATEGIES

Carrie Hsin-wen Tseng & Shelley Ching-yu Hsieh

8.0. Introduction

In the previous chapter, we investigate the metaphorical expressions of the stock market jargons and find that the SD of stock market maps onto eleven TDs: sport contest, show business, marriage, politics, fortune telling, emotion, age, people's value, superior force, temperature, and outlook on life. In this chapter , we continue our research on the stock market jargons and further target the collocations of *gu3* 股 'stock' and *shi4* 市 'market' and expect to observe cognitive strategies at work through a comparison between the works of Chung, Ahrens and Sung (2003), Huang (2009) and the present study.

This study is divided into three sections. First, a discussion of the collocations of *gu3* 股 'stock' and *shi4* 市 'market' is presented in 8.1. Second, we compare the research findings in three works in 8.2. At the end is a conclusion in 8.3.

8.1. Collocation with Metaphors

By examining the collected tokens of stock market jargon, we find that *gu3* 股 'stock' and *shi4* 市 'market' can be collocated with various kinds of domains to extend metaphorical meaning. We first discuss *gu3* 股 'stock' collocated with six domains then *shi4* 市 'market' collocated with two domains.

8.1.1. *The Collocations of Gu3* 股 *'Stock'*

The value of stocks influences the profits of investors. Thus, *gu3* 股 'stock' can be used to describe human values or comment on conditions which may be either positive or negative in six domains. *Gu3* 股 'stock' in different collocations can have various implications. Mostly, their core meanings emphasize positive or negative, and high or low values. The collocations with *gu3* 股 'stock' are categorized into six domains: food, natural phenomena, body parts of animals, value, objects, and disease.

8.1.1.1. *Food*

In the stock market, all the investors hope that their stock values will rise higher and higher so that they can sell them at higher prices. However, in the food market, the prices of *shui3jiao3* 水餃 'dumpling' in (1), *ji1dan4* 雞蛋 'egg' in (2), and *suan1mei2* 酸梅 'sour-plum' in (3) are less than 5 NT dollars for each one and always remain cheap. In this sense, the cheap food items that never increase in value, when mapped into the target domain of *gu3* 股 'stock,' are usually applied to describe bad stock values as indicated in (1) to (3). Similarly, the food in (1) to (3) are mapped into the TD of humans, as they are usually applied when describing people in bad states. Further, we also suggest that *gu3* 股 'stock' with food collocations tends to be conceptualized as negative concepts.

(1) *shui3 jiao3 gu3* 水餃股 'dumpling-stock = penny stock'
(2) *ji1 dan4 gu3* 雞蛋股 'egg-stock = valueless stock'
(3) *suan1 mei2 gu3* 酸梅股 'sour-plum-stock = valueless stock'

8.1.1.2. *Natural Phenomena*

Natural phenomena of temperature, sunrise, sunset, volcanic eruption, and so on, are closely tied to our daily lives. The attributes of these natural phenomena can induce both physical and emotional feelings. Various specific attributes of these natural phenomena can be utilized as vehicles to conceptualize one domain in terms of another. For example, *leng3* 冷 'cold' and *re4* 熱 'hot' are the two basic physical feelings that relate to temperature. In a metaphorical sense, *leng3* 冷 'cold' collocated with *men2* 門 'door' is conceptualized as the concept of unpopularity, whereas *re4* 熱 'hot' collocated with *men2* 門 'door' is conceptualized as the concept of popularity. Hence, in (4), *gu3* 股 'stock' collocated with *leng3men2* 冷門 'unpopular' is understood metaphorically as the stock being unpopular, which means that investors are unwilling to buy it. Conversely, in (5), *gu3* 股 'stock' collocated with *re4men2* 熱門 'popular' is understood metaphorically as the stock being popular, and means that investors are willing to buy it. Additionally, as sunsets mark the end of a day, *xi4yang2* 夕陽 'sunset' is conceptualized as something that is going to end. Thus, in (6), *gu3* 股 'stock' collocated with *xi4yang2* 夕陽 'sunset' is comprehended metaphorically as stock value that is going to end, never to reach another high peak.

(4) *leng3 men2 gu3* 冷門股 'cold-door-stock = unpopular stock'
(5) *re4 men2 gu3* 熱門股 'hot-door-stock = popular stock'
(6) *xi4 yang2 gu3* 夕陽股 'setting-sun-stock = sunset stock'

8.1.1.3. *Body Parts of Animals*

Animal collocations are frequently found in Chinese expressions that often refer to the appearance of humans and to their personality (Hsieh 2001–2009); for instance, *jian1zui3hou2sai1* 尖嘴猴腮 'sharp-mouth-monkey-cheek' and *lang2xin1gou3fei4* 狼心狗肺 'wolf-heart-dog-lung.' Human appearance and personality represent one's assets, and assets stand for value. For example, we have *long2 tou2* 龍頭 'dragon-head' collocated with *gu3* 股 'stock' as shown in (7) *long2 tou2 gu3* 龍頭股 'cock stock.'

The dragon in Chinese culture is regarded as a sainted sign. This fixed expression suggests a leading stock—the head—with a high price, and its performance has an influence on other stocks. That is, the rise and fall of this stock may be important when making an analysis of the overall situation in the stock market. Another animal body part, *niu2pi2* 牛皮 'cowskin,' is considered to be a strong material. In (8), *gu3* 股 'stock' collocated with *niu2pi2* 牛皮 'cowskin' is conceptualized as the stock's value being stable.

(7) *long2 tou2 gu3* 龍頭股 'dragon-head-stock = cock stock'
(8) *niu2 pi2 gu3* 牛皮股 'cow-skin-stock = stable stock'

8.1.1.4. *Value*

Value plays a prominent role in economic activity. The rise and fall of stock value may be used by investors to predict a company's future. For example, in (9), *gu3* 股 'stock' collocated with *gao1jia4* 高價 'high value' is applied to conceptualize that the stock has a high price. Likewise, in (10), *gu3* 股 'stock' collocated with *zhong1jia4* 中價 'normal price' is applied to mean that the stock has an normal average price. Finally, in (11), *gu3* 股 'stock' collocated with *di1jia4* 低價 'low price' suggests that the stock has a low price. From the above mappings, we also find that *jia4* 價 'value' has levels, hence it is often used with gradable adjectives, for instance, *gao1* 高 'high,' *zhong1* 中 'average,' and *di1* 低 'low.'

(9) *gao1 jia4 gu3* 高價股 'high-value-stock = stock with high price'
(10) *zhong1 jia4 gu3* 中價股 'average-value-stock = stock with normal price'
(11) *di1 jia4 gu3* 低價股 'low-value-stock = stock with low price'

8.1.1.5. *Objects*

In our environment, we are surrounded by a wide range of objects. When we want to make abstract concepts less abstract, we use these concrete objects. For example, *di4lei2* 地雷 'landmine' is an explosive military weapon hidden under the ground that unexpectedly kills enemies. Thus, in (12), when *gu3* 股 'stock' is collocated with *di4lei2* 地雷 'landmine,' we can understand that *di4 lei2 gu3* 地雷股 'landmine stock' is stock that becomes valueless without warning. Similarly, because *le4se4* 垃圾 'trash' is unwanted waste material, in (13), when *gu3* 股 'stock' is collocated with *le4se4* 垃圾 'trash,' we know that *le4 se4 gu3* 垃圾股 'junk stock' is an undesirable stock with an extremely low price. Finally, in (14), *gang1tie3gu3* 鋼鐵股 'steel stock' originally referred to the stock of a company whose main product was steel, or steel-related. Sometimes, however, due to the hard attribute of *gang1tie3* 鋼鐵 'steel,' *gang1tie3gu3* 鋼鐵股 'steel stock' has a metaphorical implication used to describe humans who are considered to have a stable social status or value, no matter how the circumstances around them change.

(12) *di4 lei2 gu3* 地雷股 'landmine-stock = landmine stock'
(13) *le4 se4 gu3* 垃圾股 'trash-stock = junk stock'
(14) *gang1 tie3 gu3* 鋼鐵股 'steel-stock = steel stock'

8.1.1.6. *Disease*

Gu3feng1 股瘋 'crazy for the stock market' and *gu3ai2* 股癌 'stock cancer' do not refer to the stocks, but rather are formed in daily conversation to describe investor addiction to the stock market. *Feng1* 瘋 'crazy' and *ai2* 癌 'cancer' are two symptoms leading to an unhealthy mind and body respectively. In (15) and (16), *gu3* 股 'stock' collocated with *feng1* 瘋 'crazy' and *ai2* 癌 'cancer' can be mapped onto the TD of humans to describe that these people are stock-market obsessed.

(15) *gu3 feng1* 股瘋 'stock-insane = crazy for stock market'
(16) *gu3 ai2* 股癌 'stock-cancer = stock cancer'

8.1.2. *The Collocations of Shi4* 市 *'Market'*

Shi4 市 'market' is an economic structure that allows buyers and sellers to exchange any type of goods. *Shi4* 市 'market' is considered to be an abstract domain, hence it needs certain specific collocations to make the market more concrete and meaningful, e.g., *hua1shi4* 花市 indicates a market for flowers, and *yu2shi4* 魚市 says this is a fish market. *Shi4* 市

'market' collocated with different domains are used to describe the current trends of the stock market and of tradable items. The collocations of *shi4* 市 'market' are classified into two types as in the examples illustrated below.

8.1.2.1. *Animal*

As stated earlier, animal collocation is commonly used in Mandarin expressions. Often, the animal's characteristics, or in this case, decide the properties of the collocation. In stock market jargons, *niu2shi4* 牛市 'bull market' and *xiong2shi4* 熊市 'bear market' are loan words from the west. These two expressions are commonly applied in Mandarin, suggesting animals are one kind of collocations co-appear with *shi4* 市 'market.' *Niu2* 牛 'bull' swings its horns upward when it strikes, while *xiong2* 熊 'bear' swats at things with its paws in a downward motion. With this sense of the animal's behavior, in (17), *shi4* 市 'market' collocated with *niu2* 牛 'bull' is conceptualized as a rising stock market, whereas in (18), *shi4* 市 'market' collocated with *xiong2* 熊 'bear' is conceptualized as a falling stock market.

(17) *niu2shi4* 牛市 'bull-market = bull market'
(18) *xiong2shi4* 熊市 'bear-market = bear market'

8.1.2.2. *Orientation*

The opposing orientation upward/downward, when correlated with our physical and cultural experiences, can be used to express metaphorical concepts. The locative *shang4* 上 'up,' in (19), collocated with *shi4* 市 'market,' is conceptualized as the stock is still being traded on the stock market, whereas the locative *xia4* 下 'down,' in (20), collocated with *shi4* 市 'market' is conceptualized as the stock is no longer being traded on the stock market. The locative collocations with *shi4* 市 'market' conform to the Orientational Metaphors (Lakoff and Johnson, 1980: 16) in which HIGH STATUS IS UP and LOW STATUS IS DOWN, GOOD IS UP and BAD IS DOWN.

(19) *shang4shi4* 上市 'up-market = the stock for sale'
(20) *xia4shi4* 下市 'down-market = the stock not for sale'

8.2. Comparison with Other Studies

Now we will turn to discuss whether any similar or dissimilar concepts are shared by the research on stock market jargons of this study and the works of Chung, Ahrens, and Sung (2003) and Huang (2009). In addition, we will see if any arguments are proposed in relation to some aspects of the conceptual system. First, the chain-producing aspect of metaphor will be explored in 8.2.1. Next, the principle governing the selection of a SD to a TD and a TD to a SD will be suggested in 8.2.2. After that, the prevailing mapping domain in the economics-related field will be presented in 8.2.3. Finally, the mechanism for the GCB Metaphor will be discussed in 8.2.4.

Chung and Ahrens present a series of papers on conceptual metaphors related to the stock market and the economy. In their papers, for example, Chung, Ahrens and Sung (2003) offer findings in terms of the TD of stock market by applying the framework of the CMM. Huang (2009), furthermore, proposes the conceptualization of *jin1* 金 'gold' in terms of *jin1qian2* 金錢 'money,' *zi1jin1* 資金 'capital,' and *huang2jin1* 黃金 'gold' in Mandarin by applying the frameworks of the CMM and the GCB Metaphor. The present study has presented a study of the SD of stock market mapped onto other TDs by applying the frameworks of the CMM and the GCB Metaphor.

We are motivated to make comparisons between our finding on stock market jargons with the researches of Chung, Ahrens and Sung (2003) and Huang (2009) by three major reasons. First, they all use the CMM or the GCB Metaphor as frameworks. Second, their proposed domains are relevant to the field of economics. Third, they are all corpus-based studies. For these reasons, we compare the present study with the works in Chung, Ahrens and Sung (2003) and Huang (2009), which will be discussed in the following four sections.

8.2.1. *Source Domains and Target Domains*

Conceptual metaphor consists of a SD and a TD. For conceptual metaphor, the discrimination between a SD and a TD is a must. Typically, the SD is the more physical while the TD the more abstract kind of domain (Lakoff and Johnson 1980; Kövecses 2002; Kövecses 2005). In addition, the relationship between the SD and the TD is that a SD may apply to several TDs, whereas a TD may attach to several SDs (Kövecses 2005).

Providing us with a clear picture for the following analysis, Figure 8.1 summarizes the conceptual metaphors for stock market in Chung, Ahrens and Sung (2003) and the present study. Listed in the left column of Figure 8.1, the conceptual metaphors categorized in Chung, Ahrens and Sung (2003) are the SDs of ocean water, war, storm, earthquake and person and are mapped onto the TD of stock market. On the other hand, the classification of conceptual metaphors of the stock market jargons listed in the right column of Figure 8.1 are the TDs that are mapped onto the SD of stock market, these being sport contest, show business, marriage, politics, fortune telling, emotion, age, people's value, superior force, temperature and outlook on life.

Again, considering Figure 8.1, it should be obvious that stock market can be conceptualized as both a SD and a TD. That is, a SD can function as a TD as suggested by Kövecses (2002). Next, the metaphorical process underlying "metaphor chains" (Kövecses 2002) will be illustrated with examples and figures.

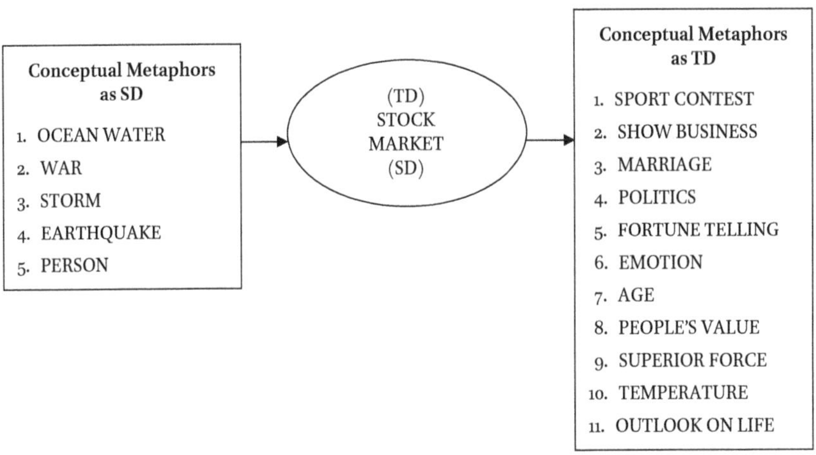

Figure 8.1. Conceptual metaphors in the domains of stock market.

As shown in Figure 8.2 on p. 136, the conceptual mappings in the metaphor chain are STOCK MARKET AS OCEAN WATER, OUTLOOK ON LIFE AS STOCK MARKET and OUTLOOK ON LIFE AS OCEAN WATER. Of these three mappings, the domain of stock market can function as both a SD and a TD. That is, the domain of stock market can be the vehicle that gets mapped onto the domains of ocean water and outlook on life to form a metaphorical chain. For example, in *qi2jian1 gu3shi4 qi3qi3fu2fu2* 其間股市起起伏伏 'its-period-stock- market-rise-rise-fall-fall = Between that (period), the stock market rises and falls,'[1] the fixed expression *qi3qi3fu2fu2* 起起伏伏 'rise-rise-fall-fall = rises and falls' appears as one of the properties of ocean water. In this sense, *gu3shi4* 股市 'stock market' is

[1] This example is given in Chung Ahrens and Sung (2003).

realized metaphorically as ocean water; specifically, STOCK MARKET AS OCEAN WATER.

For the conceptual mapping of OUTLOOK ON LIFE AS STOCK MARKET, let us take *mai3kong1ma4ikong1 de zhi4hui4* 買空賣空的智慧 'buy-empty-sell-empty-POSS.-intelligence = the basic human concept of how to deal with risks' as an example. In this sentence, *mai3kong1mai-4kong1* 買空賣空 'buy-empty-sell-empty = short buying short selling,' is a piece of stock market jargon that can be treated as a metaphorical expression corresponding between a SD and a TD. Thus, outlook on life is realized metaphorically as stock market.

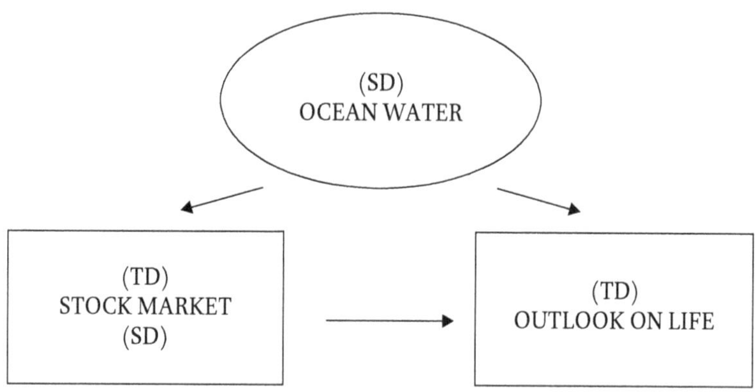

Figure 8.2. Metaphor chain formed by conceptual mappings.

Now, let us turn to the conceptual mapping of OUTLOOK ON LIFE AS OCEAN WATER. Take the following sentence for example: *ren2sheng1 de chao2qi3chao2luo4* 人生的潮起潮落 'The tide rises, the tide falls in life.' The whole sentence can be conceptualized in terms of OUTLOOK ON LIFE as a TD and OCEAN WATER as a SD. In this case, OUTLOOK ON LIFE is realized metaphorically as OCEAN WATER. Similar evidence of such a metaphorical chain is also found and presented in Figure 8.3.

As can be seen in Figure 8.3, the conceptual mappings in the metaphor chain are STOCK MARKET AS STORM, POLITICS AS STOCK MARKET and POLITICS AS STORM. As an example, consider *zai4du4 long3zhao4 zai4 quan2qiu2 gu3shi4 feng1bao4* 再度籠罩在全球股市風暴 '(something) was again covered by the storm of the worldwide stock market,'[2] which produces the conceptual mapping of STOCK MARKET AS STORM.

[2] This example is given in Chung, Ahrens and Sung (2003).

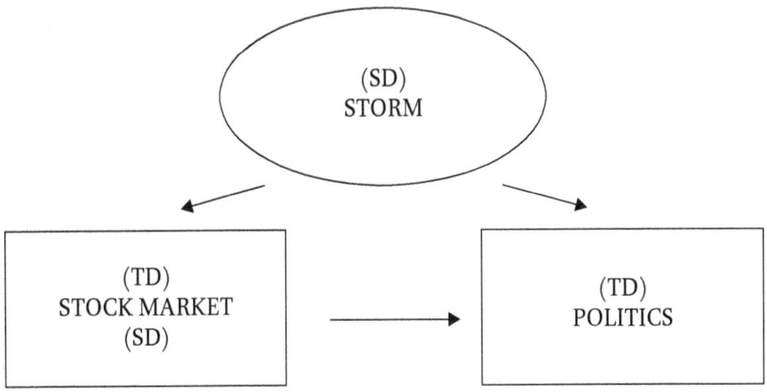

Figure 8.3. Metaphor chain formed by conceptual mappings.

Also, STOCK MARKET can function as a SD, as when we read in the newspaper *bei3 gao1 ping2pan2 min2jin4dang3 shi4qi4 zhi3die2hui2sheng1* 北高平盤 民進黨士氣止跌回升 'Taipei-Kaohsiung-equal-tray-DPP-morale-stop-fall back-raise = The party's approval ratings between Taipei and Kaohsiung are even, therefore the DPP's morale is coming back.' In addition, storm can function as a SD that gets mapped onto politics as a TD: for instance, *zheng4 zhi4 feng1 bao4* 政治風暴 'politics-wind-violence = political storm.' Thus, the conceptual mapping of POLITICS AS STORM is performed.

8.2.2. *Conceptual Metaphors*

Underlying concepts enable us to observe the motivation humans conceptualize one domain in terms of another. This section discusses if, in the stock market domain, the conceptual metaphors collected from Chung, Ahrens and Sung (2003) and the findings of the stock market jargons in the present study have any shared underlying concepts. In addition, we will see if there is any particular principle governs the underlying motivation for the selection of a SD to a TD and a TD to a SD.

In Figure 8.1, we looked at conceptual metaphors in the TD of stock market in Chung, Ahrens and Sung (2003), and the conceptual metaphors in the SD of stock market in the present study. The TD of stock market is mapped onto the five SDs of conceptual metaphors—ocean water, war, storm, earthquake and person. The SD of the stock market maps onto the eleven TDs of conceptual metaphors—sport contest, show business, marriage, politics, fortune telling, emotion, age, people's value, superior force, temperature and outlook on life.

After comparing the conceptual metaphors in Chung, Ahrens and Sung (2003) and the present study, we find that certain conceptual metaphors produced from the opposite mapping domains may share the same underlying concepts: specifically, competition and up and down as shown in Table 8.1.

Table 8.1. The shared underlying concepts in the domains of stock market.

Conceptual metaphors	Underlying concept
SPORT CONTEST AS STOCK MARKET STOCK MARKET AS WAR	COMPETITION
AGE AS STOCK MARKET TEMPERATURE AS STOCK MARKET EMOTION AS STOCK MARKET STOCK MARKET AS OCEAN WATER	UP AND DOWN

As presented in Table 8.1, sport contest and war, from opposite mapping domains, overlap with the same underlying concept of competition by (21) and (22) show respectively. Similarly, age, temperature, emotion, and ocean water, from opposite mapping domains, overlap with the same underlying concept of UP AND DOWN shown by (23) to (26). As discussed above, such shared underlying concepts can also account for why and how metaphor chains may be produced. In what follows, the notion of the shared underlying concepts will be demonstrated with examples.

(21) *2006 shi4 jie4 tuan2 ti3 zhuo1 qiu2 sai4*
2006 世 界 團 體 桌 球 賽
2006 world team table tennis competition
kai1 di1 zou3 gao1 tai2wan1 dui4 ke4 e4 luo2 si1
開 低 走 高 台灣 隊 克 俄羅斯
start low go high Taiwan team subdue Russia
'The competition of 2006 World Team Table Tennis is going from bad to good and Taiwan defeats Russian team.'

(22) *Gu3 shi4 ru2 zhan4 chang3*
股 市 如 戰場
Stock market similar battlefield
'The stock market is a battlefield.'

(23) *xia4tan4* 下探 'dip'; Function
Xiao1 fei4 nian2 ling2 xia4 tan4 tai2 wan1 LV
消 費 年 齡 下 探 台 灣 LV
Consumption age down detect Taiwan LV

xiao1 fei4 li4 shi4 ya4 zhou1 NO.2
消 費 力 是 亞 洲 NO.2
consumption power is Asia NO.2
'The age of consumers is getting younger and younger, and Taiwan is ranked number 2 in Asia for the consumption of LV products.'

(24) *Ming2 wen1 du4 liu1 hua2 ti1 xia4 tan4* 12 *du4*
明 溫 度 溜 滑 梯 下 探 12 度
tomorrow temperature slide down detect 12 degree
'The temperature will drop to twelve degrees tomorrow.'

(25) *Xin1qing2 zhi3 die2 hui2 sheng1*
心 情 止 跌 回 升
Mood stop fall back raise
'The mood is going from bad to good.'

(26) *Nan2 han2 gu3 shi4 ze2 shi4*
南 韓 股 市 則 是
South Korea stock market on the other hand is
xiao3 zhang3 ju2 mian4[3]
小 漲 局 面
small rise condition
'The stock market in South Korea rose a little.'

Additionally, an interesting finding also emerges by comparing the underlying concepts in Chung, Ahrens and Sung (2003) and the present study. As shown in Figure 8.4, the underlying concept of risk is mapped onto the TDs of marriage and politics. That is, in the SD of stock market, the underlying concept of risk is shared by the TDs of marriage and politics.

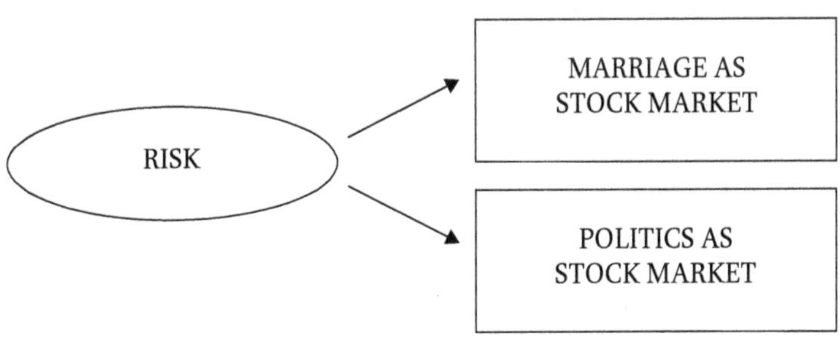

Figure 8.4. The shared underlying concept of risk.

[3] This example is collected from Chung, Ahrens and Sung (2003).

Similarly, as can be seen in Figure 8.5, in the SD of stock market, the underlying concept of up and down gets mapped onto the TDs of emotion, age and temperature. Considering Figures 8.4 and 8.5, it is worth noting that the different TDs tend to be conceptualized as the same SD with the same underlying concept. However, this is not the case in Figure 8.6.

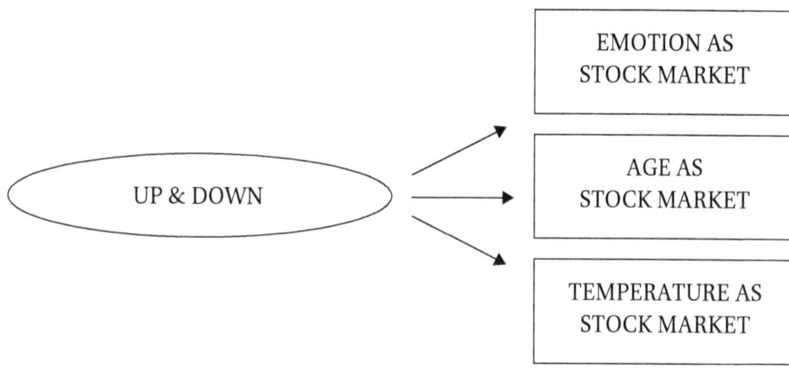

Figure 8.5. The shared underlying concept of up and down.

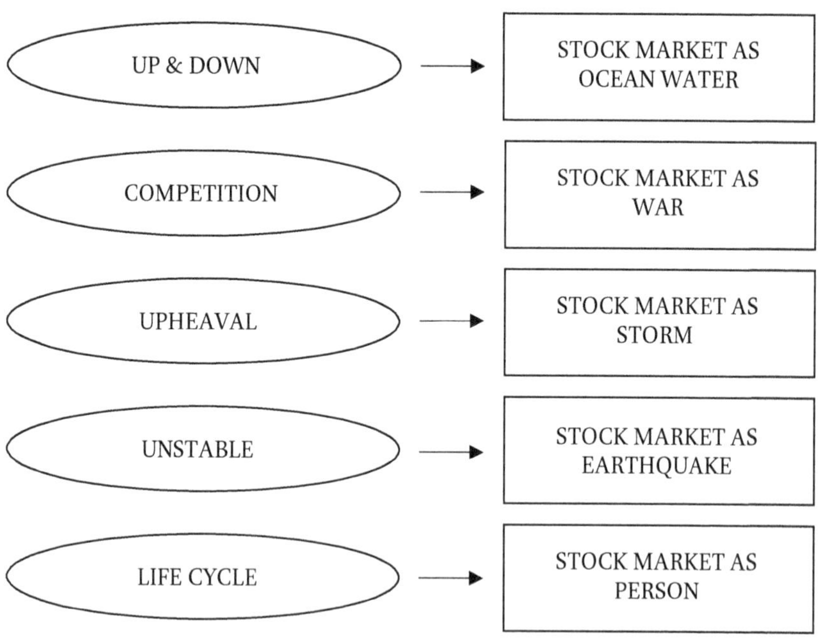

Figure 8.6. The different underlying concepts.

In contrast, as is shown in Figure 8.6, the single TD of stock market tends to be realized metaphorically as different SDs with different underlying concepts. In the TD of stock market, for example, the underlying concept of up and down gets mapped onto the SD of ocean water. Another example is illustrated by the underlying concept of life cycle which gets mapped onto the SD of person.

The present study has observed that the same SD may map onto different TDs with shared underlying concepts and a single TD may be mapped onto different SDs with different underlying concepts. Ahrens (2002) has similar findings. It suggests that the SD-TD mappings in abstract reasoning are complex and interwoven after researching on different types of linguistic data.

8.2.3. *Prevailing Mapping Domain*

Concepts can serve as a SD or a TD based on their own specific attributes. This section discusses if any prevailing mapping domain can be found in stock-market-based language.

After examining the works in Chung, Ahrens and Sung (2003) and Huang (2009), we can be certain that the conceptual metaphor of human overlaps in the mapping domains. Chung, Ahrens, and Sung (2003) demonstrate STOCK MARKET AS A PERSON, and Huang (2009), *jin1qian2* 金錢 'money' and *zi1jin1* 資金 'capital' as human. Based on the above findings, we will also examine if the present study shares the same conceptual metaphor of human. In the present study, six conceptual metaphors in the SD of stock market—fortune telling, emotion, age, people's value, superior force and outlook on life—overlap in the human level of the GCB Metaphor hierarchy shown in Table 8.2 Consequently, we can conceptualize HUMAN AS STOCK MARKET. This result suggests that the conceptual agent, human, can function as the SD and TD of stock market. It also serves as the TDs of *jin1qian2* 金錢 'money' and *zi1jin1* 資金 'capital.'

On the other hand, if we take a look at the tokens for each conceptual metaphor overlapping in the human level of the GCB Metaphor, the total number of tokens for the six conceptual metaphors is 485,[4] which is 37.22% of the total number of tokens. In this case, the human level plays a prominent role in the SD of stock market.

[4] There are 1303 TDs of all the conceptual metaphors corresponding with the SD of stock market.

Table 8.2. Conceptual metaphors in the human level.

Conceptual metaphors as stock market	Tokens
FORTUNE TELLING	54
EMOTION	46
AGE	38
PEOPLE'S VALUE	254
SUPERIOR FORCE	66
OUTLOOK ON LIFE	27
TOTAL	485

Table 8.3. The ratio of humans as source domain.

Conceptual metaphors	%
STOCK MARKET AS A PERSON	14.07%
JIN1QIAN2 AS HUMAN	37%
ZI1JIN1 AS HUMAN	27%

As just mentioned, human can be mapped onto the TDs of stock market, *jin1qian2* 金錢 'money,' and *zi1jin1* 資金 'capital.' Table 8.3 presents the ratio of human as SD in the different TDs of stock market, *jin1qian2* 金錢 'money' and *zi1jin1* 資金 'capital.' When conceptualizing stock market, 14.07% of the instances get mapped onto person, *jin1qian2* 金錢 'money' 37% and *zi1jin1* 資金 'capital' 27%. After comparing the metaphorical interpretations of the three FLEs in the three research works, we see that the HUMAN level is the prevailing mapping domain in the economics-related field.

Furthermore, closer examination of Table 8.2 and Table 8.3 reveals that human is conceptualized as a SD and a TD; therefore, we arrive at the finding that *human* tends to be employed more in the SD than in the TD. In other words, HUMAN tends to be used in a more concrete SD in metaphorical mapping due to its attributes. This phenomenon, known as personification is a common metaphorical mapping process in the cognitive system (Ungerer and Schmid 2006: 126). Kövecses (2002: 50) also points out that personification is a metaphorical device that helps us comprehend other aspects of the world by knowing ourselves. Not only the metaphorical mapping process of personification apply to *stock market, jin1qian2* 金錢 'money' and *zi1jin1* 資金 'capital,' but it also applies to *economy* and *euro* (Charteris-Black 2000; Chung, Ahrens and Huang 2003; White 2003; Charteris-Black and Musolff 2003). As has been made clear above, it is notable that human conceptualization is the prevailing mapping domain in the economic related field.

8.2.4. *The Levels in the Great Chain of Being Metaphor*

The GCB Metaphor proposed by Lakoff and Turner (1989) is a cognitive-based vertical hierarchy which organizes conceptual metaphors in a certain domain from top to bottom. This section focuses on conceptual metaphors applied to the GCB Metaphor in both Huang (2009) and the present study.

As presented in Huang (2009: 76–80), the six levels in the GCB Metaphor for the TD of *jin1qian2* 金錢 'money' (from top to bottom) are: supernatural power, humans, animals, plants, complex objects and natural physical things.[5] As demonstrated in the present study, the three levels in the GCB Metaphor for the SD of stock market (from top to bottom) are: society, humans and natural physical things. The highest level in the basic GCB Metaphor reaches its limit at humans, whereas the extended GCB Metaphor moves its metaphorical level higher from humans up to the relations of society, universe and god. Therefore, the two domains of

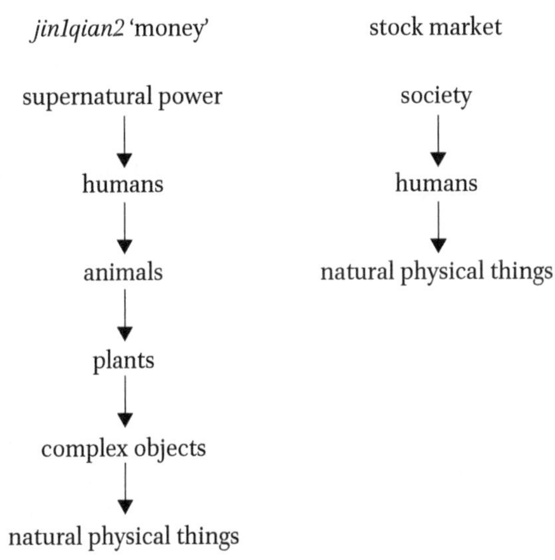

Figure 8.7. *Jin1qian2* and stock market in the GCB Metaphor.

[5] Natural physical things are like rivers, water, wind, and so on.

jin1qian2 金錢 'money' and stock market in the GCB Metaphor are apparently attributed to the extended GCB Metaphor instead of the basic GCB Metaphor because their metaphorical levels all ascend from human up to society and supernatural power, respectively as shown in Figure 8.7.
With respect to the process of the GCB Metaphor, the conceptualizations in the SD of stock market proceed from a higher SD to a lower TD. On the other hand, the conceptual metaphors in the SD mapped onto the TD of *jin1qian2* 金錢 'money' are supernatural power, human, prey, plant, commodity, machine, medicine, dirty object,[6] and water. The majority of the conceptual metaphors overlap in the five levels of supernatural power, humans, animals, plants and complex objects from top to bottom. Only the conceptual metaphor water overlaps in the sixth level of natural physical things. In the hierarchy of the GCB Metaphor, the TD, *jin1qian2* 金錢 'money,' overlaps in the fifth level of complex objects. Thus, it should be noted that *jin1qian2* 金錢 'money,' which is the TD in the lower level of the hierarchy, is conceptualized as the conceptual metaphors, i.e. the SDs, in the upper level of the hierarchy. That is to say, the conceptualizations in the TD of *jin1qian2* 金錢 'money' tend to proceed from a higher SD to a lower TD.

As has been observed, in the extended GCB Metaphor, the two domains of stock market and *jin1qian2* 金錢 'money' work in the same direction, but organize the extended GCB Metaphor levels in different ways. This result suggests that in the GCB Metaphor's metaphorical process, the different kinds of domains can form a different kind of GCB Metaphor vertical hierarchy, but may share the same conceptualization direction—a higher SD to a lower TD or a lower SD to a higher TD, in the GCB Metaphor's metaphorical process.

8.3. Conclusion

The present study has two research goals. First, we discussed the collocations of *gu3* 股 'stock' and *shi4* 市 'market.' Second, we compared the finding of Tseng (2010) with the works of Chung, Ahrens and Sung (2003) and Huang (2009). It was found that *gu3* 股 'stock' tended to be collocated with the fields of FOOD, NATURAL PHENOMENA, BODY PARTS OF ANI-

[6] As in Chapter 4, example (26) *jin1qian2 fu3hua4 ren2 xin1* 金錢腐化人心 'money-rot-people-heart = money rots human beings' hearts' is one example of *JIN1QIAN2* AS DIRTY OBJECT.

MALS, VALUE, OBJECTS and DISEASE; however, *shi4* 市 'market' tended to be collocated with the fields of ANIMAL and ORIENTATION.

Additionally, in light of the present study and in comparison with the works of Chung, Ahrens and Sung (2003) and Huang (2009), the cognitive operations behind metaphorical processes have been observed. First, the cognitive operation of the metaphorical chain is produced when as a SD becomes a TD. For example, STOCK MARKET AS STORM, POLITICS AS STOCK MARKET and POLITICS AS STORM.

Second, the conceptual mappings produced from the opposite mapping domains may share the same underlying concepts; for example, EMOTION AS STOCK MARKET and STOCK MARKET AS OCEAN WATER both share the same underlying metaphorical concepts of up and down.

Third, different TDs may use the same SD for the same reason, for example, EMOTION AS STOCK MARKET and AGE AS STOCK MARKET are structured by the reason of up and down. As opposed to the above-mentioned operations, a single TD must use different SDs for different reasons, as in STOCK MARKET AS WAR and STOCK MARKET AS PERSON which share the different reasons of competition and life cycle, respectively.

Fourth, human conceptualization is the prevailing mapping domain in the economic-related field as we can see from HUMAN AS STOCK MARKET, STOCK MARKET AS A PERSON, *JIN1QIAN2* AS HUMAN and *ZI1JIN1* AS HUMAN. Finally, different domains can organize the vertical hierarchy of the GCB Metaphor in different ways, but may share the same conceptualization direction. For example, the SD of stock market and the TD of *jin1qian2* structure the vertical hierarchy of the GCB Metaphor with different levels, but share the same conceptualization direction—a higher SD to a lower TD.

PART TWO

IN GERMAN AND MANDARIN CHINESE

CHAPTER NINE

FINANCIAL LINGUISTIC VERBS IN GERMAN

Shelley Ching-yu Hsieh

9.0. Introduction

Based on economic metaphors (White 2003) and the elements of semantic frame (Fillmore and Atkins 1992), this study presents the three German FLE verbs *kaufen* 'buy,' *verkaufen* 'sell' and *bezahlen* 'pay' in newspaper usage (see examples (a) and (b)). The research goal is to explore German culture and social cognition through the commercial activities that the three verbs show. The data are taken from the German *Corpus Search, Management and Analysis System* (COSMAS II) and *Deutscher Wortschatz.* Mandarin data is used as a comparison.

(a) Die Bilanzdefizite werde das Klinikum aus den Rücklagen <u>bezahlen</u>, versicherte der Interims-Chef. [M06/FEB.09424 Mannheimer Morgen, 04.02.2006]
'The clinical center will <u>pay</u> the budget deficit out of the reserved fund, which was confirmed by the interim manager.'

(b) Der Optimismus müsse wachsen, "dass die Dinge, die wir erfinden, auch zu guten Produkten werden, die wir in der ganzen Welt in größer werdenden Märkten <u>verkaufen</u> können". [M07/JAN.00011 Mannheimer Morgen, 02.01.2007]
'optimism must grow, that the things, which we invent will become good products and can be <u>sold</u> on all markets that become bigger and bigger around the world.'

This chapter is divided into three sections. We first introduce the methodology and data sources, including FLEs in language and semantic frameworks in 9.1, the three verbs of the FLEs and life-form in 9.2, Elements of commercial transaction frame in 9.3, and a conclusion in 9.4.

9.1. Methodology and Data Source

The present research is based on economic metaphors (White 2003) and the notion of Frame Semantics (Fillmore and Atkins 1992). White's approach (2003) has been reviewed in Chapter 1. We now briefly introduce Frame Semantics as proposed by Fillmore and Atkins (1992) in Chapter 2 in order to link it with the research framework of this study. Fillmore and Atkins put forth the theory of Frame Semantics claiming that it is linked to people's comprehension process; specifically, how we understand meanings in context. During this process, lexical meaning and grammatical characteristics "both with information about related words and with our general cultural knowledge about the world" (Goddard 1998: 69) work together in one's comprehension. The meaning of a word can be understood only against a background frame of experience, beliefs, or practices that "motivate the concept that the word encodes" (Fillmore and Atkins 1992). They give this set of verbs as an example: *buy, sell, charge, pay, cost,* and *spend.* To understand any of these verbs, one needs to understand a complete 'commercial transaction frame.'

In any given society, this frame is a complex yet compact linguistic base for words such as *buy, sell,* and *charge.* People who do not have this linguistic frame in mind will not understand the meaning of *buying* and *selling.* Tarzan, for example, would have such difficulty. More precisely, it is by means of the compositionality of the concepts in the related words and the background knowledge of society that we comprehend the words and expressions used in daily life.

Likewise, to understand the verbs *kaufen* 'buy,' *verkaufen* 'sell' and *bezahlen* 'pay' in German requires a complete commercial transaction frame in speakers' minds. This commercial transaction frame defines the six commercial verbs and enables us to further investigate concepts other than economical ideas carried by these verbs.

Elements of the commercial transaction frame include TWO PERSONS, POSSESSION, and ECONOMIC SYSTEM (agreement, money, social value). We will focus on two Elements: persons and possession, in order to examine the concepts these three FLE verbs—*kaufen, verkaufen* and *bezahlen*—convey in the German society as revealed in the newspaper corpus.

From an anthropological perspective, Keesing (1981) points out that culture is an ideational system representing the pattern of social behavior and social communication of a specific social group. Culture is a generalization, and it is therefore impossible for two individuals to have the same perception of any given culture. According to Nostrand's (1978, see Stern 1993) Emergent Model, "culture" involves extensive topics, including language, paralanguage, body language, value systems, contemplating habits, the shared assumption of reality, and so on. This study will investigate German culture linguistically from the points of the three FLE verbs.

Our data are taken from the German *Corpus Search, Management and Analysis System* (COSMAS II) (Institut für Deutsche Sprache 2008), *Deutscher Wortschatz* (Universität Leipzig 1998–2008), and Google search. The main data are newspaper articles searched in COSMAS II. *Deutscher Wortschatz* is used to locate the significant or frequent collocations of the verbs. Google search enables us to reassure the validity of some data.

9.2. The Three FLE Verbs and Life-Form

There are 5677 tokens that were retrieved from COSMAS II: *kaufen* 2,810, *verkaufen* 2,631, and *bezahlen* 236 from 2006 to 2007. Looking into the context of the data and observing grammatical subject of the sentence in which the verb occurred, the most frequently occurring subjects are presented in Table 9.1 below. As we can see from the table, 'person' is the most often used subject for all three verbs, followed by 'organization,' 'group,' and 'pronoun.' Some examples are given below. It should be noted that 'group' is often a representation of the plural form of 'persons,' such as *die Reisenden* 'tourists' in (3a) and *die Westeuropäer* 'west-Euopean' in (3b). So too are 'pronoun' such as *wer* 'who' and *keiner* 'none.'

Table 9.1. Most frequent subjects of the 3 FLE verbs.

Subject	*kaufen*	*verkaufen*	*bezahlen*
Person	35.27%	44.55%	32.07%
Organization	8.21%	13.86%	11.60%
Group	15.94%	9.41%	22.36%
Pronoun	30.92%	8.91%	10.34%

(1) person
  a. *Schüler* <u>bezahlen</u> 8 Euro.
     '*pupils* <u>pay</u> 8 Euro.'
  b. kann *ein Anleger* maximal Anteile im Gegenwert von 5000 Euro <u>verkaufen</u>.
     '*one investor* can <u>sell</u> shares up to a maximum of 5.000 Euro counter value.'

(2) organization
  a. ... will *der Kreisverband* das Grundstück zwischen Industrie- und Dieselstraße kaufen
  '*The local union* will buy the estate located between Industry- and Dieselstreet.'
  b. *Das japanische Unternehmen*... der Konsole im ersten Jahr 6 Mio. Geräte verkaufen.
  '*The Japanese company*... sell 6 Million of the consoles in the first year.'

(3) group
  a. ... müssen *die Reisenden* allerdings bezahlen.
  '... however the *passengers* have to pay for it.'
  b. *Die Westeuropäer* kaufen wieder Autos, allen voran Dieselmodelle.
  '*People from western Europe* buy cars again, especially cars with diesel.'

(4) pronoun
  a. *Wer* Kindersachen verkaufen möchte, muss sich allerdings vorab...
  'People, *who* want to sell things for children, have... in advance.'
  b. ... *keiner* tut einen Dienst, ohne einen Preis zu bezahlen.
  '... *nobody* does a service without paying a price for it.'

Moving on from the data collection, we now concentrate on two elements of the commercial transaction frame: PERSONS and POSSESSION. White (2003), as we reviewed in Chapter 1, found that the scenario of economic activities agrees with the life cycle progression, of birth, zenith, decline, and death. We therefore searched our data for this aspect. The most frequent grammatical subject of the sentence in which the three FLE verbs occurred is 'person'—a life-form. 'Group' and 'pronoun,' as mentioned above, are often other forms of 'person' as well. We then searched *Deutscher Wortschatz* (1998–2008) for the most frequent collocations related to these two aspects. Additionally, more representations of life-form are found (as shown in Table 9.2). Example (5) points out *Zertifikate* 'certificates' and (7) *verrückt* 'crazy,' *lächerlich* 'absurd, laughable' show human emotion, while *dumm* 'stupid,' *will* 'will' present human mind.

Table 9.2. The representation of life-form.

	kaufen		*verkaufen*		*bezahlen*	
	left	right	left	right	left	right
Human being	1136	329	896	286	1065	–
Identity	78	–	120	–	–	–
Responsibility and order	–	275	–	317	106	4494
Emotion	–	52	–	–	–	–
Mind	–	26	505	–	–	–

(5) identity: Anleger sollten nur *Zertifikate* kaufen, deren Funktionsweise....
'Investors should only buy *certificates* when they understand their function....'

(6) responsbility: dass die Bürger, die das Ganze bezahlen *sollen*, kein Klagerecht haben....
'that the citizens, who *should* pay for all this, have the right to sue....'

(7) emotion: zwischen 20 und 40 aus allen Schichten kaufen wie *verrückt*, manche 20 Tüten auf....
'people between 20 and 40 years old of all classes buy like *crazy*, some of them 20 bags....'

(8) mind: wir nicht die Absicht haben, uns für *dumm* verkaufen zu lassen, scheitert dieser Wunsch
'we have no intention to let us be taken for a *fool*.... this wish fails.'

Focusing on two elements of the commercial transaction frame, PERSONS and POSSESSION, the data shows that these elements can reveal social change and modern products. The element PERSONS can be two companies, political parties, or associations (see example 2). As for the element POSSESSION, the basic needs of human beings are evident and remain unchanged (*Brot* 'bread,' *Fleisch* 'meat,' *Torten* 'cake'), while modern products (*Auto* 'car,' *Grundstück* 'property,' *Euro* 'euro,' *EC-Karte* 'EC-card,' *online* 'online'), and investment (*Euro* 'euro,' *Aktien* 'stocks') also figure prominently in the data and enjoy high frequency in *Deutscher Wortschatz* as significant collocations of the three verbs given. The next section explores the cultural implications implied by the collocations (now objects and adjectives) of the three German verbs and compares it to that found in Mandarin.

9.3. Cultural Implication

The significant left and right collocations of the three FLE verbs also reveal different buying and selling activities in modern society when compared to the old days. For example, in modern German society, *Autos* 'autos' rank second in *verkaufen* (frequency = 3.09%) and third in *kaufen* (353 2.08%). *Aktien* 'stocks,' *Internet* 'internet,' and *online* 'online' are also significant collocations for *kaufen* and *verkaufen*. As *Deutscher Wortschatz* shows, *bezahlen* 'pay' is often collocated with *Strafe* 'punishment' (0.85%), *Rechnung* 'bill' (1.28%), and *Leben* 'life' (0.6%). These collocations indicate burdens in life as they are revealed by *bezahlen* 'pay.'

We now compare German with Mandarin Chinese. The Mandarin data shows that, as in Germany, modern products like PCs and CDs are similarly popular articles for trading. However, we found a special Chinese philosophy or thinking that is different than that found in German culture. For example, up to the present, some Chinese scholars still consider making a living with their knowledge an act of selling (see example 9). We should know that the traditional Chinese scholars were noble and incorruptible. That is, they believed it was their duty or mission to offer their knowledge to the whole world to make it better. They considered their knowledge a kind of virtue to be contributed, not traded. Thus, it would be vulgar to make a living by selling their knowledge because their virtue should be of benefit to all, not just for themselves or a small number of certain individuals.

In addition, the selling of 'natural products' is something worth mentioning because it was not found to be a significant collocation of *kaufen, verkaufen* or *behzahlen* in *Deutscher Wortschatz*. According to Hsieh's (2009c) study on the comparison between the financial adjectives, *arm* 'poor' in German and *pin2* 貧 'poor' in Mandarin, Chinese usually associates *pin2* with the concepts of nature or human being, while Germans associate *arm* with the concepts of human sensation and society. The differences between *arm* in German and *pin2* in Mandarin reflect the different philosophies and religious beliefs of these two peoples. Chinese speakers have been strongly influenced by the philosophy of Taoism, which advocates that heaven, earth and human beings are a unity in which these three parts closely connect to and rely strongly on one another to make the world harmonious. The idea that human beings are nature, and nature is human beings, is reflected in the language Chinese people use. On the other hand, the use of *arm* in German reflects the Christianity, capitalism, and pragmatism of German society. In medieval times, religious doctrines taught Germans to be ascetic and abandon any yearnings for stimulation of the bodily senses. However, this kind of religious teaching was oppressive and caused people to feel deprived. Therefore, the association of German *arm* with physical sensation reflects Germans' rebellious thought against asceticism.

Turning now to the trading activity of *Aktien* 'stocks' (frequency = 2.03%) (example 10) and *Börse* 'stock exchange' (0.61%) are much more active in German than in Taiwanese society (in Mandarin the frequency is 0.35%). While German *Auto* enjoys the highest frequency in German commercial activity, food trading is the most popular (6.77%) in Taiwan.

Furthermore, the significant collocations *lassen* 'let' (18.39%) and *dürfen* 'may' (4.82%) in German do not show up as significant collocations in our Mandarin data. It could be a consequence of syntax and verbal systems of using light verbs, or it may indicate the Germans are much more law-abiding.

The emotion and mindset revealed in the Mandarin data is different from that in the German data. On one hand, the Taiwanese seem to be more fond of buying and selling than the Germans, as examples *xi3huan1* 喜歡 'like' in (11) and *ai4* 愛 'love' in (12) indicate. Nevertheless, the significant collocations also show Taiwanese conservatism and caution in trading as *bu4gan3* 不敢 'dare not' in (13) indicates.

On the other hand, the attitude toward economic activity can also be observed in the German data. *Kaufen* usually appears with emotive terms, such as *verrückt* 'mad,' *lächerlich* 'ridiculous,' *lieber* 'prefer,' while *verkaufen* is usually followed by expressions that are related to mental states, such as *dumm* 'stupidly.' Furthermore, the Germans call on reason as *kaufen* is often collocated with *möchte* 'would like' (334 4.29%), *können* 'can' (1889 24.26%), *bewusster* 'consciously' (0.57%). *Möchte* 'would like' shows will as well as hesitation, *können* 'can' reminds ability, *bewusster* 'more consciously' suggests mindfulness.

From observing the context of the three verbs, we found that there is room to modify the commercial transaction frame proposed by Fillmore and Atkins (1992). The concept and elements in the frame are changed from the concept of financial and commercial transaction to a description of the organizational structure of human society. In other words, these verbs originate from the concept of financial and commercial transaction, but focus on describing the organizational structures of human society, such as group, organization, and society, under rational economic behaviors. That is, these verbs are, on the surface, concerned with economics, but actually they return to the description of organizational structure of human society.

(9) *Zhe4 xie1 zhuan1 jia1 shi1le ye4 zhi3 hao3 yi3 mai4*
這 些 專 家 失了 業 只 好 以 賣
These experts out of job have to by sell
zhi1 shi4 ji4 neng2 wei2 sheng1
知 識 技 能 為 生
knowledge skill make a living
'These specialists lost their jobs, ... have to sell their knowledge and technique to make a living.'

(10) ... Börse offen ist, kann der Konzern *Aktien* kaufen so viel er will und von wem auch immer.
'... stock exchange has opened, the company can buy *shares* as many as he wants, no matter from whom.'

(11) *mai3 shu1 de yuan2 ze2 shi4 mai3 zi4 ji3*
買 書 的 原 則 是 買 自 己
Buy book POSS. Principle be buy one's
xi3 huan1 de
喜 歡 的
like
'The principle for buying books is to buy what he himself likes.'

(12) *li4 ru2 nü3 ren2 ai4 mai3 yi1 fu2 na3 tian1*
例 如 女 人 愛 買 衣 服 那 天
for instance woman love buy clothes one day
jiu4 hui4 meng4 jian4 zi4ji3 bei4 yi1 fu2
就 會 夢 見 自己 被 衣 服
will dream oneself passive clothes
mai2 qi3 lai2
埋 起 來
be buried
'Such as women love to buy clothing, some day will dream of themselves being buried by clothes.'

(13) *jie2 guo3 wo3 lian2 dong1 xi1 dou1 bu4 gan3 mai3*
結 果 我 連 東西 都 不 敢 買
As the end I even thing all dare not buy
'At the end I dare not to buy anything.'

9.4. Conclusion

Based on economic metaphors (White 2003) and the elements in semantic frame (Fillmore und Atkins 1992), this study presented the three German FLE verbs, *kaufen, verkaufen* and *bezahlen*, in newspaper discourse to examine German economic activity, social cognition and culture. The collocations of these verbs prove that the commercial transaction frame (Fillmore and Atkins 1992) is the fundamental semantic frame underlying the three German FLE verbs *kaufen, verkaufen* amd *bezahlen*. The element PERSONS that these verbs collocate with not only indicate modern business and financial activities, but also describe the underlying organization of human society in modern Germany because the element PERSONS is the subject of the verbs that cover people, organizations and groups. In other words, these verbs rather than merely expressing the concepts of financial commercial activities, actually emphasize human social structure. On the other hand, the element POSSESSION reveals not only the objects that Germans buy, sell, and pay for nowadays, but also the values of the people, especially when compared with data in Mandarin Chinese.

Furthermore, the additional check for the significant left and right collocations in *Deutscher Wortschatz* also reveals types of popular merchandise, that the Germans call on reason when purchasing, and that they are law-abiding. Whereas the Chinese collocations reveal a conservative mentality and an adherence to traditional literati thought that originated from feudal society.

Since the economic crisis has spread worldwide, financial-related expressions have recently become a popular research topic in linguistics. This research exploring three German verbs reveals that language discloses human's perception. By reviewing considerable amounts of semantic data, we find the cultural value and model of cultural cognition embedded in German.

CHAPTER TEN

GESCHÄFT IN GERMAN NEWSPAPER REPORT

Shelley Ching-yu Hsieh

10.0. Introduction

Geschäft 'business' in (a) to (c) found in two German newspapers represents different economic concepts and cultural values. In (a), life form (such as humans or animals) is the SD for comprehending the movement of business in the market (only life forms can *laufen* 'walk, be progressing'). Religious power is involved in running business, therefore *Gnade* 'mercy, grace' in (b), and the concept of *Sklaverei* 'slavery' are found in the business domain (c).

(a) ...hatte die Bussparte aus dem *laufenden* *Geschäft* 13 Millionen Euro Verlust eingefahren.
[Braunschweiger Zeitung, 12.03.2008]
'...the bus branch would have brought in the loss of 13 million Euro from the ongoing (walking) business.'
(b) das *Geschäft* ist *gnadenlos*: Alte Trainer, heisst es....
[Galler Tagblatt, 04.01.2008]
'Business is cruel (merciless, graceless): Old trainer, is called....'
(c) ... berichten, die vom *Geschäft* mit der *Sklaverei* profitierten.
[Galler Tagblatt, 08.01.2008]
'...reported, it is benefited from business with the slavery.'

Though much research has been done on FLEs, such as those we reviewed in Chapter 2, little has investigated German *Geschäft* 'business' in contrast to its counterpart in Chinese.

The present study attempts to unravel the cultural interpretations behind *Geschäft* 'business' by examining its use in German newspapers. The German data are gathered from *Corpus Search, Management and Analysis System* (COSMAS II, Institut für Deutsche Sprache 2008) and *Deutscher Wortschatz* (Universität Leipzig 1998–2008). The Mandarin Chinese data are collected from *Academia Sinica Balanced Corpus Mandarin Chinese* (Chen and Huang 2001). The theoretical background is financial expressions in language (White 2003) and the CMM

(Ahrens 2002). By comparing *Geschäft* in German with *shenglyi4* 生意 'business' in Mandarin, the hidden values of these words and phrases are expected to be revealed, thus benefitting linguistics, cultural studies, and pedagogical uses.

This chapter is divided into three sections. First, we introduce the theoretical framework in 10.1. Second, we the analysis of *Geschäft* in German and that of *shenglyi4* in Mandarin are demonstrated in 10.2 in which the data of *Geschäft* is presented first and followed by the contrast between German and Mandarin. Third, the CMM and the semantic frame are applied in 10.3 to further manifest our research results and unravel the different cognition of doing business in German and Mandarin. A conclusion is given in 10.4.

10.1. Theoretical Framework

White (2003) claims that metaphor helps our understanding of language (see Chapter 1 for a review). Here we will briefly introduce the CMM (Ahrens 2002) again to provide the research framework of this study.

Based on the Contemporary Theory of Metaphor (Lakoff and Johnson, 1980; Lakoff, 1993) Ahrens (2002) proposed the CMM (as introduced in Chapter 2), which was revealed by progressing through a series of five steps when analyzing metaphors as they were generated by informants. First, the informants generated all the examples about a proposed TD based on their linguistic intuition. Second, the generated examples with similar SDs were grouped. Third, each SD was checked so that conceptual real-world knowledge regarding each SD would be generated. Fourth, novel expressions gathered during Step 1 were filtered out. Fifth, the informants map their conceptual knowledge of the SD, which is based on the three questions in step three, to the abstract TD. Based on the analysis of metaphorical expressions, the underlying reason, or what is referred to as the Mapping Principle, can be postulated. The Mapping Principle describes the underlying reason, i.e. the logic of why and how a TD uses a particular SD. As an example, the Mapping Principle for IDEA AS BUILDING is formulated as "Idea is understood as building because buildings involve a (physical) structure and ideas involve an (abstract) structure" (Ahrens, 2002: 279).

Moreover, Ahrens, Chung and Huang (2003: 36) propose that "each source-TD pairing will have a prototypical instance of mapping as evidenced by an individual lexical item that is highly frequent as compared with other mappings." In other words, the most frequent lexical item of each conceptual mapping verifies the postulation of a Mapping Principle.

The CMM strengthens the functions of Contemporary Theory of Metaphor, and differs from other models in some aspects. For example, it distinguishes three types of metaphor—entities, qualities and functions. Furthermore, it also explicitly predicts the processing of these metaphors. In conclusion, the CMM facilitates an understanding of the processes involved in conceptual metaphors.

10.2. *Geschäft* in German Newspapers

The first step in applying the CMM to our data is to collect data from the above corpora, which constitutes the linguistic intuition of native speakers. In total, 8456 instances of German *Geschäft* were collected from COSMAS and 160 *Geschäft* collocations were collected from *Deutscher Wortschatz*. For Mandarin, 289 instances of *shenglyi4* were collected from *Academia Sinica Balanced Corpus Mandarin Chinese*. In addition, 253 *shenglyi4* collocations (from the same corpus) were collected. Table 10.1 summarizes the collection of data.

The second step in applying the CMM to our data is to group the generated examples based on the similarity of the SDs. We group the raw data based on the similarities of the collocations according to both their micro and macro levels. A macro level is a SD that is mapped onto *Geschäft*. For example, *florierendes* 'blooming' in *florierendes Geschäft* 'prosperous business' (1) is the micro level—'the growing of plants.' *Geschäft mit dem*

Table 10.1. The collection of the data.

Lexemes	*Geschäft*		*shenglyi4*	
Corpora	COSMAS	Deutscher Wortschatz	*Academia Sinica Balanced Corpus Mandarin Chinese*	
Collected data	Instances with the lexeme	Collocations appearing before or after the lexeme	Instances with the lexeme	Collocations appearing before or after the lexeme
Quantity	8456 instances	160 kinds	289 instances	253 kinds

Tod 'business with the death' in (2) is the micro level—'activities of living organisms.' Furthermore, we group (1) and (2) into a macro level—"life cycle." The *ihrem* 'their' in *ihrem Geschäft* 'their business' (3) and *unserem* 'our' in *unserem Geschäft* 'our business' are both possessive pronouns referring to people and they classified into the macro level—"ownership."

Table 10.2 presents the top ten macro levels in German and Mandarin. We exclude determiners and punctuations from the percentage of each macro type. The following sections will discuss the linguistic phenomenon and cultural values revealed by these data, first German, and then Mandarin.

(1) Die Hoffnungen auf ein *florierendes* Geschäft waren berechtigt. [St. Galler Tagblatt, 28.03.2008]
'Hopes for a prosperous (blooming) business are justified.'

(2) ...und Werbeeinblendungen ihr Geschäft *mit dem Tod* machen will. [Nürnberger Nachrichten, 17.06.2008]
'...and want to make the business with death by finding in advertisements.'

(3) ...diese Neuigkeiten in Kürze in *ihrem* Geschäft zu präsentieren. [St. Galler Tagblatt, 04.04.2008]
'...to present these news in their business soon.'

10.2.1. *The Conceptual Mapping Model of* Geschäft

In Table 10.2, it is not surprising to see the SDs, like "union/cooperation," "quality," "operation," "timing," and "product" because they are natural components of business, but we observe the differences between German and Mandarin, which will be discussed in 10.3.2. Our investigation, in terms of the CMM, will probe the macro levels "space" (frequency 3939, 6.4%) and "life cycle" (frequency 3291, 5.4%) in the German data and "size" and "movement" in Mandarin data.

For the German data, the top two SDs are "union/cooperation," and "operation," whereas in the Mandarin data, they are "quality," and "situation and consequence." In this section, we will first present "union/cooperation" and "operation" in German examined in terms of the CMM followed immediately by the top two SDs in Mandarin in section 3.2.

Examples (4)–(6) are instances of "union/cooperation": *Auf Gegenseitigkeit* 'one another' (4); *in Nordosteuropa* 'in Northeast Europe' (5); and *im weltweiten* 'around the world' (6). All highlight the German businessmen and bankers' emphasis on "union/cooperation." Now we analyze this

Table 10.2. The macro level of the collocation of *Geschäft* in German and of *shenglyi4* in Mandarin.

Geschäft	Examples	(%)	*Shenglyi4*	Examples	(%)
union/ cooperation	mit, auf Gegenseitigkeit	29.8%	quality	old, bad, good, not bad	10.5%
operation	betreibt, machen, operativen, operative	15.1%	situation and consequence	hard, busy, untouchable	7.7%
ownership	unserem, seines, ihrem, eigene	9.5%	degree	more and more, the most, quite	4.9%
quality	gutes, schlechtes, hartes, besseres	7.4%	product	computer, pen, frame, porcelain	4.6%
profit	profitables, lukrativen, lohnendes,	7.0%	growth	thriving, prosperous, expand	4.3%
space	in Osteuropa, im Ausland, außerhalb,	6.4%	reason and consequence	thus, therefore, hence, so	4.0%
timing	späten, frühen	5.7%	size	big, small	4.0%
life cycle	mit dem Tod, florierte, boomt, fortzuführenden	5.4%	movement	come and go	3.7%
situation and condition	stabilere, schwieriges, riskantes	2.7%	result	to close a deal, finish, make a bargain	3.4%
development	stieg, läuft, entwickelt, ausbauen	2.6%	quantity	many, none, no	3.4%
Total		100%	Total		100%

top collocation of *Geschäft* in terms of the CMM. Our understanding of the world is that a group of two or more people or organizations agree to a goal, establish mutual trust, cooperate and work for the goal. The union created for the sake of business is usually under a contract confined by law. Table 10.3 lists the CMM analysis of the salient macro level "union/ cooperation" for the collocation of German *Geschäft*.

(4) Es habe sich um ein Geschäft *auf Gegenseitigkeit* gehandelt.
[Nürnberger Nachrichten, 14.04.2008]
'It has to do with the business among one another.'

(5) …*in Nordosteuropa*, wo die Bank ihr Geschäft weiter ausbauen wird. [Braunschweiger Zeitung, 18.01.2008]
'In Northeast Europe where the banker would like to promote their business…'

(6) …neuer Chiphersteller, der *im weltweiten* Geschäft mit Komponenten für Mobiltelefone und….
[VDI Nachrichten, 18.04.2008]
'The new chip manufacturers, they and the businessmen around the world and the components of cell phones and….'

(7) Ziel der FDP sei es nicht, ins *operative* Geschäft einzugreifen….
[St. Galler Tagblatt, 16.01.2008]
'The aim of the FDP party is not to get involved in running business….'

Step 4 in applying the CMM to our data is to retain the conventional FLEs generated in Step 1 and filter out novel FLEs. This step is not necessary for this study and is not included because we investigate reports gathered from newspaper corpora and the most frequently occurring collocations.

Step 5 in applying the CMM to our data is to analyze the FLEs that actually do the mapping between the SD (e.g., BUILDING in IDEA AS BUILDING) and TD (e.g., IDEA in IDEA AS BUILDING). Each action listed in Table 10.3 is necessary when doing business. Take the entities that are involved in business between the businessman and the customer, for example in this case: shared goal, agreement, ability or financial capability. The businessman first has the product. The customer shows an interest in the product (hence, a shared goal). Both of them agree on the quality, quantity, and price of the product, a process that might involve compromise (hence, agreement). Then the businessman is able to sell the product, and the customer is able to buy it (hence, ability or financial capability).

Table 10.3. The salient macro level "union/cooperation" (*Geschäft*).

Union/ cooperation	What entity does the SD have?	shared goal, agreement, ability or financial capability
	What characteristics does the entity in the SD or the TD have?	mutual trust, cooperation
	a. What function does the SD have? b. What do people do to (or within) the SD?	a. mutually benefit each other b. to decrease each other's burden, to have certain benefits, and get more growth in business

As for the characteristics of "union/cooperation," based on the trust between the businessman and the customer, to pay and to sell (cooperation) makes the deal. For function, both the businessman and customer have benefits: one gets the money, whereas the other gets the product. In this case, both decrease each other's burden, receive certain benefits, and the businessman is able to grow their business in the market (hence, growth in business). The customer on the other hand gains more knowledge (if this product were a book) or improves an interpersonal relationship (if the product they buy is, say, a flower given as a gift to someone else). However, if the two sides united and cooperating in a business venture are the shareholders or partners at branches, then the entity, quality and function are required in doing business. What differs is that the product may not be delivered via money, but rather offered via one's effort, such as the branch of a business organization being capable of running a business.[1]

Now consider the second most frequent SD "operation" (example 7). The entities of a business operation are wealth, ability, manpower, customers, products, goals, time, involvement, strategy, and so on. All these elements make the "operation" possible. However, the business might make good or poor profits because of different owners' abilities, such as their strategies or the way the company operates. The company might have different pay or profit sharing and distribution scales due to different amounts of monetary investments and manpower. The company might have long-term and short-term plans because of different goals and business hours. Differences might also result from the owners' involvement. Running a business involves the behaviors and activities of well-organized operations, investment of manpower and efforts, profit-making, goal-setting, time budgeting, and so on.

Therefore, when investigating the entity, quality, and function of the SDs that are mapped onto the TD *Geschäft* 'business,' we found that the aspiration to run a business is closely related to economic activities because running a business involves the acts of arrangement and also the operations of enterprises. The entities of running a business are correlated with the fundamentals of economic activities and components, such as money, manpower, customers, etc.

---

[1] Different wordings might be used by different researchers for the presentation of the analysis like those in Table 10.3.

What is significant is that business is goal-oriented, which takes time for the goal to be realized, and is human controlled. In other words, from the German viewpoint, *Geschäft* can be managed, arranged, and controlled. Furthermore, it requires money, ability, manpower, customers, products, goals, time, involvement, and strategies. Moreover, *Geschäft* is a human activity with goals, by which people make profits. Table 10.4 demonstrates the CMM analysis of the salient macro level "operation" for the collocation of German *Geschäft*.

In 10.2 we mentioned the special SDs in German, "space" and "life cycle," presented in Table 10.1. We now discuss their characteristics. First, space, which has length, width, and height, can be a location, an area, or a distance. It can be open wide, like field or sky, or enclosed, like houses or boxes. It also has the property of being big, small, wide, narrow, far, or near. Humans determine and shape the dimensions of the space they use to suit their activities.

From our analysis of the entity, quality, and function of "space," we learn that the mapping onto "space" can be a location, such as a country or region, as *in Osteuropa* 'in Northeast Europe' demonstrates (5). "Space" not only limits but provides room for *shenglyi4/Geschäft* activities. For example, *weltweite* 'world wide' in (6) indicates the area is not just wide and open, but ubiquitous.

Moreover, people use "space" to promote or limit the range of the *shenglyi4/Geschäft* activities, internationally, abroad, within, and so on. Here we see that when the "space" as the SD maps onto the TD, it refers to the location or the range of the *shenglyi4/Geschäft* activities. Table 10.5 illustrates the CMM analysis of the macro level "space" for the collocation of German *Geschäft*.

Table 10.4. The salient macro level "operation" (*Geschäft*).

Operation	What entity does the SD have?	money, ability, manpower, customers, products, goals, time, involvement
	What characteristics does the entity in the SD or the TD have?	good/bad, long-term/ short-term/ multi-goal/ single-goal, a little amount of money, diligent/ at will
	a. What function does the SD have? b. What do people do to (or within) the SD?	a. help people to benefit via economic activities b. set goals, invest manpower and material resources, make schedules

Table 10.5. The salient macro level "space" (*Geschäft*).

Space	What entity does the SD have?	Location, length, width, distance, area
	What characteristics does the entity in the SD or the TD have?	big, small, broad, far, near, open, enclosure
	a. What function does the SD have? b. What do people do to (or within) the SD?	a. it provides and limits the range for activities. b. it uses space and limits the range of certain space.

"Life cycle" is another of the top ten SDs. The entity of life cycle is life form, such as humans, animals, and plants. In addition, during the time span of a life cycle, living organisms have various characteristics, such as being energetic, lifeless, alive, dead, aging, etc. A life cycle is bound by the limits and the vitality of the living organisms at different times. Humans can manage their lives according to their life cycle. For example, they learn, work, get married, and have babies when they are young. Also, they avoid taking the risks of exceeding their physical limits. For instance, to avoid getting hurt, people take a break, have sleep, and arrange their retirement when they are old.

Table 10.6. The salient macro level "life cycle" (*Geschäft*).

Life cycle	What entity does the SD have?	living organism, time, life mechanisms, life cycle
	What characteristics does the entity in the SD or the TD have?	energetic, lively, lifeless, alive, dead, aging, (alive, dead, old, reproductive)
	a. What function does the SD have? b. What do people do to (or within) the SD?	a. it shows the life cycle and the limit of the ability of the living organisms at different times, in which the vitality of the living organism is highlighted. b. people arrange appropriate activities based on the life cycle, such as learning, getting married, having babies, and, retiring.

We learn that German treats *Geschäft* as a living organism, a plant that can grow. Therefore it blossoms, as in *floriert* 'blooming' (1) and dies, as in *mit dem Tod* 'with the death.' (2) However, it has its duration, such as *fortgeführten* 'continued.' We can see that *Geschäft* is a living organism because it is energetic and vital (such as *boomend* 'booming, prospering'). Our Chinese data show that *sheng1yi4* is also a living organism with living properties (such as *sheng1zhang3* 生長 'growth'). From the vitality shown in the SD, we can see the living activities and properties in the TD. Table 10.6 presents the analysis of the salient macro level "life cycle" for the collocation of German *Geschäft*.

10.2.2. *A Comparison with* Sheng1yi4

The macro level of the SD "quality" (see Table 10.2) can refer to that of products and services. The characteristics of such quality can be good/bad, delicate/rough, excellent/poor, etc. The function of quality is to identify the value of the product. The quality of the product can be controlled, managed, chosen, decreased and improved. As shown in our data, both German and Mandarin place a high emphasis on, and strive for quality. Both languages treat *sheng1yi4/Geschäft*, in this case, the concept of business, as a product or a service. The mapping onto the TD is quality-oriented as shown in German by *vermiesen* 'spoil,' *schmutziges* 'dirty,' *gutes* 'good,' *eigentlichen* 'one's own,' *politischen* 'politic,' and in Mandarin by *bu2cuo4* 不錯 'not bad' (example 8), good, stupid, real, special, still in. These characteristics are the standards a product is judged by, which allows people to control and manage the quality of a product. For example, *du2men2-desheng1yi4* 獨門的生意 'specific business,' *pei2qian2desheng1yi4* 賠錢的生意 'running a business that is losing money' and *pei2ben3desheng1yi4* 賠本的生意 'running a business that is losing capital.' Or to improve the quality as in *besseres* 'better business,' and choose the product as in *re4men2desheng1yi4* 熱門的生意 'popular business.' Table 10.7 demonstrates the CMM analysis of the salient macro level "quality" for the collocation of Mandarin *sheng1yi4*.

(8) *sheng1 yi4* *bu2 cuo4* *ba?*
生 意 不 錯 吧?
Business not bad INT.
'Is the business not bad?'

Table 10.7. The salient macro level "quality" (*sheng1yi4*).

Quality	What entity does the SD have?	Product, service
	What characteristics does the entity in the SD or the TD have?	good, bad, delicate, rough, excellent, poor, etc.
	a. What function does the SD have? b. What do people do to (or within) the SD?	a. the standards by which people judge the value of the product. b. control, manage, choose, improve, lower

(9) *ren2 ren2 kan4 hao3 wen3 zhuan4*
人 人 看 好 穩 賺
Everyone to have confidence definitely make profits
de sheng1 yi4 peng4 bu4 de2
的 生 意 碰 不得
POSS. business untouchable
'The business everyone has confidence on is untouchable.'

(10) *Dang1 bing1 liang3 nian2 ran2 hou4 cun2 le*
當 兵 兩 年 然 後 存 了
Army service two years then save ASP
yi4bi3qian2 kai1shi3 xiao3 sheng1yi4
一筆錢 開始 小 生意
some money start small business
'After serving in the army, he saved some money and started a small business.'

(11) *Gong1 si1 bi3 jiao4 jian4 kang1 de tai4du4 ying1 gai1*
Company more healthy attitude should
公 司 比較 健康 的 態度 應該
shi4 jiang1 qi2 sheng1 yi4 wang3 lai2 yu3 da3 guan1si1
是 將 其 生 意 往 來 與 打 官 司
be use its business interaction and to litigate
fen1 kai1 chu3li3
分 開 處理
separately to deal with
'A healthier attitude for a company is to deal with the business interaction and the litigation separately.'

(12) …kürzlich sogar die dritte Generation im *Geschäft* einsteigen.
[St. Galler Tagblatt, 29.05.2008]
'Nowadays, the third generation even steps into the business management procession'

In German, the entity of the SD "situation and condition" (see Table 10.2) is usually an event, a question, a presupposition, or a possibility. The quality

Table 10.8. The salient macro level "situation and consequence" (*sheng1yi4*).

Situation and consequence	What entity does the SD have?	event, problem, presupposition and possibility
	What characteristics does the entity in the SD or the TD have?	difficult, simple, busy, easy, etc.
	a. What function does the SD have? b. What do people do to (or within) the SD?	a. to explain the event, provide the evaluation of the event, or refer to it. b. to deal with/address it, or presuppose it

of the SD might be difficult, simple, busy, easy, and so on. The function of the SD is to illustrate the development of a certain event, the possibility of the event, to enable people to deal with the event, to solve the problem and make presuppositions about the current condition.

Here, we observe that *sheng1yi4* is an event that may give rise to problems. These problems might cause some presuppositions and possibilities to arise, as indicated by the Mandarin: *yao4shi4* 要是 'what if,' *zhi3yao4* 只要 'as long as,' and *bu2dan4* 不但 'not only.' Meanwhile, when dealing with the problems, we see the quality of *sheng1yi4* could be *kun4nan2* 困難 'difficult,' *jian3dan1* 簡單 'simple,' *mang2lu4* 忙碌 'busy,' *rong2yi4* 容易 'easy,' or *peng4bu4de2* 碰不得 'untouchable' (example 9).

The following conditions help us to estimate the risk (*riskantes* 'risk'): *stabilere* 'stable,' *schwache* 'weak' and *mühsames* 'tiresome' in German, and *nan2* 難 'difficult,' *mang2lu4* 忙碌 'busy' in Mandarin. But people can try to deal with the problem, or find it hard to be dealt with, as in *peng4bu4de2* 碰不得 'untouchable.' Table 10.8 presents the CMM analysis of the salient macro level "situation and consequence" for the collocation of Mandarin *sheng1yi4*.

Two special SDs in Mandarin are "size" and "movement" since they seem not to have to do with business at a glimpse. A concrete object can have "size" for it has a physical measurable extent. The quality of it could be large/small (as listed in Table 10.9), long/short, wide/narrow, tall/short and so on. The function of "size" is to mark the extent, which helps to distinguish how big the object is. The size of objects is subject to being changed by either expansion (larger), or contraction (smaller).

However, when examining the Mandarin data, we found that the mapping from the SD to the TD is fixed. That is, *sheng1yi4*, in Mandarin, does

Table 10.9. The salient macro level "size" (*shenglyi4*).

Size	What entity does the SD have?	object, extent, measurement
	What characteristics does the entity in the SD or the TD have?	large, small, long, short, wide, narrow, tall, short
	a. What function does the SD have? b. What do people do to (or within) the SD?	a. to mark the extent and show the scale b. to contract, to enlarge

not have the property of length, width, or height, but only "size," in terms of large and small. It is treated as an object with the property of large and small, by which the scale of *shenglyi4* is attributed, such as *zuo4yi2geda4/xiao3shenglyi4* 做一個大/小生意 'run a big/little business.' Table 10.9 presents the CMM analysis of the salient macro level "size" for the collocation of Mandarin *shenglyi4*.

Let us examine the last SD "movement." Only a few data were identified as belonging in this macro level, and they appear in both German and Mandarin. Furthermore, it is observed that "movement" and space are correlated. To move requires a movable object and space for the object to move in. Within any given space, there is a certain distance between the object and the goal. The "movement" itself has a direction and speed, which can be fast or slow, and is driven by others, or its own free will or motivation. The function of the "movement" is to move someone or something from place A to place B. Generally, people can choose the location, speed, and direction of the "movement" to be, and people also have the free will or motivation to move.

However, our data show that German and Mandarin have different linguistic interpretations of "movement." In German, *einsteigen* 'involve in' and *zurückziehen* 'withdraw' are juxtaposed after *Geschäft*, and the object that moves is not *Geschäft*, but a person or company, such as *die dritte Generation im Geschäft einsteigen* 'the third generation steps into the managing group' (example 12). Here, *Geschäft* is the space in which the object moves, and the "movement" has a direction as it moves inwards (*einsteigen*), or backwards (*zurückziehen*). Furthermore, people have the free will to move.

On the contrary, *shenglyi4* in Mandarin is attributed as a moving object that can come and go, as in *shenglyi4wang3lai2* 生意往來 'business interaction.' It has direction too, e.g., *shenglyi4shang4men2* 生意上門 'business comes visit' and *shenglyi4hui2lai2le* 生意回來了 'business comes back.' However, free will and motivation are not observed. Only

Table 10.10. The salient macro level "movement" (*shenglyi4*).

Movement	What entity does the SD have?	movable object, space, distance, outside force, self-driven force, free will, direction, motivation
	What characteristics does the entity in the SD or the TD have?	fast, slow, far, near, direction (east, west, south, north, left, right, up, down, inward, outward)
	a. What function does the SD have? b. What do people do to (or within) the SD?	a. locate someone or something at an appropriate place. b. determine the speed and direction

the direction and driving force are found. Table 10.10 presents the CMM analysis of the salient macro level "movement" for the collocation of Mandarin *shenglyi4*.

As presented in the above analysis, we see that time and space are important notions in *shenglyi4* and *Geschäft*, and how *shenglyi4* and *Geschäft* are controlled and operated by human will. However, Germans and Taiwanese operate business differently, in that human's power over *Geschäft* is highlighted in German, whereas Mandarin treats *shenglyi4* as having its own will and is thus free from human volition, though people can set the extent, control the quality and presuppose and deal with the events. We will discuss this further in 10.3.2.

10.3. Results and Discussion

The analysis above illustrates that (1) the macro levels of the collocations of *Geschäft* in German and *shenglyi4* in Mandarin show the different viewpoints of Germans and Taiwanese towards business, and (2) the relation between the macro levels of the collocations, the CMM, and the semantic frame.

10.3.1. *German and Mandarin Speaker's Different Assumptions towards Business*

Based on the salient macro and special SDs, German and Mandarin speakers have different assumptions towards business.

Though the SDs, such as "space" and "life cycle," are seemingly not related to business, the German reporters do use them to attribute the German financial economic reporting (i.e. the collocations of *Geschäft*). The way Germans operate business has shown that they have a subconscious awareness that people are integrated together. Germany is located in the center of Europe, and although overwhelmed by the financial crisis just as the other countries are, their sense of being a member of the global village urges them to cooperate with others. This is made evident by the most frequent SD "union/cooperation" (frequency 18264, 29.3%).

When the euro was adopted in 1999, Germany was an economically powerful nation and did not need to give up its previous currency, the Deutsch Mark (DM), to use the euro. The use of euro has impaired the growth and state of German economics. Li (2007) points out that after the euro was adopted, the Deutsch Mark lost its predominance in the market, and interest rates were no longer lower or better than those of other European Union members. Affected by the value of the euro, economic growth in Germany has become restricted. The evaluation of the euro directly influences German exports (WAZ New Media 2012). Moreover, according to statistics given by the Council for Economic Planning and Development (2006), Germany's GDP growth rate was 3.2% in 2000, but decreased to 0% in 2002, and −0.2% in 2003. The economic growth of Germany relies heavily on the Export Department, and even though the evaluation of the euro has had a harmful influence on German exports, Germany continues using the euro (see also European Financial Stability Facility 2011).

Perhaps this situation results from the following reasons: the confidence in economics and finance, Germany's geographical location, and the responsibility and sense of guilt for starting World War II. Germans feel responsible and dishonored for starting WWII, and ceremonies are held every year in order to remind their people of the lesson they have learnt. Germans not only do not hide the mistakes, but teach their young generation about the past and hope the young generation learns from it. Books for teenagers in city libraries can be found everywhere with stories or novels on the topic of WWII, which contain reflections on what Germans did.

On the other hand, "union/cooperation" in German data illustrate that Germans emphasize the cooperative relationship between people, groups, and nations. The use of the macro level "life cycle" also suggests Germans' humanism, as they respect human nature or values in running businesses. Thus we found in the macro levels of *Geschäft* collocations, that *Geschäft* is "space" (i.e. revealed by the micro levels 'large,' 'small,' 'wide,' 'far,' 'near,' 'open'), and that business is a life with human nature, as shown in *Geschäft* is "life cycle," like 'being alive,' 'dead,' 'aging,' and 'reproductive.'

Nevertheless, no such linguistic phenomena are observed in Mandarin. As shown in the macro SD "size" and "movement," *shenglyi4* 'business' is viewed as a solid object, which has size, moves, and can be touched, as shown in the macro levels of "size" ('large,' 'small,' 'long,' 'short,' 'wide,' 'narrow,' 'tall,' 'short').

Our data is in line with the research results of economists. For example, according to Ringer (1996), how Germans manage their business is more humanistically governed when compared to that of the English and American models, which are individualized with much more freedom and stress on commercial pursuits. Egelhoff and Frese (2009: 80) note that Germans have endeavored to make the Labor Standards Act and social security systems. During 1920s and 1930s, Germans developed a set of government-supervised plans that were integrated into the strategies for local industrial management (Fischer 1987; Herrigel 1996). A significant breakthrough took place when a central association controlled directly by the government was founded. This association not only dealt with balancing the profits between labor and capital, but also built the model in which labor and capital cooperate (Egelhoff and Frese 2009: 80). Human rights are guaranteed by health care, elderly annunities, unemployment benefits, detailed labor laws, institutional negotiations, and the sharing of ownership. All these reveal Germans' respect for human nature and values in doing business.

Compared with Germans, Mandarin speakers interpret business more conservatively. Hsieh (2009b) examined the German verbs, *kaufen* 'buy,' *verkaufen* 'sell' and *bezahlen* 'charge' and compared them with those in Mandarin. She found that Taiwanese people are reluctant to be businessmen if they can choose being scholars because the Mandarin data show that speakers keep the traditional thought that scholars still enjoy a better social reputation. Here, we give (13) below as an example, "selling their knowledge" shows the contradiction and unwillingness of the people. Moreover, Hsieh (2009c) investigated the cultural values through the concept of *poor* in Mandarin and German. She pointed out that whereas Germans are deeply influenced by Christianity, Mandarin speakers have the philosophy that men are an integral of nature and men should let things take their natural course. We see the conservative thoughts of this cultural group in doing business.

(13) *zhe4 xie1 zhuan1 jia1 shi1 le ye4,... zhi3 hao3 yi3 mai4*
這 些 專 家 失了業，只 好 以 賣
These experts out of job have to by sell
zhi1 shi4 ji4 neng2 wei2 sheng1
知 識 技 能 為 生
knowledge skill to make a living
'These specialist lost their jobs,... have to sell their knowledge and technique to make a living.'

10.3.2. *Conceptual Mapping Model and Semantic Frame*

The analysis above shows the compatibility of the macro levels of business (*Geschäft* and *sheng1yi4*) in both languages, semantic frame of commercial transaction, and the CMM. We have introduced semantic frame in chapter 2. The theory of semantic frame proposed by Fillmore and Atkins (1992) is consistent with the process of comprehension, by which people understand how a term is used. For example, all verbs make sense in the commercial transaction frame involving a scenario: "in which one person acquires control or possession of something from a second person, by agreement, as a result of surrendering to that person a sum of money. The needed background requires an understanding of property ownership, a money economy, implicit contract, and a great deal more." (Fillmore and Atkins 1992: 78)

Let us take a closer look at the elements in the commercial transaction frame, which involves the following concepts: both sides that make the deal (both sides of the "union/cooperation"), an amount of money (the entity of "operation," which possesses financial capability), an agreement (both sides agree to the quality, quantity, and price of the product), the concept of "ownership" (reflected in 'possessives'), knowledge about economic structures, contracts, etc. We see that the components of the frame are similar to the macro levels presented in Table 10.2.

In other words, the collocations of *Geschäft* in German and *sheng1yi4* in Mandarin work within the semantic frame. Practicality, "quality," "benefit," "result," and "quantity" are the notions of business and trading in economics. Therefore, we can integrate the commercial transaction frame with the *Geschäft* semantic extension given by Universität Leipzig online database (Deutscher Wortschatz 1998-2008) in Figure 10.1, the commercial transaction frame is marked blue.

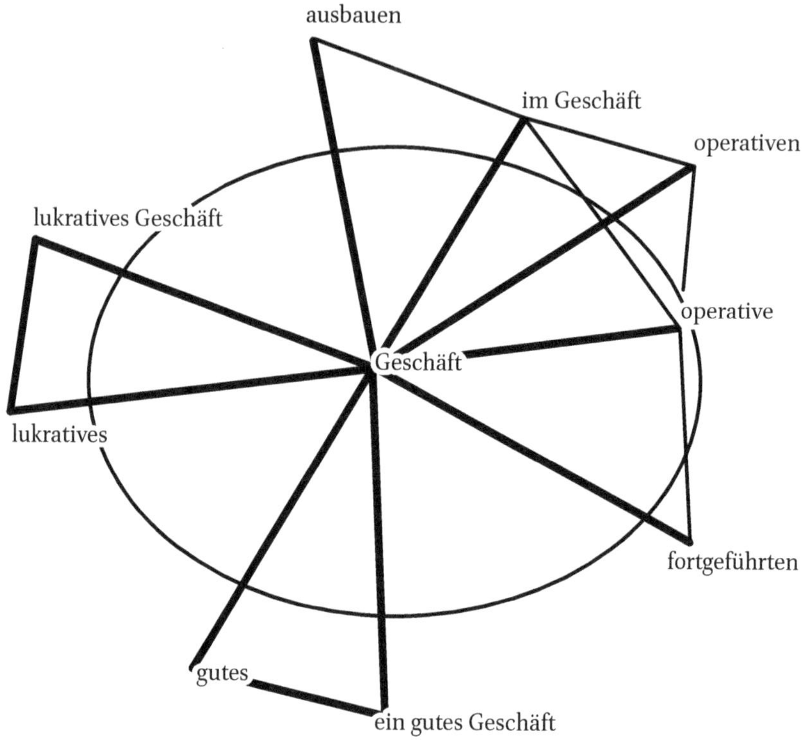

Figure 10.1. The salient collocations and semantic frame of *Geschäft*.

10.4. Closing Remark

Taking linguistic data from *Corpus Search, Management and Analysis System* (COSMAS II) and *Deutscher Wortschatz*, we examined how *Geschäft* is attributed in German newspaper reporting and compared it with *sheng1yi4* in Mandarin. The CMM proposed by Ahrens (2002) and economic metaphors proposed by White (2003) are the fundamental framework of this study. Germans emphasize cooperation (*auf gengenseitigkeit* 'with one another,' *mit dem Ausland* 'with the abroad,' 29.8%), and the principle of running business (*betreibt* 'run,' *machen* 'make,' *operativen* 'operative,' etc., 15.1%). They have a strong sense of responsibility in being a member in the global village. On the other hand, people in Taiwan view business as an object. They are eager for business (opportunistic, hit, to lose money, to die), stress "quality" (old, poor, good, not bad), and "result" (prosperous, sluggish, failed, exuberant).

CHAPTER ELEVEN

THE FINANCIAL LINGUISTIC EXPRESSIONS IN EMBODIMENT

Shelley Ching-yu Hsieh

11.0. Introduction

Previous chapters proved that ECONOMY IS LIVING ORGANISM like humans, animals, or plants are pervasive in language. The usage of living organism, or life forms, like *tiger* or *flower* drew linguists' attention because "the importance of the use of animal and plant names characterizes the relationship between the segments of human society" (Radcliffe-Brown 1929 in Lévi-Strauss 1963: 1). As a matter of fact, animals and plants are vivid and memorable and thus offer concrete image banks for languages to generate fixed expressions able to capture and compose mankind's fleeting moments into words (Hsieh 2009a: 224).

This chapter investigates FLEs in embodiment. An embodiment expression is defined as an expression with one or more life-form names, such as that of human beings, body parts, emotions, animals, and plants (Hsieh 2009a: iv). For example, *wu3gu3feng1deng1* 五穀豐登 'five-grain-plenty-mount = to have a good harvest of all grain crops; great outcome,' *Flohmarkt* 'flea market = flea market' and *alle seine Schäflein beisammen haben* 'all-one's-little sheep-together-have = to have all one's sheep around; to collect or control all of one's assets or valuables.' Again, we will compare Mandarin and German. Data are collected from embodiment corpora: *Plant Chinese Corpus, Animal Chinese Corpus, Plant German Corpus* and *Plant German Corpus* (Hsieh 2009a). There are totally 418 tokens in Mandarin and 262 tokens in German abstracted from the corpora for this study.

The purpose of this chapter gives a closing chapter for this book on FLEs. Meanwhile, we hope to provide a broader view of the study of the FLEs by presenting the rich overlap of the FLEs in embodiment in order to invite further research in this concern.

We will first present the FLEs in terms of animal and plant vehicles to see which vehicles and which FLEs are most or least expressed. Further, the data will be analyzed by means of linguistic financial judgment and hierarchy of concepts (Ungerer and Schmid 2006). The research questions asked are: (1) Which FLEs render more expressions, and which, the least in embodiment vehicles? (2) How is the different distribution of linguistic financial judgment and hierarchy of concepts in both languages? And, (3) what cultural features are presented in the data?

The main bulk of this chapter is organized in the following way. After an introduction, section 11.1 is a general presentation of the data we have collected, in which we first show the FLEs that specific vehicles are involved, and then go on to compare Mandarin and German data concerning salient FLEs. Section 11.2 analyzes the data in terms of their linguistic financial judgment and hierarchy of concepts. Section 11.3 deals with the cultural features of these the FLEs. At last, section 11.4 gives suggestions for further study.

11.1. The Financial Linguistic Expressions in Embodiment

In this section, the data will be presented to see which FLEs render more FLEs and which render the least. Then some salient FLEs will be focused on to compare their distribution in Mandarin and German.

11.1.1. *Financial Linguistic Expressions and the Metaphorical Vehicles*

In Mandarin, the FLEs that constitute more expressions are 'money' (64 expressions), 'poor' (56), 'profit' (52), 'job' (40), and 'rich' (25). In opposite, the FLEs that have the least expressions are 'economy' (1), 'salary' (1), 'stock' (1), 'management' (2), 'office' (3), etc.

Let us first take a look at the FLEs that are expressed with animal vehicles. 'Money' has been the FLE that renders the most (64) expressions (see Table 11.1 below). Besides the animal vehicles, like *pig, bull* or fowl such as *hen, duck, bird* and *eagle*, the ancient Chinese mythological creatures such as *dragon* and *phoenix* are used to express 'money' in some ways. On the other hand, 'money' is expressed through plant vehicles, such as *vegetable, fruit, rice, tea, wood, bamboo, flower*, and *grass*. The *appearance* or characteristic of certain plants, for example, pod and the sting of the plant can also refer to 'money.'

The FLE 'poor' has the second most (56) expressions. Vehicles such as *dog, tiger, leopard, wood* and *grass*, also parts of the plant, such as the branches and roots, are used to convey the idea of 'poor.'

Table 11.1. The animal/plant vehicles for the financial linguistic expressions in Mandarin and German.

FLEs	Animal vehicles	Plant vehicles
Chinese		
money (64)	pig, bull, dog, horse, hen, duck, bird, eagle, dragon, phoenix.	vegetable, fruit, rice, tea, woods, bamboo, flower, grass, pod, the sting of the plant.
poor (56)	dog, tiger, leopard, horse, pig, deer, fish, dragon, crow, phoenix, rooster, frog, snail.	wood, grass, fruit, leaf, fern, branches, roots.
profit (52)	bull, sheep, hare, mouse, elephant, donkey, fish, bear, bird, duck, hen, dog, fly, snipe, clam, sparrow, cicada, mantis.	wood, fruit, flower, grass, rice, vegetable, seedling, branches, seedling.
job (40)	bull, horse, donkey, pig, cat, turtle, phoenix, cuttlefish.	wood, grass, kudzu vine, fruit, flower, vegetable, cereal.
German		
money (22)	cat, cow, hare, mouse/mice, monkey, pig, rooster.	branch, cone, hay, leaf, lilac, moss, oat, pepper, wood.
worth (19)	donkey, sparrow, pigeon.	bean, bud, chanterelle, cinnamon, fruit, hazelnut, lawn, leafstalk, lentil, nut, pea, pear, stalk, tobacco, turnip, cabbage.
profit (14)	fish, livestock, wolf.	flower, rose, fruit, grain, wheat.
poor (13)	dog, hen, horse, mouse, animal.	bean, cabbage, grain, herb or leaf, stick, straw, wood.
rich (12)	dog, hen, fish.	fruit, bean, flower, hay, pepper, thorn, tree, vegetable.

Fruit and flowers are often used to express 'rich' and 'success' and will be further discussed in section 11.2.1.

Hunting is a customary practice in Germany since the past. Hunting was one of the most popular activities for the royal family or the nobles. Dogs played an essential role in tracking and chasing animals. In order to do this, they are trained professionally and fed well and these could have caused them to be associated with richness. In fact, it is common to see that there are dogs present in the paintings of a royal family or the nobles.

In Table 11.2 below we give some animal examples for the salient FLEs in Mandarin and German.

Table 11.2. Salient financial linguistic expressions in terms of animal vehicles.

FLEs	Vehicles	Examples
Mandarin Chinese		
money	pig	*huo3dao4zhu1tou2lan4 qian2dao4gong1 shi4ban4* 火到豬頭爛, 錢到公事辦 'fire-reach-pig-head-overcook, money-reach- public-affairs-handle = to satirize that officials handle business only if they receive money'
	dog	*gou3pi2gao1yao4* 狗皮膏藥 'dog-skin- paste-medicine = dog skin plaster; quack medicine'
	horse	*ma3diao4* 馬吊 'horse-hang = a card game'
	bull	*tan1qian2mai3lao3niu2* 貪錢買老牛 'desire-money-buy-old-cow = to condemn people who are keen on gaining petty advantages'
poor	tiger	*hu3e4feng2ren2shi2 ren2qiong2qi3dao4 xin1* 虎餓逢人食, 人窮起盜心 'tiger-hungry- come-human-eat, human-poor-case-steal- heart = the embarrassed look of someone who is cornered and does not care about a sense of honor or of shame'
	pig	*fu4ren2du2shu1qiong2ren2wei4zhu1* 富人讀書, 窮人餵豬 'wealthy-person-study, poor-person-feed-pig = describes the disparity between the rich and the poor'
	horse	*ren2qiong2zhi4duan3 ma3shou4mao2chang2* 人窮志短 馬瘦毛長 'people-poor- ambition-short horse-thin-hair-long = poverty chills ambition; poverty stifles ambition'
	snail	*wu2ke2gua1niu2(zu2)* 無殼蝸牛(族) 'no-shell-snail (tribe) = people who are not capable of purchasing houses'
profit	sheep	*yang2mao2chu1zai4yang2shen1shang4* 羊毛出在羊身上 'sheep-hair-produce-on-sheep-body-upon = after all, the wool still comes from the sheep's back; in the long run, whatever you're given, you pay for'
	fish	*fang4chang2xian4diao4da4yu2* 放長線釣大魚 'release-long-line-catch-big-fish = throw a long line to catch a big fish, adopt a long-term plan to secure something big'
	bird	*yi4shi2liang3niao3; yi4shi2er4niao3*; 一石兩鳥; 一石二鳥 'one-rock-two-bird = kill two birds with one stone; to gain two advantages by a single move'
	chicken	*tou1ji1bu4zhao2shi2ba3mi3* 偷雞不著蝕把米 'steal-chicken-not-success-lose-handle-rice = try to steal a chicken only to end up losing the rice; go for wool and come back shorn'

Table 11.2. (*cont.*)

FLEs	Vehicles	Examples
job	cow	*huang2niu2* 黃牛 'yellow-cattle = cheat'
	horse	*qi2ma3zhao3ma3*(or *qi2lü2zhao3ma3*) 騎馬找馬 (or 騎驢找馬) 'ride-horse-seek-horse (or ride-donkey-seek-donkey) = look for a horse while sitting on one; hold on to one job while seeking a better one'
	cuttlefish	*chao3you2yu2* 炒魷魚 'fry-cuttlefish = to be fired'
	cat	*ye4mao1zi* 夜貓子 'night-cat-suffix = owl; a person who goes to bed late'
rich	horse	*ren2wu2heng2cai2bu4fu4 ma3wu2ye3cao3 bu4fei2* 人無橫財不富, 馬無野草不肥 'people-no-horizontal-money-not-rich, horse-no-grass-not-fat = the importance of luck'
	fish	*yu2mi3zhi1xiang1* 魚米之鄉 'fish-rice-of-hometown = a land of fish and rice; a land of abundance'
	pig	*fei2zhu1* 肥豬 'fat-pig = a fat person; fatty'
	turtle	*jin1gui1xu4* 金龜婿 'gold-turtle-husband = a son-in-law from a wealthy or politically influential family; a rich son-in-law.'
money	cow	*die Kuh muß man melken* 'the-cow-must-one-milk = one must milk the cow; this person is a good source of money'
	hare	*den Hasen laufen lassen* 'the-hare-run-let = to let the hare run; to spend the money liberally'
	pig	*Schweinegeld* 'pig money = a lot of money'
	mouse	*keine Mäuse mehr haben* 'no-mice-more- have = have no more mice; no money, no bread/brass'
worth	donkey	*jmdn. hat der Esel im Galopp verloren* 'someone-has-the-donkey-in-gallop-lost = someone has lost the donkey in the gallop; someone is unacceptable or not worth considering'
	sparrow	*ein Spatz in der Hand ist besser als eine Taube auf dem Dach* 'a-sparrow-in-the-hand- is-better-than-a-pigeon-on-the-roof = a bird in the hand is worth more than two in the bush'
profit	fish	*(den Fisch) an der Angel haben* '(the-fish)-on-the-fishing rod-have = to have that fish on the fishing rod; to be sure of that profit'
	livestock	*Kleinvieh macht auch Mist* 'small livestock-makes-also-manure = many a mickle makes a muckle'
	wolf	*jeder ist des anderen Wolf* 'everybody-is-a-other-wolf = everybody is a wolf to the other one; everybody thinks of his own profit only'

Table 11.2. (*cont.*)

FLEs	Vehicles	Examples
poor	dog	*Es ist schwer,einem so treuen Gefährten wie einen Hund zu finden; hat ein Armer ihn aufgezogen,so wird er keinem Reichen je folgen* 'it-is-heavy, a-so-faithful-companion- as-a-dog-to-find; has-a-poor-it-raised, so- will-it-no-rich-ever-follow = it is difficult to find a as faithful companion as a dog; if a poor has raised it, it would not ever follow the rich'
	hen	*das Ei unterm Huhn verkaufen müssen* 'the-egg-under-hen-sell-must = must sell the egg under hen; to be very poor and forced to sell everything'
	horse	*vom Pferd auf den Esel kommen* 'from- horse-onto-the-ass(donkey)-come = come from horse onto the ass; to become poor'
	mouse	*arm wie eine (Kirchen)maus* 'poor-like-a-(church)mouse = very poor'
rich	dog	*Es ist schwer, einem so treuen Gefährten wie einen Hund zu finden; hat ein Armer ihn aufgezogen, so wird er keinem Reichen je folgen* 'it-is-heavy, a-so-faithful-companion- as-a-dog-to-find; has-a-poor-it-raised, so-will-it-no-rich-ever-follow = it is difficult to find as faithful a companion as a dog; if a poor has raised it, it would not ever follow the rich'

As we can see from Table 11.2, *huo3dao4zhu1tou2lan4, qian2dao4gong1shi-4ban4* 火到豬頭爛, 錢到公事辦 'fire-reach-pig-head-overcook, money-reach-public-affairs-handle' uses the animal vehicle *pig* to express the satire that officials feel happy seeing money, and handle business only if they receive money. Using the vehicles *dog, gou3pi2gao1yao4* 狗皮膏藥 'dog-skin-paste-medicine' is a plaster for rheumatism, strains, contusions, etc., formerly spread on dog skin, but now usually on cloth. Such a dog skin plaster is just quack medicine used to cheat money. *Ma3diao4* 馬吊 'horse-hang' where the vehicle *horse* is used, refers to a card game played in the 16th century, possibly the forerunner of mahjong, for gambling to hopefully win money.

To express poorness, the animal vehicle *tiger* expresses *hu3e4feng-2ren2shi2 ren2qiong2qi3dao4xin1* 虎餓逢人食，人窮起盜心 'tiger-hungry-come-human-eat, human-poor-case-steal-heart,' which contrasts the hunger of an otherwise strong tiger and a poor person, the tiger will eat whatever it encounters, also humans, whereas the poor will inevitably steal. This expression thus describes the embarrassed look of someone who is cornered and does not care about a sense of honor or of shame.

In German, for 'money,' *cow* is used as in *die Kuh muß man melken* 'the-cow-must-one-milk' meaning one must milk the cow; this person is an excellent milk cow, a source of money. The vehicle *hare* is used as in *den Hasen laufen lassen* 'the-hare-run-let' where to let the hare run refers to spending money liberally. And *Schweinegeld* 'pig money' uses the vehicle *pig* as an intensifier to describe the amount of the money, so the expression means 'a lot of money.'

For the FLE 'worth,' *sparrow* is used as in *ein Spatz in der Hand ist besser als eine Taube auf dem Dach* 'a-sparrow-in-the-hand-is-better-than-a-pigeon-on-the-roof; a bird in the hand is worth more than two in the bush.' The vehicle *Spatz* can also be replaced with *Sperling* and pictures the same idea. For 'profit,' *livestock* is used as in *Kleinvieh macht auch Mist* 'small livestock-makes-also-manure = many a mickle makes a muckle' where "A penny saved is a penny earned" is expressed. That is, economy in trifles will ensure abundance after all.

In Table 11.3 below we give some plant examples for the salient FLEs in Mandarin and German.

Table 11.3. Salient financial linguistic expressions in terms of plant vehicles.

FLEs	Vehicles	Examples
Mandarin		
money	wood	*guan1cai2ben3* 棺材本 'coffin-capital = the money to buy one's own coffin'
	bamboo	*qiao1zhu2gang4* 敲竹槓 'knock-bamboo-pole = to take advantage of someone when you have discovered a vital weakness of theirs'
	lotus	*he2bao1* 荷包 'lotus-bag = wallet'
	tea	*fan4lai2zhang1kou3 cha2lai2shen1shou3* 飯來張口, 茶來伸手 'rice-come-open-mouth, tea-come-reach out-hand = someone who is dependent on others in life'
poor	thorn	*jing1chai1bu4qun2* 荊釵布裙 'thorns as hairpin and skirt made of coarse cloth = a woman's plain dress'
	fleabane	*peng2hu4weng4you3* 蓬戶甕牖 'fleabane-door-urn-window = a very poor household'
	root	*jiao2cai4gen1* 嚼菜根 'chew-vegetable-root = to bear hardships'
	vegetable	*hu2xing2cai4se4* 鵠形菜色 'swan-shape-vegetable-color = skinny and weak due to hunger'

Table 11.3. (*cont.*)

FLEs	Vehicles	Examples
profit	firewood	*ben3xin1* 本薪 'original-firewood = the basic salary'
	flower	*cha1hua1* 插花 'insert-flower = to gain something by participating in others' activities'
	rice	*xian1xia4mi3 xian1chi1fan4*, 先下米, 先吃飯 'first-down-rice, first-eat-meal = those who take action first will profit first'
	grass	*tu4zibu4chi1wo1bian1cao3* 兔子不吃窩邊草 'rabbits- do not-eat-nest-side-grass = rabbits do not eat the grass near their lair to protect their home from being seen; one does not harm his close ones or neighbors'
rich	firewood	*shuang1xin1jia1ting2* 雙薪家庭 'double-firewood-family = a couple who both has an income; a family with two salaries'
	grain	*wu3gu3feng1deng1* 五穀豐登 'five-grain-plenty-mount = to have a good harvest of all grain crops'
	kudzu	*bei1ge2* 杯葛 'cup-kudzu = to boycott'
	taro	*tang4shou3shan1yu4* 燙手山芋 'scald-hand-mountain- taro = things that are troublesome and which others do not wish to handle'
German		
money	branch	*Geld abzweigen* 'money-branch off = money branch; to divert money away from its main channel for some other purposes'
	leaf	*Geld wie Laub* 'money-like-leaves = stacks of money, money to burn'
	pepper	*Wo Geld genug ist, tut man den Pfeffer an die Suppe* 'where-money-enough-is, do-one-the-pepper-at-the- soup = where there is enough money, they put pepper to the soup; rich people are wasteful'
	lilac	*Flieder* 'lilac = money'
worth	bean	*keine Bohne wert* 'no-bean-worth = worthless'
	chanterelle	*Keinen Pffferling wert sein* 'no-chanterelle-worth-be = to be worth not a chanterelle; to be worthless'
	leafstalk	*keinen Pappenstiel wert sein* 'no-leafstalk-worth-be = not to be worth a paper stalk; not to be worth anything'
	hazelnut	*etwas ist keine gelöcherte/hohle Haselnuß wert* 'something-is-no-empty/cracked-hazelnut-worth = something is not worth for an empty hazelnut; something is worthless'

Table 11.3. (*cont.*)

FLEs	Vehicles	Examples
profit	bean	*kalte Bohnen* 'cold-beans = poor people's food'
	grain	*es steht wie armer Leute Korn* 'it-stands-like-poor-people-grain = it stands like the grain of poor people; it looks a poor sight'
	stick	*am Stock gehen* by-stick-go = to walk by a stick; to be ill/in a bad financial situation'
	straw	*Von der Feder/Bettfeder aufs Stroh kommen* 'from-the- feather/bed-feather-on-the-straw-come = to get from the (bed-)feather onto the straw; to be reduced to poverty'
poor	fruit	*die Frucht* 'the-fruit = outcome derived from something'
	grain	*dieses Korn ist auf guten Boden gefallen* 'this-grain-is-from-good-ground-fallen = this seed fell into good ground; this was a worthwhile investment'
	wheat	*Seinen Weizen scheren* 'one's-wheat-shear = to cut one's wheat; to make profits'
rich	fruit	*etwas wird Frucht tragen* 'something-will-fruit-bear = something will be successful'
	bean	*Er hat viele Bohnen im Sack* 'he-has-many-beans-in-sack = he has got a lot of beans in his sack; he is or seems to be rich'
	flower	*blumenreich* 'flower rich = in a flowery way'
	hay	*Heu in den Stiefeln haben* 'hay-in-the-boots-have = to have hay in one's boots; to be financially well off'

Table 11.3 presents that to express the FLE 'money' the plant vehicle *wood* is used such as *guan1cai2ben3* 棺材本 'coffin-capital' referring to the money used to buy one's own coffin, which means the very basic capital that one holds. *Tea* is also used, as in *fan4lai2zhang1kou3, cha2lai2shen1shou3* 飯來張口, 茶來伸手 'rice-come-open-mouth-tea-come-reach out-hand' saying that someone who only knows how to enjoy life, but not the work or terms behind the comfort of enjoyment, actually indicates someone who is dependent on others in life.

In German, *branch* can relate to 'money' and express *Geld abzweigen* 'money-branch off' meaning that 'to divert money away from either its main, previous or accustomed channels for some other purposes.' Germans tend to use certain plant vehicles to mean least of value, e.g., *bean, chanterelle, leafstalk* and *hazelnut*, in Table 11.3, all are such cases.

When something is worth even less than these vehicles, they are almost worthless.

On the other hand, *grain* is used to express 'poorness' as in *Dieses Korn ist auf guten Boden gefallen* 'this-grain-is-from-good-ground-fallen.' When the Germans say 'this seed fell into good ground,' it means 'this was a worthwhile investment.' This analogy could be derived from the Bible in Mark 4:8. Many of the above examples convey cultural specific attributes and will be further discussed in section 11.4 below.

For those FLEs that consist merely of less than three expressions, the Mandarin animal vehicles are *dragon, crane, livestock, sheep, horse, dragon*, and *warbler*. Plant vehicles are *rice* and *grass*. In German, animal vehicles are *bull, rooster, flea, animal, pegasus*, and *cat* and plant vehicles are *pea, fruit, apple, tree*, and *lemon*.

In this section, we presented the data with the categories of salient financial domains. We further compare the Mandarin and German data in the next sections.

11.1.2. *A Brief Comparison Between Chinese and German*

We now compare some similarities and differences in the Chinese and German data. We will talk about the most popular FLE 'money,' some vehicles that render FLEs with similar ideas, and compare the FLEs concerning 'success' and 'failure.'

The FLE 'money' has rendered the most expressions both in Chinese and German, which are 15% and 8% of the expressions, respectively. Further, it is found that the animal vehicle *dragon* is favored to be used to express the idea of 'money,' especially in terms of coin, in both Chinese and German, as in *Drachendollar* 'dragon-dollar,' *long2yang2* 龍洋 'dragon-money = a kind of currency which was used in Ching Dynasty' and *long2bi4* 龍幣 'dragon-money = the silver dollar coin, 8 taels in weight, minted by Emperor Wu in the Han Dynasty.'

The animal vehicles *fish* and *pig* share the same expressions in Chinese and German. *Fish* is related to 'profit.' For example, *yu2li4* 漁利 'fishing-profit = to take illegitimate profit' in Chinese and *den Fisch an der Angel haben* 'the-fish-on-the-fishing rod-have = to have that fish on the fishing rod; to be sure of a profit' in German. As for *pig* in Chinese, sayings such as *huo3dao4zhu1tou2lan4, qian2dao4 gong1shi4ban4* 火到豬頭爛, 錢到公事辦 'fire-reach-pig-head-overcook, money-reach-public-affairs-handle = to satirize that officials feel happy seeing money, and handle business only if they receive money' or *tan1qian2mai3de2zhu1po2rou4* 貪錢買得豬婆

肉 'greedy-low-priced-buy-pig-woman-meat = to condemn people who are keen on gaining petty advantages' show the relationship between *pig* and money. In German, *Schweinegeld* 'pig-money' means a lot of money.

There are quite a few FLEs that connote 'success' or 'failure' in both Mandarin and German. In terms of plant vehicles, *fruit* such as *hundertfältige Frucht tragen* 'hundredfold-fruit-bear = to bear hundredfold fruit; to be successful,' and *flower* as in *blühend* 'flourishing or thriving' can be referred to business, industry, culture or city. For 'failure,' plant vehicles such as *cactus* like *in die Kacke greifen* 'in-the-cactus-grab; to grab shit = to be without success; to make a bad business.'

In Mandarin, the following are for 'success': *bai3hua1qi2fang4* 百花齊放 'hundred-flowers-together-release = different styles of art or manners of thinking, rising, developing, and flourishing'; *ming2lie4 qian2mao2* 名列前茅 'name-listed-front-cogongrass = to be top of the rank.' For 'failure' are: *luo4hua1liu2shui3* 落花流水 'fallen-flower-flowing-water = the few injured and defeated remaining; a messy and confusing sight'; *shu4dao3hu2sun1san4* 樹倒猢猻散 'tree-topple-macaques-disperse = monkeys disperse when a tree falls; associated members run away when a family breaks apart or an institution loses power and authority.'

In terms of animal vehicles, *bee*, and *herring* refer to 'success.' For example, *Bienen braten* 'bees-bake = to bake bees; to try hard and to see little success,' and *Hier wird er keinen Hering braten* 'here-will-he-no-herring-roast = he has no herring to roast here; here he will have no success.' But *mouse* as in *mit Mann und Maus untergehen* 'with-man-and-mouse-sink = to sink with man and mouse; (of a ship' to sink with crew and cargo; (of a company) to go bankrupt' are used to indicate 'failure.' In Mandarin, the FLEs using animal vehicles to express 'success' are the following: *hong2tu2da4zhan3* 鴻圖大展 'swan goose-big-spread = a swan goose hovers in the air' means 'to carry out one's great plan; ride on the crest of success.' *Ma2que4bian4feng4huang2* 麻雀變鳳凰 'sparrow-become-phoenix = a modest girl, with outstanding performance, or to become a beauty' where obviously the *phoenix* plays the successful role. For failure: *Fei1e2pu1huo3* 飛蛾撲火 'moth-fly-into-fire = bring destruction upon oneself.' The vehicle *tiger* in Mandarin usually denotes 'great, strong, powerful,' etc. (Hsieh 2006a: 2212), however, in the FLE *hu3luo4ping2yang2bei4quan3qi1* 虎落平陽被犬欺 'tiger-fall-Ping-Yang-insulted-by-dogs,' when a tiger fell to the city Ping-Yang, it was even bullied by a dog because probably there were many dogs there. This FLE refers to a man who loses position and influence and thus may be subjected to much indignity.

We have seen a brief comparison of the FLEs 'success' and 'failure.' In section 11.2.1 below we will have a further analysis of the broader view of the financial feature success (incl. the keywords 'worth,' 'rich,' 'money,' etc.) and failure (incl. 'poor,' 'worthless,' etc.) and try to delve into the underlying associations that language users have in mind when they observe the real world to produce the FLEs.

Moreover, different animal vehicles are used to refer to legends, myths or histories to express financial ideas. This is different from culture to culture. For example, in Chinese, *ya1chao2sheng1feng4* 鴉巢生鳳 'crow-nest-birth-phoenix = ugly mother gives birth to a pretty daughter' and *pan1long2fu4feng4* 攀龍附鳳 'fasten-dragon-attach-phoenix = put oneself under the patronage of a bigwig' use the ancient Chinese mythological creatures *dragon* and *phoenix*. In German, the expressions such as *Pegasus im Joche* 'pegasus-in-yoke = a poet who has to earn his living in an ordinary job, or by writing for a profane purpose' and *Dinosaurier* 'dinosaur = a very inflexible person, office or institution' use the *Pegasus* and *dinosaur*. Section 11.4 will deal with more cultural issues.

11.2. Cognitive Analysis

This section takes a cognitive linguistic perspective to delve into the FLEs in embodiment. In 11.2.1 we examine the judgment of the financial metaphors and reveal the real world association of the expressions. In 11.2.2, the hierarchy of concepts, especially the basic level category, will be illustrated. At the end, salient distributions will be focused on.

11.2.1. *Linguistic Financial Judgment and Underlying Conceits*

When we examine the data that we have collected and see in what way they show financial features (a feature may contain several FLEs, e.g, success includes 'profit,' 'worth,' 'rich,' etc.), we found the financial features are distributed in three levels: linguistic, semantic and pragmatic. To be specific, the linguistic level is when the FLEs show financial features in the expressions themselves, such as *saubillig* 'sow cheap = extremely cheap' and *Flohmarkt* 'flea market = flea market' where 'cheap' and 'market' exhibit the financial features respectively. The ones that belong to the semantic level only give the clue when the language users know the meaning of the expressions, for example, *alle seine Schäflein* 'all-one's-little sheep = to have all one's sheep around' does not show financial features in the statement, but the language users apply this expression after acquiring its meaning: 'to collect or control all of one's assets or valuables.' The ones judged at the pragmatic level go a step further, not until the expression is used, is the financial feature shown. For example, *Dieses Korn ist auf guten Boden gefallen* 'this-grain-is-from-good-ground-fallen = this seed fell into good ground' may be in a context such as when a Christian receives inspiration, where no financial features are applied, but in a certain context it can also mean 'this was a worthwhile investment' where its financial value at the pragmatic level is given.

If we observe the distribution of the linguistic financial judgment in our data, the expressions tend to favor the semantic level in both languages (see Table 11.4).

Table 11.4. The linguistic financial judgment and the salient financial features.

Levels	Salient financial features
Mandarin	
Linguistic level (123)	money + coin = 38 buy + sell = 17 ... poor = 7
Semantic level (282)	poor = 44 profit = 44 money + coin = 32 ... less = 1
Pragmatic level (54)	poor = 27 ... money + coin = 3
German	
Linguistic level (122)	gold + silver = 20 money + coins + cash = 15 ... capital, business, share = 1
Semantic level (156)	money, cents, pennies + cash = 17 profit = 15 ... sale, office/institution, gift = 1
Pragmatic level (41)	worth = 8 money + coins = 6 ... business, dealer, unemployed = 1

*... = omitted features

Table 11.4 shows that in Mandarin, most expressions are observed at the semantic level (282), and fewer at the linguistic level (123) and pragmatic level (54). For the linguistic level, 38 expressions are found in 'money' and 'coin.' They are the most salient financial features that tend to be expressed linguistically. Besides, 17 expressions are found in 'buy' and 'sell,' but only 7 expressions in 'poor.'

In German, too, most expressions are observed at the semantic level (156), and fewer at the linguistic level (122) and pragmatic level (41). For the linguistic level, 20 expressions are found in 'gold' and 'silver.' The second most salient financial feature with 15 expressions is related to 'money,' 'coins,' or 'cash' for this level.

Below we will focus on success (incl. worth, rich, money, etc.) and failure (incl. poor, worthless, etc.) and give an attempt to signify why certain vehicles are often used for certain financial attributes.

Flowers and *fruit* are taken as popular metaphorical vehicles to express richness semantically in both Mandarin and German. They are often used to express the idea of richness. For example, *etwas wird Frucht tragen* 'something-will-fruit-bear = something will be successful,' and *bai3hua1qi-2fang4* 百花齊放 'hundred-flowers-together-release = different styles of art or manners of thinking, rising, developing, and flourishing.' From a botanical perspective, flowers are the outcome of botanic growth, an outcome which is either pleasant to humans' eyes so that they decorate their rooms or meeting zones with flowers, or can be served as food, such as a day lily. Fruit is the result of the plant and can be served as a vegetable like pumpkin, or as fruit, like berries or plums. Therefore, associated with such underlying conceits (the association between the real world and the expression), flowers and fruit are taken as popular metaphorical vehicles to express richness semantically.

Also *hay, leaf* and *moss* are widely used to express the idea of richness. For example, *Er hat Geld wie Heu* 'he-has-money-like-hay = he has great amounts of money,' *Geld wie Laub* 'money-like-leaves = stacks of money, money to burn,' *viel Moos haben* 'much-moss have = have much moss; to be rich,' and so on. The examples show that the quantity of the vehicles *hay, leaf* and *moss* are associated with the idea of richness by the German speakers. *Qiong2zhi1yu4ye4* 瓊枝玉葉 'fine-jade-branch-jade-leave = offspring of noble families' and *jin1ye4* 金葉 'gold-leaf = gold foil; wineglass' are Mandarin examples.

On the other hand, *vegetables* such as *turnip* and *cabbage, grain, bean,* and *pea* are used more to express the idea of poorness. For example, *Der ist so wenig wert wie die Rübe im Kraut* 'he-is-so-little-worth-as-the-turnip-in-cabbage = he is worth as much as a turnip in the cabbage; he doesn›t have much/enough money,' *kalte Bohnen* 'cold-beans = poor people's food,' *es steht wie armer Leute Korn* 'it-stands-like-poor-people-grain = it stands like the grain of poor people; it looks a poor sight,' and *Er mag Erbsen zählen* 'he-likes-peas-count = he likes to count peas; he is unemployed.' The reason that these vehicles are used is not based on the underlying conceit of the growth characteristics of a plant, but in terms of their being the food of the poor. In comparison with having meat, only having vegetables, especially the common ones like cabbage or beans are considered to be poor. In Mandarin, *jiao2cai4gen1* 嚼菜根 'chew-vegetable-root = to eat old-leaf vegetable' means metaphorically 'to bear hardships' because old leaves are not tasty at all. Someone who has to eat old leaves is pictured as bearing hardships.

In terms of animal vehicles, *cat, pig* and *hamster* are related to the idea of richness. For example, *Geldkatze* 'money cat = cash bag used to be worn at the waistband,' *Schweinegeld* 'pig money = a lot of money,' and *Hamsterware* 'hamster-goods = hoarded goods.' As we can see, the above examples all show financial features linguistically and the vehicles are used because the Germans associate them with the characteristics of the animal. *Geldkatze* has the *Katze* 'cats,' because cats are popular pet in Germany and they like to have them around as close as a cash bag. In *Schweinegeld* where *Schwein* 'pig' is used as an intensifier to mean 'a lot of' presumably because pigs give birth to many piglets at a time. *Hamsterware* uses the behavioral quality of a hamster in that this animal saves food for winter or for contingent use.

Yang2mao2chu1zai4yang2shen1shang4 羊毛出在羊身上 'sheep-hair-produce-on-sheep-body-upon = after all, the wool still comes from the sheep's back; in the long run, whatever you are given, you pay for,' *shou-3zhu1dai4tu4* 守株待兔 'watch-stump-wait-hare = watch the stump and wait for a hare; one who sticks to his folly and does nothing' and *yu4bang4xiang1zheng1 yu2weng1de2li4* 鷸蚌相爭，漁翁得利 'snipe-clam-mutual-compete, fish-man get-benefit = when the snipe and the clam grapple, the fisherman profits; it's the third party that benefits from the tussle' are Mandarin examples where stories about hunting hares and that of a fisherman's work are referred to.

In a word, language users associate various underlying conceits to create FLEs, whether it is the human-animal or human-plant relations (pets for companionship, cows provide milk, hens provide eggs, horses carry goods for people, etc.), the characteristics of the animals (pigs give birth to many piglets at a time, hamsters like to save food), or the growth characteristics of the plants (grains grow and give harvest, seeds fall into the fertile soil and grow).

Hsieh, Lien and Meier (2005) studied the plant vehicle *flower* in Mandarin and German, after observing the underlying conceits and found that "the linguistic frames of flowers show that German tends to focus on function by adopting usability and edibility of plants in their expressions, whereas Mandarin is inclined to perceive the outer appearance of plants and compile "visualized" Chinese expressions" (Hsieh, Lien and Meier 2005: 107). However, the functionalism in German and the visualism in Mandarin are not obvious in this study about FLEs in embodiment. The present study shows that the underlying conceits tend to associate the function, edibility, serving as a material, etc. of the animals or plants in the real world. It can be inferred that such underlying conceits are more affordable for FLEs because economy maintains exchange of merchandise in a society, which affects the demand and supply of basic human needs, eating, clothing, dwelling, etc., and other peripheral needs.

In this sense, we further suggest that it is possible that certain metaphorical vehicles (*flower, root, eagle*, etc.) or certain semantic groups of expressions (such as FLEs, and those that are sports and/or entertainment related) will draw on different types of underlying conceits to form fixed expressions. A systematic research in this regard is worth recommending.

11.2.2. *Hierarchy of Concepts*

We categorize the objects and concepts in the world subconsciously with a hierarchy in our mind and use the categories in due time and in due course. For example, Ungerer and Schmid (2006) state that there are three categories in the hierarchy of concepts: the concepts of superordinate category, basic level category, and subordinate category. In this section, we will analyze our data in terms of these three categories. The superordinate category is the key of a concept (e.g., transportation), subordinate category is the subdivisions or members of the concept (e.g., truck, bus, train for the concept of transportation), and the basic level category is what we usually refer to when covering the whole class (e.g., car for this concept).[1]

[1] For the studies on the hierarchy of concepts, see for example, Gelman and O'Reilly (1988) for children's language development, Tseung-Wong (2003) for law, management and social science, and Waldzus, Mummendey and Wenzelc (2005) for social psychology.

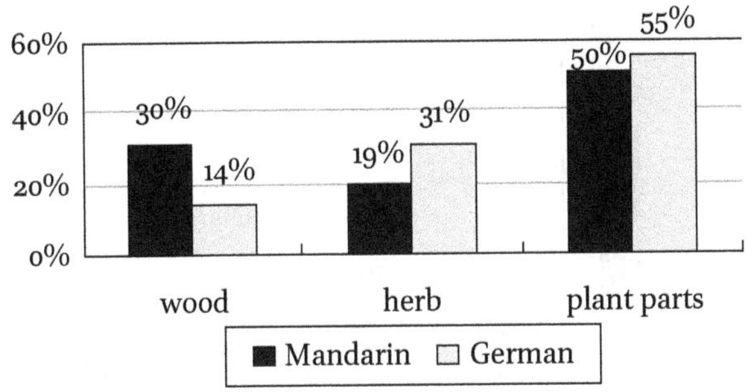

Figure 11.1. The percentage of the basic level categories in plant data.

In our study, we have two superordinate categories in the data: animal and plant. We have discussed their subordinate categories in the above sections, e.g., *dog, cat, tiger, bear* and *dragon* for animal; *apple, wheat, bean,* and *flower* for plant. In the following, we will compare basic level categories. Those for the category of plant are wood, herb and plant parts. Those for the category of animal are insects, livestock, poultry, fish, birds, wild animals and mythical animals. Figure 11.1 and Figure 11.2 give the percentages of the basic level categories in our data.

In terms of plant, as Figure 11.1 shows, there are three basic level categories: wood, herb, and plant parts. Wood includes pine, tea, apple, bamboo, etc. Herb includes rose, pepper, lotus, wheat and plant parts include root, stem, leaf, flower, fruit, seed, etc. Again, some data are not presented in this figure, such as *plant* for FLEs like *das Gewächs* 'the-plant = result; product' and *Pfifferling* 'chanterelle' for FLEs like *keinen Pfifferling für etwas geben* 'no-chanterelle-for-something-give = not to give a chanterelle for anything, to give nothing for something.'

In Figure 11.1, we see that the category of plant parts is the most popular plant metaphorical vehicle in both Mandarin and German. It occupies 50% in Mandarin data and 55% in German data. Wood ranks second in Mandarin (30%), but in German herb comes in second (31%) and outranks wood. It is reasonable that plant parts enjoys the high percentage in our FLE data because vehicles like *flower, root,* or vegetables like *cabbage, bean* are all parts of plants that people make good use of in daily life.

It is noted that some animal data are not presented for the basic level categories in Figure 11.2, such as *animal* for the FLE *Der Luxus der Tafeln ist die Not der Tiere* 'the-luxury-of the-tables-is-the-need-of the-animals = a luxurious meal is bad animals because they will be eaten there' and

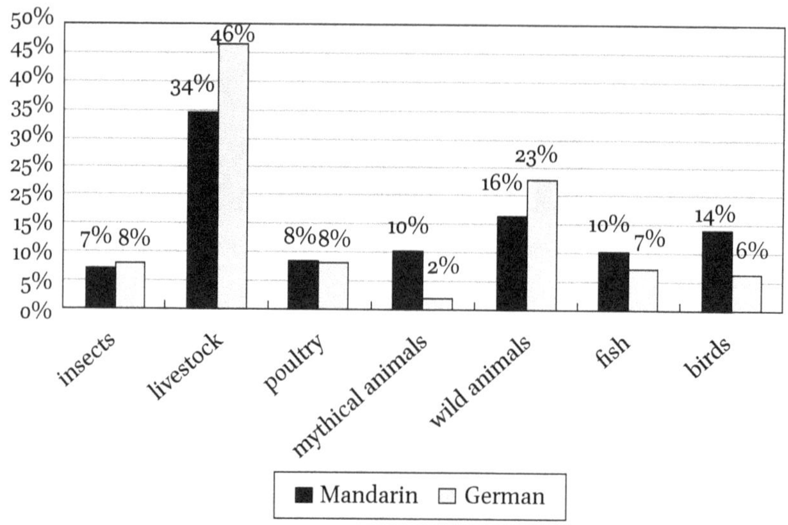

Figure 11.2. Basic level categories in animal data.

mouse for the FLE *lao3shu3hui4* 老鼠會 'rat-community = direct selling or pyramid scheme.'

In Figure 11.2, we see that livestock is the most popular animal metaphorical vehicle in both Mandarin and German. It occupies 34% in Mandarin and 46% in German data. Wild animals ranks the second, it is 16% in Mandarin and 23% in German data. On the other hand, mythical animals are the least used animal metaphorical vehicle (2%) for the Germans, while the Mandarin speakers take mythical animals (10%) more than insects (7%) and poultry (8%) into their FLEs to express financial concepts.

The expressions of insect in Chinese are unproductive and have the lowest ratio (7%), which might result from the following reasons. First, insects are small and sometimes difficult to be found. Many of the insect-related FLEs in Chinese describe the foraging behaviors of the insects, e.g., *tang2lang2bu3chan2, huang2que4zai4hou4* 螳螂捕蟬, 黃雀在後 'the mantis stalks the cicada, unaware of the oriole behind = to covet gains ahead without being aware of danger behind,' while other underlying conceits are limited. In other words, insects have low economic benefits. Second, insects seldom serve as people's staple food. Moreover, insects have neither of the other functions like laboring nor hunting for human beings.

The expressions of mythical animals in German are unproductive and have the lowest ratio (2%). Take the following FLEs as examples. *Drachendollar* 'dragon-dollar' describes the oriental dragon. *Pegasus im Joche* 'Pegasus-in-yoke = a poet who has to earn his living in an ordinary job.'

Both are of foreign origin. The latter originated from Greek mythology, and the Pegasus here has the denotation of being detached or standing aloof from the worldly affairs of the subject that does not, however, coincide with the reality of economic endeavor, just as the meaning of the expression implies. In other words, the German mythical animals are not like those in Chinese culture, which have extraordinary roles both in legend and in language. The Chinese consider the dragon their ancestor, the phoenix is capable of bringing fortune, and the unicorn can even bring sons, as the following examples indicate: *long2dechuan2ren2* 龍的傳人 'dragon's-descendant = descendant of dragon; Chinese people,' *feng4huang2 lai2yi2* 鳳凰來儀 'phoenix-come-appearance = arrival of phoenixes; an auspicious omen.' And *qi2lin2song4zi3* 麒麟送子 '*qi2lin2* delivers sons.'

11.3. Cultural Features

Proverbs or fixed expressions show culture. Take the Chinese *long2dechuan2ren2* 龍的傳人 'dragon's-descendant = descendant of dragon' and *luo4ye4gui1gen1* 落葉歸根 'fall-leaves-return-root = what comes from the soil will return to the soil' as examples. The Chinese people believe they are the offspring of the dragon, hence *long2dechuan2ren2*. The *Dragon* represents a "remarkable, valuable, important, strong, powerful, super" figure. It is sacred and inviolable (Hsieh and Kirschner 2007; Hsieh 2007; Tsai 2011). When it is the year of dragon (according to the Chinese zodiac signs), for example the year 2012, parents will plan to give birth, in the hope of having 'dragon sons and daughters.' As for *luo4ye4gui1gen2*, Chinese value their origins, their ancestor is revered and important. For Chinese culture, people can make a living away from home, traveling around the world in the prime of their life, but they like return to their native place in the end, just as the falling leaves return to the root as the expression *luo4ye4gui1gen1* says.

11.3.1. *Chinese Culture*

Most Taiwanese people have their origin in Mainland China. The FLEs point out Chinese culture. In this section, we will talk about specific Chinese cultural features expressed by our data, such as the concept of family, food, face, numbers, teachings of Confucius and Mencius, and the Doctrine of the Mean that are expressed in FLEs in terms of embodiment in Mandarin.

11.3.1.1. *About Family*

Chinese consider family to be the pillar of society. Thus, the value of *jun1jun1, chen2chen2, fu4fu4, zi3zi3* 君君，臣臣，父父，子子, that is, relationships among husband-and-wife, father-and-son or siblings are emphasized, following the teaching of Confucius in Lun yu 論語 (The Analects of *Confucius*). The maintenance of ethical relationships is essential. The FLE *chu4shi4* 畜事 'serve-livestock = to serve (parents) and raise (children)' reveals the importance of filial piety. The verb in the expression has shown the importance of one's responsibility to work in order to earn and to support his or her family.

Wang4zi3cheng2long2, wang4nü3cheng2feng4 望子成龍，望女成鳳 'hope-son-become-dragon hope-daughter-become-phoenix = to have great ambitions for one's children' reveals the high expectation of Chinese parents. Dragon and phoenix also represent the king and the queen. This expression shows that parents expect their children to be top ones in the society. Besides, the concept of inheritance also plays a vital role in family relationships. The FLE *xin1huo3xiang1chuan2* 薪火相傳 'firewood-fire-mutual-hand down' and *gan4fu4zhi1gu3* 幹父之蠱 'cover-father-POSS.-a legendary venomous insect = cover the fault of father; a son who can succeed to his father's career' refers to inheritance. The former means that even though woods have been burnt out, the flame still remains; that is, the torch of learning is passed on from generation to generation. The latter points out that a son inherits the career from his father. The connection among generations is closely related through Chinese ethical values.

11.3.1.2. *About Food*

Food culture is shown abundant in our data. For example, *wu3gu3feng1deng1* 五穀豐登 'five-grain-plenty-mount' means to have a good harvest of all grain crops. The five grains indicate the five different types of the staple foods in different parts of China produced in different climates. In the old days when the technology and knowledge were still underdeveloped, harvesting of cereals was a very important food source for the people. An expression that usually follows *wu3gu3feng1deng1* 五穀豐登 is *she4ji4an1ning2* 社稷安寧, which means foods are also bearing the responsibility to keep the society in order.

Yu2mi3zhi1xiang1 魚米之鄉 'a land of fish and rice' means 'the land of abundance,' and it originally referred to the plain at the downstream of the Chang-Jiang River (also known as the Yangtze River). Around the downstream of Chang-Jiang River, there is a rich production of rice and also a high catch of fish because of the excellent geographic environment.

Fish and rice have become the symbol of that area. Richness and peacefulness have made the Shu and Hang Provinces become the so-called "the heavens on the Earth." 魚米之鄉 represents not only the plentiful bounty of food provisions, but also the superiority of the people's livelihood and public order.

Jiao2cai4gen1 嚼菜根 'chew-vegetable-root' refers to a person who is willing to bear the hardships of a poor life, and accepts it gracefully. In Chinese food culture, the root of vegetables is cheap and normally is the food of the poor people. This expression encourages people not to be depressed because of poverty, instead one should adjust one's state of mind to be more diligent and frugal.

There are other food-related FLEs including *mi3zhu1xin1gui4* 米珠薪桂 'rice-pearl-fuel-cinnamon = rice and fuel are expensive, like pearls and cassia; high food prices,' *chai2mi3you2yan2* 柴米油鹽 'firewood-rice-oil-salt = necessities of everyday life,' and *chi1mi3 bu4zhi1mi3jia4* 吃米不知米價 'eat-rice-not-know-rice-price = someone who does not understand what is happening around him,' etc.

11.3.1.3. *About Social Face*

For Chinese, 'face' is one's self-identity, it represents individual value as well as social reputation and achievement. We will refer it as social face. To have social face means high individual value. For example, *bai3zu-2zhi1chong2, si3er2bu4jiang1* 百足之蟲, 死而不僵 'a centipede dies but never falls down.' This implies that a powerful person or old institutions die hard, or that even if one's fortune or reputation is on the wane, the outfit and appearance are still kept good. Therefore, the appearance and inner individual value are both important. In spite of living poorly, to keep the social face could be even more important because a confirmation from the community gives more confidence to one's self-identity.

In addition, the expression *jie4mi3xia4de2guo1, tao3mi3xia4bu4 de2guo1* 借米下得鍋, 討米下不得鍋 'borrow-rice-down-able-pot, ask-rice-down-no-able-pot' says that the rice borrowed is edible because it is returnable, while the rice received is not edible because it cannot be turned back anymore. The expression literally shows rice is a staple food in China; meanwhile the expression also implies the social value of face in Chinese society, that the 'face' is weighty.

Furthermore, the expression *shu4dao3hu2sun1san4* 樹倒猢猻散 'tree-topple-macaques-disperse = monkeys disperse when a tree falls; associated members run away when a family breaks apart or an institution loses power' signifies once the prestigious or the wealthy lose the advantages, people around will leave them. In the beginning, the inferior or the poor get close to the superior one because of a better reputation and value for the social face.[2] On the contrary, once the superior one loses their status, the inferior one leaves due to lack of the social face.

The interaction between host and guests of course is related to the social face. The FLE *peng2bi4sheng1hui1* 蓬蓽生輝 'fleabane-bamboo fence-produce-splendor = an important or honorable visitor adds luster to a simple house' is a modest way of a host to describe his own house. It means the presence of the guest is a credit to the host's house. *Peng2bi4* 蓬蓽 refers to an ordinary and simple house, and is a modest way to describe one's own house to show the importance of a guest. It shows how a host welcomes his guest. It not only expresses a host's pleasure, but also means the guest has given the social face to the host, or the host to the guest mutually.

11.3.1.4. *About Numbers*

The FLE *dan4de2yi2pian4ju2pi2 chi1, qie3mo4wang4ledong4ting2 hu2* 但得一片橘皮吃，且莫忘了洞庭湖 'yet-get-a-piece-tangerine- skin-eat, just-don't-forget-Dongting Lake' conveys the financial idea 'profit' and was cited in the classic Chinese novel Jin Ping Mei 金瓶梅 (The Plum in the Golden Vase)[3] originating in Dongting Lake, which abounds in tangerines. In this expression, when people eat a piece of tangerine, they will think of Dongting Lake. Literally, a piece of tangerine means the one or the only; however, a piece of tangerine represents the concept as a whole. Although one seems single in number, the meaning of one also refers to completeness, or oneness. From the perspective of culture, numbers like "one" convey underlying meanings. The use of "one" expresses the concept of completion and fullness. Therefore, this FLE also means "as soon as someone gets a tangerine to eat, he/she should remember the lake". The Chinese value the importance of entirety instead of individuality. One is widely used in the concept of wholeness.

Shi2mi3jiu3kang1 十米九糠 'ten-rice-nine-chaff' refers to people living in extreme poverty and conveys the financial idea 'poorness.' In Chinese, the pronunciation of ten is similar to that of 實 'stead.' They are homonyms. Likewise, the pronunciation of nine is similar to that of

---

[2] Liu (2010) has researched *mian* 面 in Mandarin, in which the social face is also presented.

[3] The author is *Lan Ling Xiao Xiao Sheng* 蘭陵笑笑生. This novel was first found in year 1610.

久 'forever' in Chinese. The Chinese use a decimal number system (from one to ten), the extended meaning of *jiu3* 九 'nine' and *shi2* 十 'ten' refers to a big amount. In this FLE, the literal meaning of the numbers does not mean the real number. It represents the percentage of the amount and means that though there looks like a lot of rice, but 90% of them are chaff. The decimal number system plays an important role in Chinese culture, the Chinese writing system, the square characters, is affected by decimal number system as well.

Ba1cai2 八材 'eight-materials' consists eight materials: pearl, jade, stone, wood, gold, metal, leather and feather. People can earn money after processing the materials, so the materials are taken to produce fortune. It has a significant meaning to choose exactly eight materials. The pronunciation of *ba1* 八 'eight' is similar to *fa1* 發 which means getting rich, so the number eight implies becoming rich. Thus, eight is the number that most Chinese businessmen like. For example, *yi1liu4ba1* 一六八 'one-six-eight' represents being smooth all the way, because it sounds like *yi2lu4fa1* 一路發 'being smooth all the way.' *ba1yi1ba1* 八一八 'eight-one-eight' represents being rich for it is the homonym of *fa1yi4fa1* 發一發 'boost.' Although the main purpose is not to pursue richness, "eight" is used for smooth and good fortune. The implied meaning related to homonyms is crucial (Wu 1998, Li 1999, Hsieh 2001, Chung 2004) in comprehending Chinese expressions.

Wu3gu3feng1deng1 五穀豐登 'five-grain-plenty-mount = to have a good harvest of all grain crops' presents five grains: rice, corn, wheat, beans, and millet. However, there are more than five edible grains in the Chinese area. The number five is used to represent the total number of grain due to the importance of five. The preference of five results from the five elements including wood, fire, earth, metal, and water. In Chinese philosophy, the concept of "yin and yang" forms the universe while the five elements are the main elements to form substances. These five elements generate and destruct each other. The concept of five elements is widely used, especially in substances classification. For example, the five sense organs are the eyes, mouth, heart, ears and nose. The five body organs are the liver, heart, spleen, stomach and kidneys. Similarly, five grains is an extension of the concept of five elements.

Yi4deng1long2men2, shen1jia4bai3bei4 一登龍門，身價百倍 'once-step-dragon-gate, body-price-hundred-double = vault into high society on winning the patronage of an influential or powerful person' indicates that once crossing the dragon gate, one's social value is higher. The "one" here does not imply number but the process of passing. Relatively, hundred here implies the exaggeration of number. In Chinese culture, hundred, thousand, and ten thousand are often used to describe large numbers. For instance, the hundred in *bai3hua1jiu3* 百花酒 'hundred-flowers-wine' hints at the good variety of wine. *Cheng2qian1shang4wan4* 成千上萬 'become- thousand-above-ten thousand = a lot' means "countless", and *wan4hua1tong3* 萬花筒 'ten thousand-flower-tube = kaleidoscope' also indicates large numbers.

11.3.1.5. *Teachings of Confucius and Mencius*

The FLE *qing1qiu2fei2ma3* 輕裘肥馬 'light-coat-fat-horse = soft furs and well-fed horses' refers to someone who is leading a luxurious and extravagant life. It is stated in *The Analects of Confucius* and is about the student of Confucius Gong-Xi-Chi 公西赤. While his mother is living in poverty, he is wearing fine clothes and riding on a fine horse during his diplomatic mission to Qi State. Thus, Confucius pointed out that, "Chi goes to Qi State, he is riding on a sturdy horse and wearing a fine fur coat, and I have heard all about this. A person of noble character and integrity should have helped those who are in need rather than those who are rich." *qing1qiu2fei2ma3* 輕裘肥馬 'light-coat-fat-horse = soft furs and well-fed horses' is definitely not praising a person who is elegant in dress. It actually possesses a negative meaning. It also stated Confucius's concerns and cares for the poor people and disdain for power and luxury. Through this expression, the readers can notice a contrast and comparison between richness and poorness and thus link to the thought that we should provide help and care for those who are in need and to ponder over the need to lead a luxurious and extravagant life.

Apart from the concern and care for the poor people, Confucius also promotes filial piety. For instance, there is the case of his other student, Zi-Lu, who carried rice on his back. When Zi-Lu was young, his family and he lived in poverty. He carried the rice from a hundred miles away back to his home for his parents, yet he ate only wild vegetables. When he grew up, he lived in affluence in the Chu area, but he felt sad because he could not show his filial affection towards his parents anymore since they had already passed away. In this case, Confucius said, "Zi-Lu tries his best to be filial and to please his parents while they are still alive. Also, he thinks of and misses his parents for most of the time even though they have passed away." From this, it shows the emphasis of Confucius on the relationship between the parents and children especially, as the children have to do everything they can in order to take care of their parents. This concept has greatly influenced Chinese culture and even in modern society, filial piety is still considered to be one of the standard of judging one's morality.

Hu3e4feng2ren2shi2, ren2qiong2qi3dao4xin1 虎餓逢人食，人窮起盜心 'tiger-hungry-come-human-eat, human-poor-case-steal-heart' pictures the embarrassed look of someone who is cornered and does not care about a sense of honor or of shame. In other words, it means that poverty will become the root of people to do evils or ills. It is derived from Mencius's *ji1han2qi3dao4xin1* 飢寒起盜心 'hunger and coldness will raise the intention to steal or rob.' Mencius inherited this concept from Confucius's concerns for the poor people. Mencius thinks that poverty is one of the causes of public disorder. Besides, poverty is not only an individual's problem; it is also the crisis of the whole country. So he suggests that the country should pay attention to the problem of poverty. Mencius's sympathy for the people and his reflection upon the country transformed the above mentioned FLE *Hu3e4feng2ren2shi2, ren2qiong2qi3dao4xin1.*

The other FLEs which are related to Confucius and Mencius include *li4mi3lang2li4* 粒米狼戾 'grain-of-rice-wolf-crime = the rice is spread out everywhere, which describes that food is sufficient,' *zi3jiang4lun2yu2* 梓匠輪輿 'catalpa-craftsman-wheel-carriage = a carpenter who makes wooden objects or houses, and a cart worker who makes wheels or carts,' etc.

11.3.1.6. *The Doctrine of Mean*

The Doctrine of Mean is a metaphysical philosophy. It emphasizes avoiding extremes and not to stick to the same old principles. For example, the FLE *qun2yi3fu4shan1* 群蟻附羶 'group-ant-attach-smell of sheep,' which literally means that the ants are attracted by the aroma of the mutton, so they rush up to the mutton in a crowd. It refers to a group of people who are single-minded in their pursuit of wealth. It also means that an outstanding person might invite jealousy and sabotage from the others. By this, it advises people to avoid becoming too outstanding in order to reduce fights and to lead a stable life. In other words, living in commonplace is recommended.

Another example is *wei4wan3xian1tou2su4, ji1ming2kan4zao3 tian1* 未晚先投宿，雞鳴看早天 'yet-late-first-throw-live, chicken-sound-look-early-sky.' It is based on the concept of the Doctrine of Mean and evolved into the attitude of taking precautions or making providence before it is too late. This FLE describes that tourists check in the hostel as soon as possible, before dark to avoid any possible accident during the midnight and that they wake up before the cock crows in order to reach their destination as soon as possible. When it comes to the way to handle something, the concept of the Doctrine of Mean provides a way to try to compare and contrast the options and consequences and then choose the option which has the most benefits in any given circumstance.

The other FLEs that express the Doctrine of Mean include *xiang4chi3fen-2shen1* 象齒焚身 'elephant-tooth-burn-body = an elephant is killed because of its ivory; warning against hoarding wealth,' *chou4rou4lai2ying2* 臭肉來蠅 'smelly-meat-come-fly = greedy people meet each other for benefits,' and *pan1gao1zhi1* 攀高枝 'climb-high-branch = to rise high; go to a better place; put oneself under the patronage of a big wig.'

11.3.2. *German Culture*

Let us now turn to German culture as it is revealed by the collected FLEs. We will talk about the personality, food, livelihood, custom, religion, literature and language contact.

11.3.2.1. *About Personality*

The Germans seem not to take diligence as a virtue. If we look at the examples, *Kein Gras unter den Füßen wachsen lassen* means someone is so busy that he/she 'does not allow grass to grow from the feet.' Though *Bienenfleiß* 'as diligent as a bee' dignifies diligence, it somehow has a negative connotation. *Ochsen* 'do like a cow' and *büffeln* 'do like a water buffalo' both referring to diligence or hard-working at study. They also have negative implications for *ochsen*, which is to study without fully comprehending and *büffeln*, to cram at the last minute. This attitude is contradictory to the Chinese who regard studying as the first priority as shown in *ren2-sheng1-bu4-du2-shu1, huo2-zhe-bu4-ru2-zhu1* 人生不讀書, 活著不如豬 'human-life-no-study-book, live-PART.-no-inferior-pig = a person is worse than a pig if he/she doesn't study.' Chinese parents expect their children to be dedicated to studies. They are worried about those who rust their studies because they are afraid the children will be grouped to a *fang4 niu2 ban1* 放牛班 'put-cattle-class = cowherd class; a class without interference.' However, Germans have a different point of view as suggested in *lebe glücklich, lebe froh, wie der Mops im Haferstroh* 'live-happily, live-gladly, like-the-pug-in-the-oat-straw = live as happy as a sand-boy; live happily' (Hsieh 2006b: 15).

Germans are calm and steady. Thus, this has led them to pursue the attitude of staying stable and working at an appropriate level, that is, not too busy. For instance, the FLE *emsig wie eine Biene* 'busy-as-a-bee = a hard-working person' does not acknowledge the busy working person. A stable working attitude is a common cognition for Germans and is more emphasized by them. Besides, the FLE *Die Arbeit ist kein Frosch, sie hüpft uns nicht davon* 'the-work-is-no-frog, it-hops-us-not-away = there is no hurry to do this work' illustrates that there is no need to be in a rush and hurry in working. The FLE *Arbeit und Schulden sind keine Hasen, sie laufen nicht davon* 'work-and-debts-are-no-hares, they-run-not-away = work and debts are not hares, they do not run away' states that to do a job in a hasty and disorderly manner does not help for the completion of work at all.

11.3.2.2. *About Food*

Food plays an important role in German culture too, and it is also closely linked to the economic activities. Wheat is one of the principal food that is essential in Germany. It has become the symbol of profit as we can see in the FLE *seizen Weizen scheren* 'one's-wheat-shear = to cut one's wheat; to make profits.' It shows that wheat is an important foodstuff and thus is something that the people would like to obtain or earn since it is profitable.

Besides, apples and pears are very common fruits as well as baking materials in Germany. They are popular vehicles taken into FLEs and other fixed expressions. For example, *ich geb dir eine Birnenstiel dafür* 'I-give-you-a-pear stick-for that = it is of no value to me' and (*harte*) *Birnen fortgeben und* (*faule*) *Äpfel wiederbekommen* '(hard)-pears-give away-and-(rotten)-apples-receive = to give away hard pears and receive the rotten apples; to make a bad exchange.' From these examples, it can be inferred that pears and apples are trading objects in the economic activities. Furthermore, they are also seen as the basic standard of measurement. Another example uses food to measure the value of something is *So billig wie Brombeeren* 'as-cheap-as-blackberries = as cheap as dirt; very cheap.' Again, blackberries are also a common fruit and baking material in Germany and they are cheap when in-season. Thus, this usage is created. In comparison with Mandarin, *berries* are rarely seen in our data and this has to do with the underlying conceits of the growing characteristics of the plant.

In German, certain foods are used to indicate the degree of poverty. The most common one is *Bohnen*. For example, in the expression of *kalte Bohnen* 'cold-beans = poor people's food,' beans symbolize the food of the poor, since beans are cheap and not easy to make people full, poor families would have to cook beans as their meals; therefore, beans are symbolized as the standard of measuring the value. Likewise, the FLE *Er ist nicht einer kalten Bohne wert* 'he-is-not-a-cold-bean-worth = he is not worth a cold bean; he is worthless,' the cheapness and the smallness of beans refer to someone not worth a penny. But in the expression *Er hat Bohnen* 'he-has-beans = he is a rich farmer,' a large number of beans signify wealth. Another similar expression is *Der ist so wenig wert wie die Rübe im Kraut* 'he-is-so-little-worth-as-the-turnip-in-cabbage = he is worth as much as a turnip in the cabbage; he does not have much money,' the cabbage is also taken as something to measure the value. Thus, these examples show German culture that is revealed by food-related FLEs.

11.3.2.3. *Livelihood and Custom*

Germany is located in a temperate climate zone. During the winter, the temperature can drop to around 10 degrees centigrade or even lower. Therefore, there is a high demand for wood since to warm oneself is the major concern of everyone, particularly in the old days when electric heating systems were not popular. Thus the FLE *Das ist viel Holz* 'that-is-much-wood = that is much wood; that is a lot of money or a high price.' This FLE has indicated the high value of wood and it can even be seen as money.

The *mit Zitronen handeln* 'with-lemons-deal = to deal with lemons' can be traced to a source from a folk custom. It was spoken in the area of river Rhein back in the year about 1860. The custom was that after the coffin lifters did their job in a funeral, they would each receive a lemon (Röhrich 2001: 1774). This expression is later developed to contain the meaning of 'having expected a different result; having calculated falsely.'

Marriage is another important issue in people's life, and Germans usually compare marriage with economic affairs. For example in the expression of *Freien ist kein Pferdekauf* 'courting-is-no-horse-buy = getting a wife is much more difficult than buying a horse,' it can be seen that in marriage matters, some German men consider marrying a wife to be effort-costing. Meanwhile, marriage can have to do with money, for example, *eine Kuh kaufen* 'a-cow-buy = to buy a cow; seek marriage by offering money.' Another expression, *Elefantenhochzeit* 'elephant wedding = a merger of two big companies; jumbo merger,' though it may not necessarily refer to two companies allying by marriage, the conception of "marriage" is obviously seen.

11.3.2.4. *Religion*

Christians and Catholics constitute one third of the population in Germany. Christmas is the greatest annual festival for the whole country.

The decoration of the Christmas tree is a custom and entertainment that can be done only once a year, so it represents a high value in Christmas, and what makes it more special is that it has been given political and economic meanings. The FLE *Den Christbaum schmücken* 'the-Christmas tree-decorate = to decorate the Christmas tree; political-economic presents given to possible electors in the time before Christmas' states that the Christmas tree is a kind of political-economic present given to possible electors in the time before Christmas.

Many German FLEs are cited from the Bible. For instance, *hundertfältige Frucht tragen* 'hundredfold-fruit-bear = to bear hundredfold fruit; to be successful' is from the Book of Matthew (13: 8). Below are some other examples: *dieses Korn ist auf guten Boden gefallen* 'this-grain-is-from-good-ground-fallen = this seed fell into good ground; this was a worthwhile investment' (Mark 4: 8), *Man soll dem Ochsen, der da drischt, nicht das Maul verbinden* 'one-shall-the-ox, the-there-treading out the grain, not-the-muzzle-tie = Do not muzzle an ox while it is treading out the grain' (Deuteronomy 25: 4), *Wo aber ein Aas ist, da sammeln sich die Adler* 'Wherever there is a carcass, there the vultures will gather' (Matthew 24: 28), *Sie kamen wie ein Heuschreckenschwarm* 'they-came-like-a-grashopper / locust-swarm = a multitude of people carrying away or destroying your wealth' (Exodus 10: 12), *Perlen vor die Säue werfen* 'throw pearls to pigs' (Matthew 7: 6). These well-known passages are widely used in the German language and have become part of German concepts and culture.

11.3.2.5. *Literature and Language Contact*

Some FLEs originate from literature such as *Goldesel, Goldene Gans*, which are from Grimm's Fairy Tales. While *die schlechtesten Früchte sind es nicht, an denen die Wespen nagen* 'the-worst-fruit-are-it-not, at-which-the-wasps-gnaw = the worth of something is not to be despised' is from the mythology of *Tros*. The FLE *Pegasus im Joche* 'pegasus-in-yoke = a poet who has to earn his living in an ordinary job, or by writing for a profane purpose' is written by a well-known German poet, Schiller, and it voices a concern regarding the real-life economic obstacles than can interfere with an individual's artistic hopes: even Pegasus, the flying horse of Greek mythology, needs to work with a yoke attached.

The FLEs also give some of the linguistic sources of German sayings or fixed expressions. We see expressions that can be traced back to Latin, such as *jeder ist des anderen Wolf* 'everybody-is-a-other-wolf = everybody is a wolf to the other one; everybody thinks of his own profit only' which is from Latin *homo homini lupus*. Also *etwas vor die Hunde werfen* 'something-before-the-dogs-cast = to cast something before the dogs; to cast something (valuables) before swine,' meaning something valuable is not appreciated or even recognized by the base and ignorant, is from the Latin *agnos canibus obicientes*. In addition, FLEs also exhibit the active language contact of German with other languages, such as *Papiertiger* 'paper tiger = a person or organization that looks strong and dangerous in theory, but is weak in reality' and its Mandarin counterpart *zhi3lao3hu3* 紙老虎 'paper-tiger.' Both have the same morphological structure and the same metaphorical meaning. Further, the German FLEs below are the result of contact with Spanish (Richter 2011): *Es ist schwer, einem so treuen Gefährten wie einen Hund zu finden; hat ein Armer ihn aufgezogen, so wird er keinem Reichen je folgen* 'it-is-heavy, a-so-faithful-companion-as-a-dog-to-find; has-a-poor-it-raised, so-will-it-no-rich-ever-follow = it is difficult to find as faithful companion as a dog; if a poor person has raised it, it would not ever follow the rich,' *Von seiner Würde abweichen ist wie sein Pferd gegen einen Esel tauschen* 'from-one's-dignity-deviate-is-like-one's-horse-against-an-ass-dip = to deviate one's dignity is like exchanging one's horse for an ass' are Mongolian proverbs, too. And *Ein auf Kredit gekauftes Schwein grunzt das ganze Jahr* 'a-on-credit-bought-pig-grunts-the-whole-year = a pig which is bought on credit grunts the whole year.'

We have talked about some cultural features revealed by Mandarin and German FLEs separately, but there are also similar cultural attributes in both societies. Section 11.1 mentions that in both Mandarin and German, the idea of 'poor' is expressed more than that of 'rich.' This has its cultural factors too, and in this case, similar cultural attributes in Chinese and German societies. We will now talk about the traditional way of thinking and history in these two cultures. First of all, both cultures believe that to discuss wealth and riches, especially to wish for it or openly plan for it, is to tempt fate, and possibly draw bad luck upon oneself, whereas to discuss poverty is humbler, and therefore perceived as safer. Therefore, people tend to express their poorness, insufficiency, and problems that they encounter in their daily life through objects around them like plants and animals. As Lévi-Strauss (1963) states, plants are nature's material for mankind's languages. Atran (1990: 219) shows that plant names are convenient choices for describing human society. Hsieh (2009a: 275–) believes that this is true with animals too. Rich data for the current research is thus available.

Furthermore, traditional teachings of the respective societies also play a role. Confucius's ways are taught in Taiwanese schools. Confucius taught that *fu4gui4yu2wo3ru2fu2yun2* 富貴於我如浮雲 'richness is nothing but just something which is easy come, easy go.' It is not documented whether such a concept is practiced in Taiwanese society, yet it is a teaching that people learn. In German culture, Christian teachings have imbued people with the belief that Christians have a superior sense in terms of morality. Poorness is nothing to be ashamed of. Jesus was frugal and not rich. People would actually be getting closer to Jesus and be heading in the right direction of the Christian core when in poverty. And Jesus taught that "blessed are the poor". Though the Confucian system of belief in Taiwan and the Christian teaching in Germany are not all the same, the essence of treating poorness and richness is the same.

On the other hand, due to geographical and climatical differences between Asia and Europe, different plant vehicles are used in expressing various financial concepts. For example, *bamboo, fern* and *rice*, as in the FLEs *qiao1zhu2gang4* 敲竹槓 'knock-bamboo-pole = to take advantage of someone when you have discovered a vital weakness of theirs,' *wei2jue2* 薇蕨 'fern-brake = wild plant that poor people pluck for eating,' and *yu2mi3zhi1xiang1* 魚米之鄉 'fish-rice-of-town = a land of fish and rice; a land of plenty (example 7),' arose because these are plants that can be found in China easily. But in German, *Pfifferling* 'chanterelle,' *Petersilie* 'parsley' and *Brombeere* 'blackberry' are used in FLEs such as *nicht einen Pfifferling* 'not-a-chanterelle = not a chanterelle; description of stinginess,' *sie verkauft Petersilie* 'she-sells-parsley = she sells parsley; she is a wallflower; she has not found a partner at the ball' and *so billig wie Brombeeren* 'as-cheap-as-blackberries = very cheap.'

11.4. Suggestions for Further Study

This chapter presents FLEs in the form of embodiment. After categorizing the data, we present them by means of linguistic financial judgment and hierarchy of concepts. In the final portion, this section discusses the cultural messages that the FLEs can reveal about the societies that use them.

We hope to provide a broader view of the study of FLEs and present rich FLEs in embodiment in order to invite further research in this direction. Further study can work on questions such as: Do certain animal and plant vehicles tend to be used to express certain financial concepts (e.g., birds more for richness, wild animals more for poverty)? Additionally, which financial concepts tend not to be expressed with animal and plant vehicles?

In the above we suggested that it is possible that certain metaphorical vehicles or certain semantic features (such as FLEs, sports-related expressions, and topics in entertainment) will draw upon different types of underlying conceits to form fixed expressions. A more systematic research is welcomed for a more solid conclusion. Finally, other life forms related vehicles such body-part terms (hands, eyes, etc.), emotions (anger, happiness, etc.) are also interesting issues worth exploring with the data that we have presented.

CHAPTER TWELVE

CONCLUSION

Shelley Ching-yu Hsieh

We have now come to the closing of this book. The promise of this book was to show rich FLEs in both Mandarin and German. We hope we have given an interesting perspective on the explicative power of financial expressions, showing how they reveal deep insights into a culture's symbolic value system, serving as living metaphors in that they are language we use every day and that are involved with various linguistic vehicles that are related to the real world, such as gold, the stock market, animals, and plants. In the conclusion, we will first summarize the findings of the research performed, and highlight the possible contributions of this book.

The goal of Part I is to investigate how the FLEs in Mandarin are perceived and evaluated from cognitive and cultural perspectives by the Mandarin speakers in Taiwan. Chapter 3 focuses on *huang2jin1* 黃金 'gold' and our results show that *huang2jin1* is the SD that exemplifies eight TDs: (1) The Chinese emperor, (2) solidity, (3) eternity, (4) words, (5) literary works, (6) excellence, (7) perfection, and (8) opportunity. The SD-TD pairing of *huang2jin1* is quality-oriented.

Chapter 4 shows that the metaphorical extensions of *jin1qian2* 金錢 'money.' *Jin1qian2* in the SD-TD pairings is the TD, which is contributed to by nine concrete objects: (1) supernatural power, (2) humans, (3) prey, (4) plants, (5) water, (6) machines, (7) commodities, (8) medicine and (9) dirty objects.

Chapter 5 has *yin2* 銀 'silver' as its focus. In this chapter, silver is examined in terms of *yin2* fixed expressions and metaphorical clusters. Interestingly, though the data which are analyzed are of two different types, *yin2* fixed expressions and metaphorical clusters, both have similar metaphorical mappings; that is, both of them can logically be categorized into five groupings: humans, animals, plants, objects, and natural physical things.

In Chapter 6, we focus on the conceptualization of economically disadvantaged conditions in the form of three quasi-synonyms, *pin2qiong2* 貧窮 'poor,' *pin2* 貧 'poor' and *qiong2* 窮 'poor' in a newspaper corpus from a cognitive-emergent perspective. The results show that Mandarin speakers' economic reactions transpire by means of philosophical ontology. However, though *pin2qiong2* 貧窮 'poor,' *pin2* 貧 'poor' and *qiong2* 窮 'poor' are derived from the same economic concept of 'poverty,' they have different metaphorical characteristics. For instance, *qiong2* is more widely used to describe people's impoverished situations than *pin2*, and *pin2qiong2* has fewer variations in its parts of speech.

In Chapters 7 and 8, we present research on stock market jargon. We first show that verbs are the preferred syntactic category in the SD of *gu3shi4* 股市 'stock market.' Further examining *gu3* 股 'stock' and *shi4* 市 'market' individually, we see that *gu3* tends to be collocated with the fields of food, natural phenomena, body parts of animals, value, objects and disease; whereas, *shi4* tends to be collocated with the fields of animals and orientation. In addition, the metaphor chain can be produced by the opposite mapping domain, and the different TDs may use the same SD for the same reason, while a single TD must use different SDs for different reasons. The mapping strategies contribute to our understanding of how conceptual mappings are structured by stock market jargon.

The goal of Part II is to turn the focus to a broader view of FLEs in which we collect and analyze comparative studies contrasting German and Mandarin. To study three German verbs, Chapter 9 focuses on newspaper reports. Taking data from the German *Corpus Search, Management and Analysis System* (COSMAS II) and *Deutscher Wortschatz*, the collocations of the verbs *kaufen* (buy), *verkaufen* (sell), and *bezahlen* (pay) are investigated. Data from Mandarin are used as a comparison. The results showed modern German and Taiwan commercial activities, cultural values, and underlying social organization. For example, German *Auto* enjoys the highest frequency (5.17%) in German commercial activity, while food trading is the most popular (6.77%) in Mandarin. The importance of car and food in the respective societies is exhibited.

Chapter 10 shows that German *Geschäft* and Mandarin *sheng1yi4* 生意 reflect fundamentally different attitudes towards business. Germans do business with the philosophy of racial harmony, which is shown in the frequency of the notion of "union/cooperation," which is the most frequent SD in attributing *Geschäft*, and that "space" and "life cycle" are the salient SDs that Germans prefer to use. Germans conduct business on the basis of emphasizing cooperation, especially when compared with *sheng1yi4*, which shows that 'business' in Mandarin is viewed as a solid object because it has size, it moves, and it can be touched.

In Chapter 11, we present the data with the FLEs ('rich,' 'poor,' 'job,' 'worth,' etc.) and animal (*cat, swan,* etc.) and plant vehicles (*rice, bean,* etc.). After a brief comparison between Mandarin and German, we found the linguistic financial judgment and underlying conceits of the FLEs. Also the hierarchy of concepts and cultural features given in the data were displayed. We show the rich data in this respect, and hope that it invites further studies not only of FLEs, but also research concerning embodiment.

This study has made the following contributions: we combine Mandarin with Western linguistic application, compare Mandarin and German, show cultural attributes, benefit Mandarin learning, add linguistic or cultural perspectives to the MMF series, and make observations about abundant and up-to-date linguistic phenomena.

First, we present a number of cultural attributes. Part I of this book focuses on the Mandarin speaking in Taiwan. Most Taiwanese people have their origin in Mainland China; therefore, the FLEs point to values and cultural assumptions of not only the culture in the Mandarin speaking society of Taiwan, but also Chinese culture in general. We revealed that cultural features, such as the Chinese emperor, one's promise, and one's literary works, are highly valued, as suggested by the study on *huang2jin1* 'gold' in Chapter 3. On the other hand, Mandarin speakers tend to use stock-market jargon to describe marriage negatively. We thus see that the Mandarin speakers in Taiwan lack confidence in the marriage relationship as they do in the bearish stock market.

Further, the use of FLEs reflects the eager pursuit of money, profits, and suggests the assumption that there will be a bright future in Taiwan. For instance, we see that *jin1qian2* is perceived not just positively, but powerfully, as 60% of the metaphorical expressions are mapped from the upper levels of the hierarchy in the GCB Metaphor (Lakoff and Turner 1989), such as supernatural power (13%) or humans (37%). Similarly, stock market jargon is utilized to describe people's value as positive. In line with the above, in FORTUNE TELLING AS STOCK MARKET, the orientational metaphorical concept of MORE IS UP is highlighted. The above reveal that in the culture of a Mandarin speaking society, such as Taiwan, fortune telling tends to involve positive advice, and guides people towards the brighter side of life. Even the metaphorical analysis of *pin2qiong2* in Chapter 6 indicates people's determination to fight against the bad results of a bad economy.

When we come to Part II, different cultural viewpoints towards FLEs are investigated as we analyze the conceptual metaphors applied by

Germans and Taiwanese. Germans put more emphasis on humanism and cooperation, whereas Mandarin speakers see business as an object (Chapter 10). Meanwhile, Chapter 11 reveals specific Mandarin cultural features expressed by the FLEs in terms of embodiment, such as the concepts of family, food, face, numbers, the teachings of Confucius and Mencius, and the Doctrine of the Mean. In addition, German cultural attitudes concerning personality, food, livelihood, custom, religion, literature and language contact were displayed.

Second, we compared Mandarin and German, showing some of the linguistic differences while also revealing similarities. For example, the element POSSESSION reveals not only the objects that Germans buy, sell, and pay for nowadays, but also the values of the people. The Germans are law-abiding, and they call on reason when purchasing. Whereas the Chinese collocations reveal a conservative mentality and an adherence to traditional literati thought that originated from feudal society (Chapter 9). In Chapter 11 we indicate that the expressions of mythical animals in German are unproductive and have the lowest percentage of occurrence. Related examples like *Drachendollar* 'dragon-dollar,' and *Pegasus im Joche* 'Pegasus-in-yoke = a poet who has to earn his living in an ordinary job.' Somehow, all have a foreign touch, as they either refer to Chinese currency, or are of Greek origin. However, mythical animals play extraordinary roles both in legend and in language. The Chinese consider the dragon their ancestor; the phoenix is capable of bringing fortune, and the unicorn can even bring sons, as the following examples indicate: *long2dechuan2ren2* 龍的傳人 'dragon's-descendant = descendant of dragon; Chinese people,' *feng4huang2lai2yi2* 鳳凰來儀 'phoenix-come-appearance = arrival of phoenixes; an auspicious omen.' And *qi2lin2song4zi3* 麒麟送子 '*qi2lin2* delivers sons.'

On the other hand, through the comparison between Mandarin and German, it is obvious that rich linguistic data are available in our daily-life conversation, whether they be FLEs or animal and plant embodiment expressions. Take embodiment expressions as an example: as Lévi-Strauss (1963) indicates, plants are nature's material for mankind's languages. Atran (1990: 219) shows that plant names are convenient choices for describing human society. Hsieh (2009a: 275–) further believes that this is true with animals.

Third, we revealed interesting linguistic findings. For example, metaphorical mappings conform to people's perceptions. That is, it is the most salient property that is perceived as the most notable. For instance, *jin1qian2, huang2jin1,* and *gu3shi4* have different characteristics and uses in daily-life language, which has led to different conceptualizations. The mappings between *huang2jin1* and its TDs are quality-based for its value, and chemical attributes are salient in people's perception. *Jin1qian2*, however, is function-based, for it is a tool in the market exchange, and it is the function that is salient and therefore is applied in their metaphorical use. A similar linguistic phenomenon is observed in stock market jargon for the SD-TD mappings are still function-oriented.

We also found that the conceptual mappings produced from the opposite mapping domains may share the same underlying concepts. For example, EMOTION AS STOCK MARKET and STOCK MARKET AS OCEAN WATER share the same underlying metaphorical concepts of up and down. Meanwhile, different TDs may use the same SD for the same reason; for example, EMOTION AS STOCK MARKET and AGE AS STOCK MARKET are also structured by the reasoning of up and down. As opposed to the above-mentioned strategy, a single TD must use different SDs for different reasons, as in STOCK MARKET AS WAR and STOCK MARKET AS PERSON, which share the structural logic of competition and life cycle.

Also, different domains can organize the vertical hierarchy of the GCB Metaphor in different ways, but may share the same conceptualization direction. For example, the SD of the stock market and the TD of *jin1qian2* and *yin2* structure the vertical hierarchy of the GCB Metaphor with different levels, but share the same conceptualization direction—a higher SD to a lower TD.

In addition, people's abstract reasoning conforms to cognitive economy, by which the most information is perceived with the least effort or within the least amount of time as obviously shown in the prevailing use of personification, as we can see from *JIN1QIAN2* AS HUMAN, YIN2 AS FARMER, HUMAN AS STOCK MARKET, and STOCK MARKET AS A PERSON. This is a common tendency because it eases our cognitive process and allows us to save more cognitive effort. This strategy is frequently utilized in linguistic performance and communication for people to utter and interpret information using egocentric reference systems (Waller, Lippa and Richardson 2007) and because people have the inclination to simplify information (Ungerer and Schmid 2006; Tsao, Tsai and Liu 2001; Grundy 2000).

Moreover, we found in Chapter 9 that from observing the context of the three verbs, there is room to modify the commercial transaction frame proposed by Fillmore and Atkins (1992). The concept and elements in the frame are changed from the concept of a financial and commercial transaction to a description of the organizational structure of human society.

In other words, these verbs originate from the concept of financial and commercial transaction, but focus on describing the organizational structures of human society, such as group, organization, and society, operating under rational economic behaviors. That is, these verbs are, on the surface, concerned with economics, but actually they return to a description of the organizational structure of human society.

Chapter 10 exhibits that *Geschäft* collocations illustrate various uses of metaphors in the contrast between languages. The most salient SDs of *Geschäft* in German are "union/cooperation", and "operation", whereas they are quality, and situation/consequence in Mandarin. Space and life cycle are the special SDs of *Geschäft*, whereas size and movement are those of *sheng1yi4* in Mandarin. Chapter 11 shows that in both Mandarin and German, most expressions register at the semantic level, and fewer at the linguistic and pragmatic levels. Furthermore, in Mandarin, the linguistic level, 38 expressions are found in the categories 'money' and 'coin.' They are the most salient financial features that tend to be expressed linguistically. Moreover, 17 expressions are found in 'buy' and 'sell,' but only 7 expressions in 'poor.' Whereas in German, for the linguistic level, 20 expressions are found in 'gold' and 'silver.' The second most salient financial feature, with 15 expressions, is related to 'money,' 'coins,' or 'cash' for this level. The rich meaning behind the data may inspire linguistic majors to conduct related linguistic research.

Fourth, the information revealed by this book could help inform pedagogy and contribute to language learning, especially Mandarin learning. Part I gives a picture of how FLEs in Mandarin are perceived and discloses that the speakers tend to have humans as the SDs that depict some abstract ideas. For example, it is the quality of *huang2jin1*, the function of *jin1qian2*, and the function of *gu3shi4*, that are the most salient attributes influencing their linguistic extensions. The three quasi-synonyms, *pin2qiong2*, *pin2* and *qiong2* even suggest that Mandarin speakers' economic reactions transpire by means of philosophical ontology. Based on the above, it can be seen that there is a pattern in language learning. These patterns will help learners' long-term memory when learning Mandarin.

In Part II, the contrast between German and Taiwan Mandarin enables students' understanding through collocations that reveal how these two groups of people perceive FLEs. Becoming aware of the dissimilarities in the SDs of these two examined languages helps students compare and contrast them.

Fifth, we add linguistic perspective to the MMF series. The MMF series embraces outstanding works that show the endeavors of energetic researchers and possibilities in history, literature, economic studies, Sociology, etc. under the international project *Monies, Markets, and Finance in China and East Asia, 1600–1900: Local, Regional, National, and International Dimensions*. The present book, part of the research outcome of the sub-project No. 54, titled *A Cognitive Semantic and Pragmatic Study of Mandarin Chinese, Taiwanese and German Fixed Expressions of Money, Wealth and Poverty* is one section of the main project *Monies, Markets, and Finance in China and East Asia, 1600–1900: Local, Regional, National, and International Dimensions* provides endeavors of a different type, and shows the possibility and potentiality of linguistic study in the financial economic field.

Finally, we apply Western linguistic methods and theories to Mandarin. Most of the Mandarin linguistic data in this book are analyzed in terms of theories proposed by western linguists. On one hand, we present many examples of linguistic usage, especially financial linguistic usages, that had never previously been submitted to linguistic analysis. On the other hand, we show the validity of linguistic theories that western linguists have put forth and support them in a way that demonstrates that not only do their approaches work in western languages, but also in Mandarin. Linguistic analysis can be fun and accessible in every-day life language. The linguistic uses are interesting, for example, *huang2niu2* 黃牛 that literally means 'yellow cattle,' actually refers to someone's cheating behavior. The *guan1cai2ben3* 棺材本 'coffin-capital' is the bottom line capital that one has. *Jin1tou2nao3* 金頭腦 'gold-head-brain' refers to intelligent or brilliant people. *Ta4shang4yin2he2* 踏上銀河 'step-on-silver-river' means being in show business, and *shui3jiao3gu3* 水餃股 in Chinese is 'dumpling-stock' but suggests worthless penny stocks, etc. Our research not only connects western linguistic theories with Mandarin data, but the findings also show the compatibility of some linguistic theories, such as that of the CMM and semantic frame (Chapter 10).

Since the economic crisis has spread worldwide, financial-related expressions have become a popular research topic in academic fields. This book's exploration of FLEs in Mandarin and in German reveals that language discloses human cognition and culture as well as various perceptions of the world. By examining ample data, we see Mandarin speaker's values, perceptions and cultural modes and expect to benefit Chinese linguistic research, Chinese learning, and cultural understanding.

REFERENCES

Agar, Michael. 1994. *Language Shock. Understanding the Culture of Conversation.* New York: William Morrow.

Ahrens, Kathleen, Chung, Siaw-Fong and Huang, Chu-Ren (安可思, 鍾曉芳, 黃居仁). 2003. Conceptual Metaphors: Ontology-based Representation and Corpora Driven MPs. In the *Proceedings of the ACL Workshop on the Lexicon and Figurative Language*: 35–41.

——. 2004. From Lexical Semantics to Conceptual Metaphors: MP Verification with WordNet and SUMO. In the *Proceedings of 5th Chinese Lexical Semantics Workshop (CLSW–5)*: 99–106.

——. 2002. When Love Is Not Digested: Underlying Reasons for Source to Target Domain Pairings in the Contemporary Theory of Metaphor. In the *Proceedings of the First Cognitive Linguistics Conference*: 273–302.

Alejo, Rafael. 2010. Where does the Money Go? An Analysis of the Container Metaphor in Economics: The Market and the Economy. *Journal of Pragmatics* 42(4): 1137–1150.

Alsleben, Brigitte and Scholze-Stubenrecht, Werner. (Eds.). 2002. *Duden (Band 11). Redewendungen*. Mannheim, Wien: Dudenverlag.

Atran, Scott. 1990. *Cognitive Foundations of Natural History: Towards an Anthropology of Science*. New York: Cambridge University Press.

Boers, Frank and Demecheleer, Murielle. 1997. A Few Metaphorical Models in (Western) Economic Discourse. In Wolf-Andreas Liebert, Gisela Redeker and Linda Waugh (Eds.). *Discourse and Perspective in Cognitive Linguistics*: 115–129. Amsterdam: John Benjamins.

Boers, Frank. 2000a. Enhancing Metaphoric Awareness in Specialised Reading. *English for Specific Purposes* 19(2): 137–147.

——. 2000b. Metaphor Awareness and Vocabulary Retention. *Applied Linguistics* 21(4): 553–571.

Bradford DeLong, James. 1999. Thinking Like an Economist. Retrived 15 Diciembre, 2006. from http://econl61.berkeley.edu/Teaching_folder/Econ_101b_F99/Drafts/Chs_teach.html.

Carroll, David W. 2004. *Psychology of Language*. California: Wadsworth.

Charteris-Black, Jonathan and Ennis, Timothy. 2001. A Comparative Study of Metaphor in Spanish and English Financial Reporting. *English for Specific Purposes* 20: 249–266.

——. 2001. The Comparative Study of Metaphor in Spanish And English Financial Reporting. *English for Specific Purposes* 19: 249–266.

Charteris-Black, Jonathan and Musolff, Andreas. 2003. 'Battered Hero' or 'Innocent Victim'? A Comparative Study of Metaphors for Euro Trading in British and German Financial Reporting. *English for Specific Purposes* 22: 153–176.

Charteris-Black, Jonathan. 2000. Metaphor and Vocabulary Teaching in ESP Economics. *English for Specific Purposes* 19(2): 149–165.

——. 2004. *Corpus Approaches to Critical Metaphor Analysis*. New York: Palgrave MacMillan.

Chen, Keh-Jiann and Huang, Chu-Ren (陳克健, 黃居仁) (Eds.). 2001. *Academia Sinica Balanced Corpus of Mandarin Chinese*, Version 4.0. Taipei: Academia Sinica.

Chen, Kuo-Hong (陳國弘). 1991. *The Origin of Idioms* (成語源). Tainan: Guo Hong Bookstore.

Chung, Ming-Wai (鍾明慧). 2004. *A Study of Puns in the Modern Chinese Language*. M.A. Thesis of School of Chinese. Hong Kong: The University of Hong Kong.

Chung, Siaw-Fong (鍾曉芳). 2008. Cross-linguistic Comparisons of the MARKET Metaphors. *Corpus Linguistics and Linguistic Theory* 4(2): 141–175.

Chung, Siaw-Fong, Ahrens, Kathleen and Huang, Chu-Ren (鍾曉芳, 安可思, 黃居仁). 2003. ECONOMY IS A PERSON: A Chinese-English Corpora and Ontological-based

Comparison Using the Conceptual Mapping Model. In the *Proceedings of the 15th ROCLING Conference for the Association for Computational Linguistics and Chinese Language Processing*: 87–110.
——. 2004. RECESSION: Defining Source Domains through WordNet and SUMO. In the *Proceedings of the Linguistic Society of Korea (LSK) International Conference* 2: 43–52.
——. 2005. Source Domains as Concept Domains in Metaphorical Expressions. *Computational Linguistics and Chinese Language Processing* 10(4): 553–570.
Chung, Siaw-Fong, Ahrens, Kathleen and Sung, Ya-Hui (鍾曉芳, 安可思, 宋雅惠). 2003. STOCK MARKETS AS OCEAN WATER: A Corpus-based, Comparative Study of Mandarin Chinese, English and Spanish. In the *Proceedings of the 17th Pacific Asia Conference on Language, Information and Computational (PACLIC)*: 124–133.
Chung, Siaw-Fong, Huang, Chu-Ren and Ahrens, Kathleen (鍾曉芳, 黃居仁, 安可思). 2003. Economy is a Transportation Device: Contrastive Representation of Source Domain Knowledge in English and Chinese. In the *Proceedings of the Special Session for the International Conference on Natural Language Processing and Knowledge Engineering (NLP-KE): Upper Ontology and Natural Language Processing (UONLP)*: 790–796.
Committee of Official Language Promotion (Ed.). 1994. *Chinese Mandarin Online Dictionary* (3rd edition). Taipei: Ministry of Education.
Corning, Peter A. 1995. Evolutionary Economics: Metaphor or Unifying Paradigm? *Journal of Social and Evolutionary Systems* 18(4): 421–35.
Council for Economic Planning and Development. 2006. Second: The Contemporary Economic Situation. *Taiwan New Economic NewsLetter* 1620: 12–76.
Deignan, Alice and Potter, Liz. 2004. A Corpus Study of Metaphors and Metonyms in English and Italian. *Journal of Pragmatics* 36: 1231–1252.
Egelhoff, William and Frese, Erich. 2009. Understanding Managers' Preferences for Internal Markets Versus Business Planning: A Comparative Study of German and U.S. Managers. *Journal of International Management* 15(1): 77–91.
Eubanks, Philip. 1999. Conceptual Metaphors as a Rhetorical Response. *Written Communication* 16(2): 171–199.
European Financial Stability Facility. 2011. *CFSF Newsletter* 11(3): 1–2.
Fauconnier, Gilles and Turner Mark. 1998. Conceptual Integration Networks. *Cognitive Science: A Multidisciplinary Journal* 22(2): 133–187.
Fillmore, Charles J. and Atkins, Beryl T. 1992. Toward a Frame-Based Lexicon: The Semantics of Risk and Its Neighbors. In: Lehrer Adrienne and Eva Feder Kittay (Eds.). *Frames, Fields and Contrasts*: 75–102. Hillsdale, New Jersey: Erlbaum.
Fillmore, Charles J., Paul Kay and Mary C. O'Connor. 1988. Regularity and Idiomaticity in Grammatical Construction: the Case of Let Alone. *Language* 64(3): 501–538.
Fischer, Wolfram. 1987. Europaeische Wirtschafts- und Sozialgeschichte vom Ersten Weltkrieg bis zur Gegenwart. *Handbuch der Europaeischen Wirtschafts- und Sozialgeschichte* 6. Stuttgart: Klett-Cotta.
Fluck, Hans-Rüdiger, Li, Zaize and Zhao, Qichang (Eds.). 1984. *Kontrastive Linguistik Deutsch/Chinesisch*. Heidelberg: Groos.
Fromkin, Victoria and Rodman, Robert. 1998. *An Introduction to Language*. Boston: Thomson Wadsworth.
Fukuda, Kosei. 2009. A Comparative Study of Metaphors Representing the US and Japanese Economies. *Journal of Pragmatics* 41(9): 1693–1702.
Gelman, Susan A. and O'Reilly, Anne Watson. 1988. Children's Inductive Inferences within Superordinate Categories: The Role of Language and Category Structure. *Child Development* 59: 876–887.
Gibbs, Raymond W. 1999. Taking Metaphor out of Our Heads and Putting It into the Cultural World. In: Raymond W. Gibbs and Gerard Steen (Eds.). *Metaphor in Cognitive Linguistics*: 145–166. Amsterdam: John Benjamins.
——. 2002. A New Look at Literal Meaning in Understanding What Is Said and Implicated. *Journal of Pragmatics* 34: 457–486.

Gibbs, Raymond W. and O'Brien, Jennifer E. 1990. Idioms and Mental Imagery: The Metaphorical Motivation for Idiomatic Meaning. *Cognition* 36: 35–68.

Goatly, Andrew. 2000. *Critical Reading and Writing: An Introductory Course Book*. Routledge: Taylor and Francis.

Goddard, Cliff. 1998. *Semantic Analysis: A Practical Introduction*. New York: Oxford University Press.

Gong, Shu-Ping (龔書萍). 2009. Mapping Principles and Conceptual Metaphors: A Corpus-Based Study on the *Idea* Metaphors. In the *Proceedings of the Second International Conference on Multi Development and Application of Language and Linguistics*: 33–34.

Grundy, Peter. 2000. *Doing Pragmatics*. New York: Oxford University Press.

Halliday, Michael Alexander Kirkwood. 1985/1994. *An Introduction to Functional Grammar*. London: Edward Arnold.

Henderson, Willie. 1982. Metaphor in Economics. *Economics* 18(4): 147–157.

——. 1994. Metaphor and Economics. In: Roger E. Backhouse (Ed.). *New Directions in Economic Methodology*: 343–367. London, New York: Routledge.

——. 2000. Metaphor, Economics and ESP: Some Comments. *English for Specific Purpose* 19: 167–173.

Herrigel, Gary. 1996. *Industrial Constructions: The Sources of German Industrial Power*. Cambridge: Cambridge University Press.

Hong, I-Fang (洪藝芳). 2001. "Shijing Chengyu de Fazhan Bianhua" 詩經成語的發展變化 (The Development of the Idioms in Classic of Poetry). *Zhongguo wenhua yuekan* 中國文化月刊 (Chinese Culture Monthly) 158: 19–38.

Hopper, Paul. 1987. Emergent Grammar. *Berkeley Linguistics Society* 13: 139–157.

Horn, George M. 2003. Idioms, Metaphors and Syntactic Mobility. *Journal of Linguistics* 39: 245–273.

Hsieh, Shelley Ching-Yu (謝菁玉). 2001. *Tiermetaphern im Modernen Chinesischen und Deutschen: Eine Vergleichende Semantische und Soziolinguistische Studie* (Animal Metaphors in Modern Chinese and German: A Comparative Semantic and Sociolinguistic Study). Doctoral Dissertation. Tübingen, Germany: Eberhard Karls University of Tübingen.

Hsieh, Shelley Ching-Yu and Chiu, Yuan-Ling (謝菁玉, 邱苑伶). 2005. Plant Fixed Expressions in Mandarin Chinese and English: A Cross-cultural Study on 'Trees.' In the *2004 Proceedings of Language Education International Conference*: 63–83.

Hsieh, Shelley Ching-Yu and Huang, Hsin-Mei (謝菁玉, 黃欣梅). 2008. A Cognitive Semantic and Pragmatic Study of Mandarin Chinese and German Fixed Expressions of Money, Wealth & Poverty. *Workshop on Monies, Markets and Finance in China and East Asia*. Heidelberg: Heidelberg University.

Hsieh, Shelley Ching-Yu and Kirschner, Roland (謝菁玉, 羅南德). 2007. Kultur, Denken und Sprache: Ein Vergleich der Drachen- und Phönixmetaphern im Chinesischen und Deutschen (Culture, Thinking and Language: A Study of mythical Animals in Mandarin Chinese and German). *Tamkang Journal of Humanities and Social Sciences* 29: 107–130.

Hsieh, Shelley Ching-yu and Kolodkina, Elena. 2011. Emotion Expressed with Eyes and Hands in Three Languages. In Christina Alm-Arvius, Nils-Lennart Johannesson and David C. Minugh (Eds.). *Selected Papers from the 2008 Stockholm Metaphor Festival*, 155–78.

Hsieh, Shelley Ching-Yu, Lien, Chinfa and Meier, Sebastian (謝菁玉, 連金發, Sebastian Meier). 2005. Compositionality in Plant Fixed Expressions. In: Edouard Machery, Markus Werning and Gerhard Schurz (Eds.). *The Compositionality of Meaning and Content. Volume II: Applications to Linguistics, Psychology, and Neuroscience*: 107–121. Frankfurt, Paris, Lancaster: Ontos Verlag.

Hsieh, Shelley Ching-Yu. 2006a. A Corpus Based Study on Animal Expressions in Mandarin Chinese and German *Journal of Pragmatics* 38(12): 2206–2222.

——. 2006b. German Culture in German Emotion Expressions: A Study of Animal and Plant Fixed Expressions *Studies in International Cultures* 2(1): 1–24.

——. 2007. A Diachronic Study of Dragon Lexemes in Mandarin Chinese: Lexical Change and Semantic Development. *Intergrams: Studies in Languages & Literatures* 8(1): 1–13.
Hsieh, Shelley Ching-Yu. 2009a. *Embodiment in Languages (1): Human, Animal and Plant Expressions*. Taipei: Bookman.
——. 2009b. Lebewesen und finanzwirtschaftliche Verben im Deutschen. *Lernen und Lehren: Deutsche Sprache, Literatur und Kultur*. Taipei: Fu Jen University.
——. 2009c. Was bedeutet *arm* im Chinesischen und im Deutschen. *2009 Conference of Department of English Language and Literature, SCU (Language, Literature and Culture: Integration/ Estrangement)*. Taipei: Soochow University.
Huang, Hsin-Mei (黃欣梅). 2009. *The Metaphorical Interpretation of the Financial Linguistic Expression Jin 金 'Money; Capital; Gold' in Taiwan Mandarin*. M.A. Thesis of Department of Foreign Languages and Literature. Tainan, Taiwan: National Cheng Kung University.
Huang, Hsin-Mei and Hsieh, Shelley Ching-Yu (黃欣梅, 謝菁玉). 2008. A Cognitive Linguistics Investigation into the Metaphorical and Metonymic Expressions of the Financial Word *Jin* 金 'Gold.' In the *Conference of the 11th International Symposium on Chinese Languages and Linguistics (IsCLL-11)*. Hsinchu, Taiwan: National Chiao Tung University.
Huang, Hsin-Mei and Hsieh, Shelley Ching-Yu. 2009. Taiwan Mandarin Speakers' Underlying Perception of Money: The Metaphorical Extensions of *Jin1 Qian2*. *Tamkang Journal of Humanities and Social Sciences* 38: 51–70.
Huang, Shuan-Fan (黃宣範). 1995. Emergent Lexical Semantics. In the *Proceedings of the Second International Symposium on Languages in Taiwan*: 358–385.
Institut für Deutsche Sprache. 2008. *Corpus Search, Management and Analysis System* (COSMAS II), Version 3.9. Mannheim: Institut für Deutsche Sprache, 1994–2008.
Johnson, Mark. 1987. *The Body in the Mind: The Bodily Basis of Meaning, Imagination and Reason*. Chicago: Chicago University Press.
Kessing, Roger. 1981. *Cultural Anthropology: A Contemporary Perspective*. New York: Holt, Rinehart and Winston.
Khalil, Elias L. 1998. The Five Career of the Biological Metaphor in Economic Theory. *Journal of Socio-economic* 27(1): 29–52.
Klein, Thoralf. 2007. *Geschichte Chinas von 1800 bis zur Gegenwart*. Paderborn: Ferdinand Schoningh Verlag.
Koestler, Arthur. 1964. *The Act of Creation*. New York: John Wiley.
Kövecses, Zoltán. 2000. *Metaphor and Emotion: Language, Culture and Body in Human Feeling*. Cambridge: Cambridge University Press.
Kövecses, Zoltán. 2002. *Metaphor: A Practical Introduction*. Oxford: Oxford University Press.
——. 2005. *Metaphor in Culture: Universality and Variation*. Cambridge: Cambridge University Press.
Kramsch, Claire. 1998. *Language and Culture*. New York: Oxford University Press.
Lakoff, George and Johnson, Mark. 1980. *Metaphors We Live By*. Chicago: Chicago University Press.
——. 1999. *Philosophy in the Flesh: The Embodied Mind and Its Challenge to Western Thought*. New York: Basics Books.
——. 2003/2006. *Metaphors We Live By*. Chicago, London: University of Chicago Press.
——. 1989. *More than Cool Reason. A Field Guide to Poetic Metaphor*. Chicago: University of Chicago Press.
Lakoff, George. 1987. *Women, Fire and Dangerous Things: What Categories Reveal about the Mind*. Chicago: University of Chicago Press.
——. 1990. The Invariance Hypothesis: Is Abstract Reason Based on Image-Schemas? *Cognitive Linguistics* 1: 39–74.
——. 1992. *The Contemporary Theory of Metaphor: Metaphor and Thought* (2nd edition). Cambridge: Cambridge University Press.
——. 1993. *The Contemporary Theory of Metaphor*. In: Andrew Ortony (Ed.). *Metaphor and Thought* (2nd edition): 202–251. Cambridge: Cambridge University Press.

Lea, Stephen E.G. and Webley, Paul. 2006. 'Money as Tool, Money as Drug' *The Biological Psychology of Behavioral and Brain Sciences* 29(2): 161–209.

Lee, Er (李耳). 2002. *Daodejing* 道德經 (Tao Te Ching). Annotated by Zhao Meng-fu and Xian Yu (趙孟頫, 鮮于). Hong Kong: The Commercial Press.

Lévi-Strauss, Claude. 1963. The Bear and the Barber. *The Journal of the Royal Anthropological Institute* 93: 1–11.

Li, Charles N. and Thompson, Sandra A. 1989. *Mandarin Chinese: A Functional Reference Grammar.* California: University of California Press.

Li, Cho-Jin (李秋錦). 2007. "1990 Niandai Hou Deguo Jingji Biaoxian yu Gaige" 1990年代後德國經濟表現與改革 (Germany's Economic Performance and Reform since the 1990s). *Jingji yanjiu* 經濟研究 (Economic Research) 7: 199–234.

Li, Ming-Fang (李名方). 1999. "Kua Shiji de Zhongguo Xiucixue" 跨世紀的中國修辭學 (Cross-centurial Chinese Rhetoric). Nanjing: He Nan Da Xue Publisher.

Lien, Chin-Fa (連金發). 2007. Idioms in Verb-Object Constructions. *Bulletin of Chinese Linguistics* 11(1): 187–209.

Lin, Cheng-Hua (林政華). 1984. "Shujing Chengyu Yanjiu" 書經成語研究 (The Study on the Idoms in Classic of History). *Kong Meng xuebao* 孔孟學報 (Journal of Confucius-Mencius Society of the Republic of China) 47: 27–67.

Lin, Yu-Tang (林語堂). 1999. *Lin Yutang Dangdai Hanyu Cidian* 林語堂當代漢語詞典 (Lin Yutang Chinese-English Dictionary of Modern Usage). Hong Kong: The Chinese University of Hong Kong. (http: //humanum.arts.cuhk.edu.hk/Lexis/Lindict/)

Liu, Ming-Ge and Qin, Zhi-Yun (劉明閣, 秦志勇). 2001. "Han Ying Wenhua zhong Zhiwu Fuhao Biaozheng Chayi de Fenxi" 漢英文化中植物符號表徵差異的分析 (The comparative study of plant symbols in Chinese and English Cultures). *Guilinshi jiaoyu xueyuan xuebao* 桂林市教育學院學報 (Journal of Guilin College of Education) 15(2): 58–60.

Liu, Yi-Jun (劉怡君). 2010. *The Polysemy and Grammaticalization of Mian* 面 *in Mandarin Chinese.* M.A. Thesis of Department of Foreign Languages and Literature. Tainan, Taiwan: National Cheng Kung University.

López-Maestre, María Dolores. 2000. The Business of Cognitive Stylistics: a Survey of Conceptual Metaphors in Business English. *Atlantis* XXII (1): 47–69.

McGlone, Matthew S. 1996. Conceptual Metaphors and Figurative Language Interpretation: Food for Thought? *Journal of Memory and Language* 35: 544–565.

——. 2007. What Is the Explanatory Value of a Conceptual Metaphor? *Language and Communication* 27(2): 109–126.

Morris, Morris W., Sheldon, Oliver J., Ames, Daniel R. and Young, Maia J. 2007. Metaphors and the Market: Consequences and Preconditions of Agent and Object Metaphors in Stock Market Commentary. *Organizational Behavior and Human Decision Processes* 102 (2): 174–192.

Ng, Tseung-Wong, C. 2003. Factors Linked to Identification with a Super-Ordinate Category in a Multi-Ethnic Context: The Case of Mauritius. *Law, Management and Social Sciences* 5: 1–11.

Niles, Ian and Pease, Adam. 2001. Toward a Standard Upper Ontology. In the *Proceedings of the 2nd International Conference on Formal Ontology in Information Systems*: 2–9.

Nostrand, Howard Lee. 1978. The Emergent Model Applied to Contemporary France. *Contemporary French Civilization* 2 (Winter): 277–94.

Nunberg, Geoffrey, Sag, Ivan A. and Wasow, Thomas. 1994. Idioms. *Language* 70: 491–538.

Qiu, Zhi-Pu (邱質扑) (Ed.). 1990. *Dalu he Taiwan Ciyu Chabie Cidian* 大陸和台灣詞語差別詞典 (Dictionary of Mainland and Taiwan Chinese). Nanjing: Nanjing University.

Radcliffe-Brown, Alfred R. 1929. *Structure and Function in Primitive Society.* London: Cohen & West.

Resche, Catherine. 2001. Metaphors in English for Economics. *Asp: La revue du Geras* 31–33: 239–259.

——. 2002. La Metaphore en Langue Specialisee, entre Mediation et Contradiction: Etude d'une Mutation Metaphorique en Anglais Economique. *Asp: La revue du Geras* 35–36: 103–119.

Richter, Frank. 2011. *Beolingus*. Chemnitz: Chemnitz University of Technology.

Ringer, Fritz K. 1996. *The Decline of the German Mandarins: The German Academic Community (1890–1933)*. Hanover, London: Wesleyan University Press.

Röhrich, Lutz. 1991. *Lexikon der Sprichwörtlichen Redensarten*. Freiburg: Herder Verlag.

——. 2001. *Das große Lexikon der sprichwörtlichen Redensarten* [electronic resource]. Darmstadt: Wissenschaftliche Buchgesellschaft.

Schmidt, Anja. 2003. *Kommunikationsmodelle in Shanghai: Selbstdefinition durch individuelle Sprachformen*. Altstadt, Germany: GRIN Verlag.

Schmidt, Christopher M. 2002. Metaphor and Cognition: a Cross-Cultural Study of Indigenous and Universal Constructs in Stock Exchange Report. In: Allwood Jens (Ed.). *Intercultural Communication* 5: 1–17.

Schoenemann, P. Thomas. 1999. Syntax as an Emergent Characteristic of the Evolution of Semantic Complexity. *Minds and Machines* 9: 309–346.

Semino, Elena. 2008. *Metaphor in Discourse*. New York: Cambridge University.

Šeškauskienė, Inesa and Urbonaitė, Justina. 2007. Health Metaphor in Political and Economic Discourse: a Cross-Linguistic Analysis. *Studies about Languages (Kalbu Studijos)* 11: 68–73.

Shao, Jun-Hang (邵軍航). 2008. Great Chain of Being Metaphor: Understanding and Reflection. *Journal of Shanghai Finance University* 2: 75–80.

Shi, Shi (史式). 1979. *The Study on Mandarin Chinese Idioms*. Chengdu: Sichuan People's Publishing House.

Skorczynska, Hanna and Deignan, Alice. 2006. Readership and Purpose in the Choice of Economics Metaphors. *Metaphor and Symbol* 21(2): 87–104.

Smith, Geoff P. 1995. How High Can a Dead Cat Bounce?: Metaphor and the Hong Kong Stock Market. *Hong Kong Papers In Linguistics and Language Teaching* 18: 43–57.

Smith, Kevin B. and Stone, Lorene H. 1989. Rags, Riches, and Bootstraps: Beliefs about the Causes of Wealth and Poverty. *The Sociological Quarterly* 30 (1): 93–107.

Stern, Hans Heinrich. 1993. *Issues and Options in Language Teaching*. Oxford: Oxford University Press.

Su, I-Wen (蘇以文). 2000. Mapping in Though and Language as Evidence in Chinese. *Chinese Studies* 18: 395–424.

Sun, Gui-Li (孫桂里). 2009. Animal Fixed Expressions in Mandarin Chinese and Taiwanese: Gender Differences. M.A. Thesis of Department of Foreign Languages and Literature. Tainan, Taiwan: National Cheng Kung University.

Tang, Zhi-Xiang (湯志祥). 2001. *Dangdai Hanyu Ciyu de Gongshi Zhuangkuang ji Qi Shanbian: 90 Niandai Zhongguo Dalu, Xianggang, Taiwan Hanyu Ciyu Xianzhuang Yanjiu* 當代漢語詞語的共時狀況及其嬗變: 90年代中國大陸、香港、臺灣漢語詞語現狀研究 (A Synchronic and Diachronic Study of the Lexicon in Contemporary Mandarin Chinese: Mandarin Chinese in Mainland China, Hong Kong and Taiwan in the 90s). Shanghai: Fu Dan University.

Tao, Hong-Yin (陶紅印). 2003. Toward an Emergent View of Lexical Semantics. *Language and Linguistics* 4: 837–856.

Tendahl, Markus and Gibbs, Jr. Raymond W. 2008. Complementary Perspectives on Metaphor: Cognitive Linguistics and Relevance Theory. *Journal of Pragmatics* 40 (11): 1823–1864.

Tsai, Rong-Chi (蔡蓉芝). 2004. "Shijing zhong de Chengyu Ci" 詩經中的成語詞(The Idiom Phrases in Classis of Poetry). *Jingnü xuebao* 景女學報 (Journal of Taipei Jing-Mei Girls High School) 4: 69–88.

Tsai, Wei-Lun (蔡瑋倫). 2011. *Animal Metaphors in Political and Economic Discourse: The Example of Legendary Animals*. M.A. Thesis of Department of Foreign Languages and Literature. Tainan, Taiwan: National Cheng Kung University.

Tsao, Feng-Fu, Tsai, Lee-Chung and Liu, Xiu-Ing (曹逢甫, 蔡立中, 劉秀瑩). 2001. *Shenti yu Piyu: Yuyan yu Renzhi de Shouyao Jiemian* 身體與譬喻:語言與認知的首要介面 (Body and Metaphor: The Primary Interface of Language and Cognition). Taipei: Crane.

Tseng, Hsin-Wen (曾婷雯). 2010. *Metaphors Related to Stock Jargons in Taiwan Mandarin.* M.A. Thesis of Department of Foreign Languages and Literature. Tainan, Taiwan: National Cheng Kung University.

Tseng, Hsin-Wen and Hsieh, Shelley Ching-Yu (曾婷雯, 謝菁玉). 2007. A Corpus-based Study of Stock Jargon in Mandarin Chinese and English. In the *Proceedings of 12th International Conference on Processing of East Asia Related Languages (PEARL-12).*

——. 2008. Stock Jargon in Discourses: A Corpus-based, Comparative Study of Mandarin Chinese and English. In the *Proceedings of American Association of Corpus Linguistics (AACL).*

Ungerer, Friedrich and Schmid, Hans-Jörg. 2006. *An Introduction to Cognitive Linguistics* (2nd edition). New York: Pearson Educated Limited.

Universität Leipzig. 1998–2008. Deutscher Wortschatz. Universität Leipzig: Institut für Informatik.

Vervaeke, John and Kennedy, John M. 1996. Metaphors in Language and Thought: Falsification and Multiple Meanings. *Metaphor and Symbolic Activity* 11(4): 273–284.

Waldzus, Sven., Mummendey, Amélie and Wenzel, Michael. 2005. When 'Different' Means 'Worse': In-group Prototypicality in Changing Intergroup Contexts. *Journal of Experimental Social Psychology* 41:76–83.

Waller, David, Lippa, Yvonne and Richardson, Adam. 2007. Isolating Observer-Based Reference Directions. *Cognition* 1: 1–27.

Wang, Yun-Lu (王雲路). 2010. *Zhonggu Hanyu Cihui Shi* 中古漢語詞匯史 (The History of Middle Chinese Lexicons). Beijing: The Commercial Press.

WAZ New Media. 2012. Euro-Krise bremst deutsche Wirtschaft aus. *WAZ.* 8 June 2012.

Weber, Max. 1934. *Die Protestantische Ethik und der Geist des Kapitalismus* (新教倫理與資本主義精神). Tübingen: J.C.B. Mohr.

White, Michael. 2003. Metaphor and Economics: the Case of *Growth. English for Specific Purposes* 22: 131–151.

Wu, Li-Quan (吳禮權). 1998. *Zhongguo Xiandai Xiuci Xue Tonglun* 中國現代修辭學通論 (An Introduction to Chinese Modern Rhetoric). Taipei: The Commercial Press.

Xu, Bing (徐冰). 2006. "Yingyu Jingji Yupian zhong Shengwu Yinyu Yingshe Moshi Tanxi" 英語經濟語篇中生物隱喻映射模式探析 (Study on Organism Metaphor Mapping in English Business Discourse). *Yanshan daxue xuebao: zhexue shehui kexueban* 燕山大學學報: 哲學社會科學版 (Journal of Yanshan Finance University (Philosophy and Social Science Edition)). 7(1): 20–23.

Yao, Yu-Wen and Mao, Tzu-Ching (姚瑜雯, 毛子菁). 2006. *Stories of Idioms* (成語故事). Taipei: The Eastern Publishing.

Young, Joni J. 2001. Risk(ing) Metaphors. *Critical Perspectives on Accounting* 12: 607–625.

Zhou, He and Qiu, De-Xiu (周何, 邱德修). 2004. *Guoyu Huoyong Cidian* 國語活用辭典 (Dictionary of Mandarin Chinese Flexible Usages). Taipei: Wu Nan.

Zhou, Zu-Mou (周祖謀). 1994. *Zhongguo Da Baike Quanshu Chengyu* 中國大百科全書成語 (Encyclopedia of China—Set Expressions). Beijing: Encyclopedia of China Publishing House.

Zhuang, Zhou (莊周). 1989. *Zhuangzi* 莊子 (Zhuang Zhi). Annotated by Guo Xiang (郭象). Shanghai: Guji.

INDEX

www.ingramcontent.com/pod-product-compliance
Lightning Source LLC
LaVergne TN
LVHW020635300926
849161LV00004B/714
9789004244337